Educational Policy Analysis

Educational Policy Analysis

A Quantitative Approach

James Edward Bruno

Crane, Russak & Company, Inc.

NEW YORK

Educational Policy Analysis

Published in the United States by
Crane, Russak & Company, Inc.
347 Madison Avenue
New York, New York 10017

ISBN 0-8448-0623-4
LC 74-24987

Printed in the United States of America

This book is dedicated to those things
which provide inspiration in life,
food, art, children, music, nature,
love; and most of all to the one
constant and first source of
inspiration in my life, my parents.

Contents

---

*Asterisks following headings indicate a fuller mathematical exposition of the topic which can be skipped by most readers without losing the principal objectives of each chapter.

CHAPTER 3

Multiple Linear Regression: Issues Related to Educational Problems of Prediction 69

CHAPTER 4

Discriminant Analysis: Issues Related to Educational Problems of Classification 107

CHAPTER 8

Lorenz Curve Analysis: Measurement of Inequality
in Educational Systems 229

CHAPTER 9

Delphi Techniques: Elicitation of Expert Opinion
for Setting Organizational Goals 243

Acknowledgments

I acknowledge the significant assistance of Ms. Lynn Doscher who painstakingly helped review and critique the entire manuscript. Her patience and insightful hints for presentation of the material were a major factor in seeing this project to fruition.

I also thank those who typed the manuscript, Ms. Lanng Tamura, Ms. Christine Tesfay, and the Communications Processing Center at the University of California at Los Angeles.

Finally, I would like to thank Dr. J. Ward Keesling, Assistant Professor, Graduate School of Education, UCLA, for reviewing, presenting, and suggesting revisions for Chapters 2, 3 and 4; and Dr. John McCall, Professor, Department of Economics, UCLA, for his suggestions concerning the content of Chapter 5.

I am grateful to the Literary Executor of the late Sir Ronald A. Fisher, F.R.S., to Dr. Frank Yates, F.R.S., and to Longman Group Ltd., London, for permission to reprint Table III from their book *Statistical Tables for Biological, Agricultural and Medical Research* (6th edition, 1974).

Preface

There is great emphasis placed upon quantitative methods and policy oriented research in graduate schools of education. The principal aim of this book is to provide the policy analyst (whether a student, planning to pursue a career in education, or a practitioner already in the field) with a clear, concise discussion of what I consider "basic" tools and techniques that provide the foundation for performing studies dealing with educational policy. This book can serve as a supplementary text to standard empirically oriented statistics courses in graduate schools of education or as a basic text for a course in quantitative analysis for educational policy and planning. Such courses now exist at the University of California at Los Angeles, and many colleges and universities are in the process of developing program areas specifically entitled "Educational Policy and Planning."

Placing in one volume the quantitative techniques and methodologies in which educational policy analysts should be knowledgeable is an impossible task. In fact, even organizing a framework or scheme to fit these various techniques into some logical, coherent order is extremely demanding. I have confronted the issue by including a broad range of those techniques that either have the highest potential in terms of application or else are used in sufficient frequency by policy analysts to be elevated to a status of standard techniques in a repertoire that might also include lesser used, more limited methodologies. Since this book was written principally as a standard reference for policy-making personnel in school districts, institutions of higher education, and research organizations, discussions of the techniques emphasize applications and policy relevance. Many of the more mathematical, theoretical foundations for these quantitative methodologies, therefore, had to be sacrificed. The book is directed at educational policy makers and planners, not mathematicians, statisticians, or operations research specialists. The book, however, does contain the essential expository development of the theoretical foundations for each of these techniques. These technical discussions can be found in the *starred sections* and can be skipped by most readers without losing the principal objectives of each chapter. References found for each chapter (located at the back of the book) are, for the most part, divided into educational policy applications and general theoretical reference works in keeping with the parallel exposition of the text.

Lesser used analytical techniques, such as Markov chain analysis, Monte Carlo methods, and advanced multivariate techniques, did not seem appropriate for inclusion here. This is mainly because there are other excellent specialized books on these subjects if the policy analyst is sufficiently interested, and also because the length of the book would have to be increased inordinately.

The heavy emphasis placed here on applications and policy relevant interpretation of computer results reflects my own experience in teaching both graduate and undergraduate courses as well as my experiences when I was a student. These experiences indicate that essential features and potential use of the techniques are often lost in technical details. It is my hope that motivation derived by a clear understanding of the potential of the techniques developed and applied to problems in educational policy and planning will be sufficient for the student to learn, on his own and in greater depth, the finer technical details. The modest technical foundations for the quantitative techniques discussed in the chapters are meant only to further the reader's understanding of the concept. The technical foundations are presented with a minimum use of high level mathematical concepts and as mentioned previously are placed in separate starred sections which can be overlooked with little loss of information to the reader concerning the potential application of the technique to educational policy and planning. The serious reader, of course, will want to go into greater depth and will want to learn more about a specific technique. Finally, the appendix contains various statistical tables frequently used in educational policy research such as F tables, a chi square table, t tables, and a table of random numbers. The tables are cited throughout the book for testing statistical significance.

Now that I have discussed those general elements of the book that support its overall objectives, I will direct my attention to each chapter and examine how the chapters are organized.

I chose to view educational policy making and planning as two separate functions requiring a different set of methodologies, even though a large number of the methods discussed are applicable to both functions.

Chapter 7 on linear programming presents to the reader some knowledge of the most widely used optimization technique and discusses its use in educational problems of resource allocation and management. The application of linear programming, discussed in Chapter 7, deals with policy issues surrounding the design of teacher salary schedules to illustrate the utility of this technique in dealing with problems of conflict resolution as well as resource allocations.

Chapter 6 on PERT is included because the coordination of activities to complete assigned tasks seems to form a large part of the responsibilities of a policy analyst in educational institutions. In addition, many federal granting agencies require either a Gantt or PERT chart of activities to be included as part of the grant proposal.

Lorenz curve analysis and Delphi techniques, Chapters 8 and 9, are included for two reasons. First, they are extremely important methodologies that have significant relevance to education. In Lorenz curve analysis, we are interested in obtaining quantitative measures of the distribution of power or wealth. Obviously the technique can be used in situations where evaluation of alternative plans for resolving some educational inequity, such as school busing plans to eliminate school segregation, is needed. Delphi technique is excellent for strategic planning and goal setting in educational organizations. This technique permits the systematic elicitation of expert opinion concerning future goals of the organization or events which might affect the organization itself. Its use in setting organization goals for education and examining future educational configurations is already well documented and established in the literature and in actual practice.

Second, most educational references with which the policy analyst comes into contact with do not devote chapters to these important techniques in sufficient detail to demonstrate their use in education. Thus, these powerful methodologies, even though they have wide applicability in education, are not exploited to full advantage, both because the visibility of these techniques is low and because formal instruction in their use is fragmented.

Chapter 2 is a brief review of univariate and bivariate statistics, provided mainly to lay the groundwork for subsequent chapters. The reader not familiar with these techniques should refer also to the statistics texts in the bibliography for more detailed explanations.

Chapters 3 and 4 on multivariate analysis need no justification for inclusion in a book on quantitative techniques for educational policy and planning. Regression and discriminant analysis are basic requisite techniques or "tools of the trade" for research that ultimately might influence policy. Regression is an especially important technique used in the great majority of educational policy and planning studies. Multivariate techniques, because they are able to systematically consider a multitude of variables, can yield important policy relevant insights to the analyst. In essence, if the problem area concerns prediction, then regression is the appropriate methodology; if the problem addresses discrimination or classification, then discriminant analysis is appropriate. Canonical correlation, used in situations where one has multiple output as well as input variables, is also discussed in Chapter 4 on discriminant analysis. Each of these chapters on multivariate analysis contains illustrative examples and places heavy emphasis on the policy relevant interpretation of the computer printouts from various software packages.

As the discipline of economics makes more contributions to education, it will be essential for policy analysts to develop a fundamental understanding of important economic theories and their potential applications to education. In Chapter 5, on microeconomic theory, two economic theories are discussed along with their possible contributions to educational policy and planning. These economic theories are human capital theory and production function theory. Human capital theory is an excellent framework for analyzing and studying how people or governments make choices concerning the level of their investment in educational expenditures. Production theory provides valuable information about the way resources should be allocated in an educational system.

Finally, Chapter 1 places the entire book in logical perspective. The principal theme in this chapter is that educational research practices, which later form the basis for educational policy and planning, are coming under closer scrutiny, especially from the courts. Simplistic, traditional methods for performing educational research will no longer suffice, especially when the research is directed at complex problems which might be related to societal notions of equal opportunity. A case is then made for why these newer sophisticated methods should be understood by educational policy analysts. A brief analysis of a RAND report concerning what we have learned from the research on schooling is also presented. With a grant from the President's Commission of School Finance, this ambitious RAND project attempted to summarize from five different research paradigms the research findings of numerous studies and relate these findings to educational policy. Chapter 1 also examines the evolution of research theory in education from both the econometric and psychological perspectives. It is hoped that the reader will be able to visualize the two great forces that seem to shape the direction of educational research and how both of these great social science disciplines, psychology and economics, have adapted to modern demands for more policy-oriented research.

My recommendation to the reader is that the chapters be read carefully, paying particular attention to the illustrative applications. Chapter 2 is helpful before reading Chapters 3 and 4. The remaining chapters can be read in any order.

Special attention is given here to readers who have minimal backgrounds in statistics, mathematics, and economics and who desire merely to develop and understand these techniques to facilitate communication with more technically specialized personnel. For these "generalists" most of the fundamentals can be gained by careful reading of all sections except the starred sections (there greater technical detail is presented) in each chapter.

One final word about general strategies for mastering the material found in this book for both "generalists" and "technical specialists": Read the chapter first, then think it out and try to conceptualize its meaning; if possible, attempt to use the technique in a particular situation by making up a small problem. Often the best way to learn these techniques is to begin to apply them to real world situations.

The application of quantitative methods to educational policy and planning is both a science and an art. I have tried to present the straightforward scientific elements of these techniques. The art of application, however, cannot be taught. Only by developing a rapport with these sophisticated techniques and knowledge of their limitations, as well as their potentials, can the policy analyst or planner achieve the art of application. An old proverb speaks of luck as being where preparation meets opportunity. The opportunity for a successful application of these techniques must be met with a thorough knowledge and preparation of the fundamentals. Providing this basic knowledge in quantitative analysis is the principal aim of this book.

James E. Bruno
June, 1976

Chapter 1

Emergence of Quantitative Analysis in Education

1-1 INTRODUCTION

"Nothing has been found (in terms of educational practices) that consistently and unambiguously makes a difference in student outcomes" (Averch et al. 1972).

The above statement concerning the state of knowledge in educational research was found in a recent RAND research study submitted to the President's Commission on School Finance. The task of the RAND study was to summarize current educational research findings from various perspectives or research paradigms and extract their implications for educational policy. The fact that no consistent findings that make a difference in student outcomes emerged from this massive in-depth review of the education research literature is quite discouraging and poses a major challenge to school policy makers and those who study the education phenomenon.

The results of the RAND study were a radical departure from the education folklore and should stimulate tremendous controversy. While one might disagree about specifics, certainly the spirit of the report seems valid. Much educational research, in spite of the millions of dollars invested, does not give the educational policy makers insight into making decisions. For example, suppose you were an educational policy maker, how would you make decisions based upon reports of studies summarized in the RAND report?

1. Comparisons of television and live classroom instruction reveal no consistent differences. Of 393 experimental comparisons, 255 showed no difference, 83 favored televised teaching, and 55 favored conventional teaching.

2. Comparisons of college teaching methods showed no consistent differences. For example, of 88 comparisons of lecture versus discussion, 45 favored lecture and 43 favored discussion.

3. Comparisons of classroom climate showed no consistent differences between learner-centered (democratic) classrooms and teacher-centered (authoritarian) classrooms. Eight studies favored the teacher-centered approach, 11 favored the learner-centered approach, and 13 found no difference.

These mixed findings possibly reflect the complex nature of the phenomenon of education, or possibly the ineffectiveness of educational research methods. The lack of consistent findings is most likely due to both reasons with elements of rapid change in societal goals and values insuring this elusiveness in attempting to model educational phenomena.

Probably the one constant feature that makes the study of education so complex is the change in the expectations and functions of each of the participants in education—teacher, student, administrator, and society (Bruno 1973). For example, students over the last decade seem to have changed from:

Materialistic orientation (preparation for high status job)	to	Idealistic orientation (wanting to enjoy education—although this might be changing back again)
Dropping out of school when unmotivated	to	Staying in school to graduation

Parental influence on attitudes toward schooling	to	Peer dominated influence on attitudes toward schooling

Teachers also seem to have changed their function in educational organizations from:

Idealistic orientation (extra work with no compensation)	to	Materialistic orientation (payment for extra work)
Professional association memberships	to	Union memberships
Ready acceptance of innovations to help students	to	Resistance to innovations that might threaten job security
Team with administrators to promote educational quality	to	Adversaries to administration and competitors for limited funds
Autonomy in the classroom	to	Accountability for student outcomes

Administrators have also changed their role in educational organizations from:

Education team philosophy where all are equal	to	Education manager
Emphasis on human relations skills	to	Emphasis on analytical skills and skills in management
Autonomy in the school organization	to	Fiscal accountability

Finally, the catalyst for the above changes is change which seems to be occurring in basic societal values. The codified form of societal values is the law. The radical changes in how courts view school and schooling have affected every aspect of school organization from school finance to student rights and teacher liability. In essence, the courts have changed their standards of judging educational practices from the basis of their reasonableness to the standard of strict scrutiny (since educational practice affects a student's entire life). In fact, some legal historians have concluded that the courts have actually assumed administration of the schools (Hogan 1972).

It becomes extremely difficult, therefore, to formulate long-term policy or perform research on schools with the social environment in a state of increasingly rapid change. To confront this challenge there have been notable changes in educational research practices:

Traditional Educational Research		*Modern Educational Research*
Qualitative	to	Quantitative analysis with heavy use of computer
Empirical analysis	to	Policy related analysis
Establishment research (research generally supporting school positions)	to	Anti-establishment research (alternatives to schools and school practices)
Single discipline research centered in psychology and education methods	to	Interdisciplinary research bringing together economics, sociology, and anthropology methods
Psychometric dominated research	to	Econometric dominated research

While the foregoing notions of how schooling and research methods have changed might be considered simplistic, certainly no one would argue that educational research practices and methods are now coming under closer societal scrutiny. This is especially true from the perspective of the courts. The emphasis of funding agencies has also reflected these changes and has shifted from basic empirical education research to more policy oriented educational research. In this and succeeding chapters, an attempt will be made to document this shift and to present the educational analyst with tools and techniques for conducting policy directed educational research to reflect this more sophisticated standard expected by society.

1-2 PARADIGMS FOR STUDYING THE EDUCATION PHENOMENA

Before presenting the various quantitative tools and techniques for performing educational policy analysis, it is important to understand exactly what methods are used for studying education and what policy-relevant findings, if any, have emerged from these fundamentally different approaches. The RAND study for the President's Commission on School Finance employed the following methodology for dealing with this problem. First, individual studies were examined in detail for internal validity (sample size, appropriate use of statistics, research design, etc.). These individual studies in one approach were then examined for consistent findings and the results summarized. Each of the five research paradigms were examined; then the findings in each approach were compared and the conclusions for educational policy were extracted. The schematic in Figure 1-1 summarizes the RAND methodology.

The five research paradigms used in the RAND study were (1) input–output, (2) process, (3) organizational, (4) evaluation, and (5) experiential.

In the input–output paradigm, statistical analysis is employed in an ex post facto cross-sectional design and student educational outcomes are made a function (usually employing predictive models) of various resource inputs. This is represented schematically in Figure 1-2.

The objective of research using the input–output paradigm is to examine how student outcomes are explained by various resource inputs. The Coleman Report is one important example of an educational study employing the input–output paradigm. In this study student verbal scores were related to school district resource inputs. Variations in the way students achieve across schools was

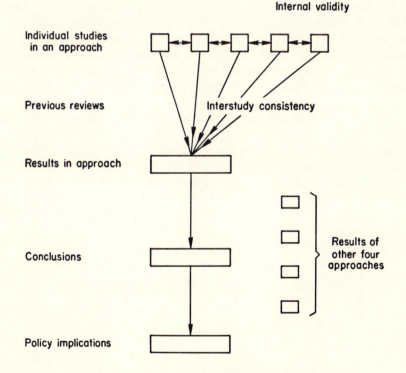

Figure 1-1. Evaluation of research findings for educational policy.

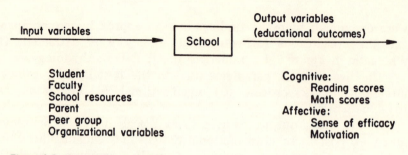

Figure 1-2. Input–output paradigm.

then explained by these resource inputs. The input–output paradigm also has both cost benefit considerations and organizational efficiency as an implicit goal. This paradigm will be explained in greater detail when we examine educational production functions in Chapter 5.

In the process paradigm, research is directed more toward how learning takes place, given resource inputs at some controlled, predetermined or given value. The major focus examines the significance of how instructional resources are applied to students and how students respond to these resources. This paradigm is represented schematically by Figure 1-3. Studies typical of experimental-control group designs of experimental psychology, such as studies comparing television instruction to live lecture presentations, are examples of the process paradigm for examining the educational phenomenon.

The organizational paradigm has the basic premise that educational effectiveness is not a result of the optimal combination of inputs such as the input–output paradigm would suggest, nor is it the result of the treatment that the process paradigm would suggest. Rather, this approach to studying educational effectiveness is predicated under the assumption that organizational structure and

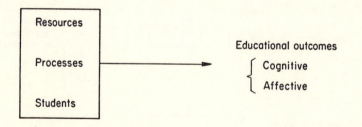

Figure 1-3. Process paradigm.

shape determine effectiveness and that this amorphous body can be distorted to produce effectiveness by outside societal demands. Innovations that produce effectiveness in education occur as a result of history, outside political pressure, and social–legal forces. Studying rigidities, organizational patterns, and incentives for the organization becomes the major research areas for this paradigm. This approach is represented schematically by Figure 1-4.

This research paradigm generally employs the case study. An in-depth study of school desegregation for a particular school district is a typical example. The issues dealt with by the organizational paradigm are by design almost totally policy related and utilize tools and techniques of economics, sociology, political science, and psychology to perform the required analysis.

During the period 1960–1970, the federal government took a strong role in attempting to alter educational outcomes—especially educational outcomes of culturally disadvantaged, low-achieving students. The next research paradigm is classified under the general heading of the evaluation paradigm. In this approach the effects of broad, usually large-scale, educational interventions are studied to examine their effects upon student outcomes. The principal objective is to influence school policy related to these individuals and increase student performance. This approach is viewed in Figure 1-5.

From the standpoint of the federal government, the focus of the evaluation paradigm is to find what works, then attempt to

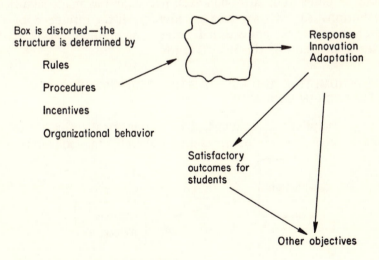

Figure 1-4. Organizational paradigm.

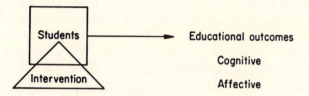

Figure 1-5. Evaluation paradigm.

apply the methods elsewhere. Title III program evaluations are an excellent illustration of evaluation studies, and Project Head Start was probably the single most important study utilizing this paradigm.

Finally, many reformers in education feel that the only "real" policy issue in education, which should be the sole concern of policy makers in education, is how schooling affects students. This paradigm, the experiential approach, focuses on shaping schools to respond to student needs (see Figure 1-6). The research, therefore, is focused on observing students' behavior, especially their happiness. The alternative school movement in America is a direct result of this interest in shaping school organizations around students.

Table 1-1 summarizes aspects of each research paradigm in terms of findings, types of researchers characteristic of the paradigm, and areas of principal concern.

We have not learned a great deal in the past 100 years or so of research in education. Although each paradigm has made significant contributions to its own area of inquiry, little influence of this research on general educational policy has resulted—at least this was the conclusion of the RAND study.

1-3 PSYCHOMETRIC AND ECONOMETRIC PERSPECTIVES TO RESEARCH IN EDUCATION

The two disciplines that seem to have the greatest influence on the direction and scope of present research in education are

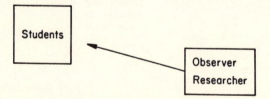

Figure 1-6. Experiential paradigm.

Table 1-1. What We Have Learned About the Schools Using Different Research Approaches

Research paradigm	Principal concern	Researchers	Results
Input–output paradigm	How resource inputs are related to school district outputs (production function)	Economists	Production functions seldom explain student outcomes very well Background factors consistently dominate Little evidence that school resources influence student outcomes when background variables are controlled
Process paradigm	Improve the way education takes place—examine the processes and methods by which resources are applied	Educational psychologists, curriculum specialists, sociologists	Many findings, but usually no benefit cost analysis, and, until recently, no aptitude treatment interaction (see Section 1-3)
Organizational paradigm	Case study—educational practice a reflection of history, social demand, and organizational change; how these factors impinge on the various decision makers and affect their behavior	Political scientists	Innovations in large school systems based upon exogenous shocks Difficult to assess validity or reliability of studies since most are nonquantitative
Evaluation paradigm	Examinations of the effects of large-scale interventions in the school systems and how they affect student outcomes	Evaluation research methodologists, statisticians	Virtually without exception, all national comparative education programs have shown no beneficial results Large fadeout of results Level of funding not sufficient for success
Experiential paradigm	Student centered; how the system affects students; the reform literature	Sociologists, philosophy of education, former teachers, radicals	Many observations, no empirical data School focus on unimportant objectives Student learning cannot take place in authoritarian environment Substance of educational practice is irrelevant Children should not be required to attend school

psychology and the more recent arrival, economics. While a large amount of the conceptual, theoretical, and actual measurement research for education has been developed in psychology, much of the modeling in terms of causality has been developed in economics. Neither of these disciplines, however, has a single theory for studying the phenomenon of education. For example, psychology can deal with individual measures or group measures (learning theory) or the interaction between learning and individuals. The economist, on the other hand, while more interested in the deductive rather than inductive nature of psychological research, is interested in finding the underlying structure for causal relationships between variables. Such a causal model for student achievement is depicted in Figure 1-7. The economist can also examine education from two perspectives: either as a basic investment problem using human capital theory or from a resource allocation viewpoint utilizing production theory.

The psychological research dealing with the individual as the center typically is based upon the group mental tests of Binet and aptitude tests for purposes of guidance, admission, and placement. The goal for this type of research is to maximize prediction of

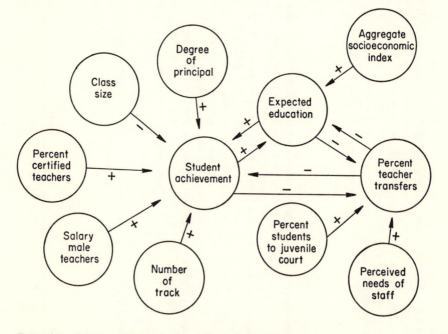

Figure 1-7. Causal models in education. *Note*: Expected signs on arrows.

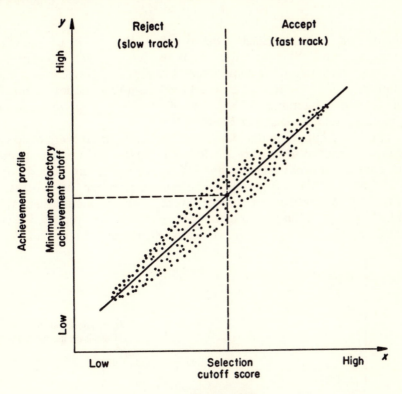

Figure 1-8. Learner-centered psychological research. *Source:* Levin and Snow (1973). Reprinted by permission of the publisher, from *Emerging Issues in Education: Policy Implications for the Schools,* edited by James E. Bruno (Lexington, Mass.: Lexington Books, D.C. Heath and Company, 1973).

success in some program regardless of the method of instruction used. The concept of fast and slow tracks in educational settings is derived from this type of "individual-based" psychological research. This branch of psychological research in education is shown in Figure 1-8. In essence, a mental test x, which has been shown to have a positive relation to achievement (y-axis) after instruction, is given before instruction. By a priori deciding what level of achievement is considered satisfactory, a cutoff point score is established for the selection test (x-axis) to divide future applicants into those accepted and those rejected, or, what is more common for public schools today, into fast and slow tracks. In most cases, the nature of instruction between x and y is ignored by the measurement psychologist; for example, learning or instructional variables are constant, only the students are different.

Another emphasis in experimental educational psychology is

research on learning itself. Based upon the work of Dewey, Thorndike, and Skinner, the focus is to improve educational practices based upon the experimental analysis of learning and the systematic manipulation of instructional stimuli in order to maximize average learning. This area of psychological research is represented schematically in Figure 1-9.

The basic experimental design for learning-centered educational research is that students are randomly separated into experimental and control groups. At the end of some treatment period, the groups are compared in order to determine whether the treatment group has a statistically higher average achievement than the control group. Thus, in Figure 1-9, it might be reported that treatment *A* resulted in statistically significant higher average

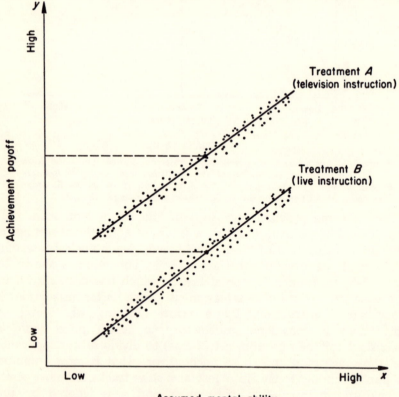

Figure 1-9. Learning-centered psychological research. *Source:* Levin and Snow (1973). Reprinted by permission of the publisher, from *Emerging Issues in Education: Policy Implications for the Schools,* edited by James E. Bruno (Lexington, Mass.: Lexington Books, D.C. Heath and Company, 1973).

achievement than a comparable control group. In essence, this psychological approach assumes that individual student differences are constant while instructional stimuli vary.

Thus, while individual-centered psychometric methods ask what kind of individual is most likely to succeed in a particular educational setting (measurement of learner), group-centered psychometric methods ask what kind of instructional method is best in a particular educational setting (measurement of learning).

To combine the best features of measurement-of-the-learner psychological research with measurement-of-learning psychological research, Cronbach and Snow (1969) have developed a technique called aptitude treatment interaction (ATI). Aptitude treatment interaction employs a graph similar to learner-centered psychological research but considers all learners, slow as well as fast, in addition to the average learner for comparisons of groups and conclusions. According to Levin and Snow, the ATI problem can be stated as:

> Assume that an educator is interested in a certain set of educational outcomes and has various alternative educational programs or treatments to consider. His question is: In what manner do the characteristics of learners affect the extent to which they attain the outcomes from each of the treatments that might be considered? Or, considering a particular learner: What outcome will each treatment produce? (Levin and Snow 1973, p. 286).

The results shown on the ATI graph, Figure 1-10, indicate that treatment *A* (live instruction) is better for lower ability students than it is for higher-ability students. Treatment *B* (television instruction), on the other hand, is better for higher-ability students, in terms of achievement payoff. The intersection of the two lines marks the point on the ability continuum at which students could be divided for assignment to different treatments, for this particular learning situation.

While there are three principal areas in which psychologists perform research on education, economists studying education, as previously mentioned, typically can be divided into two areas—those viewing education as an investment and those viewing education basically as a resource allocation problem.

The human capital economists, who will be discussed in greater detail in Chapter 5 on microeconomic theory, examine human investment as a direct counterpart to physical investment. The basic premise of human capital economists is that dollars invested

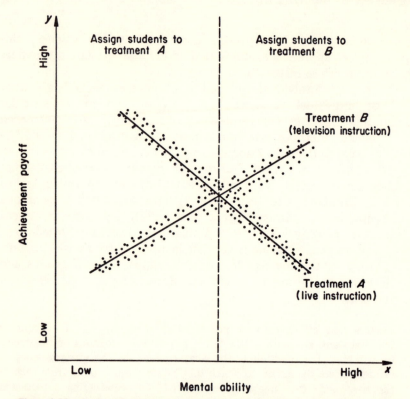

Figure 1-10. Aptitude treatment interaction psychological research. *Source:* Levin and Snow (1973). Reprinted by permission of the publisher, from *Emerging Issues in Education: Policy Implications for the Schools,* edited by James E. Bruno (Lexington, Mass.: Lexington Books, D.C. Heath and Company, 1973).

in education produce higher productivity. Therefore, people seek additional schooling whenever the future earnings are greater than the cost to the individual of obtaining the schooling. In this manner, all the basic tenets of physical investment such as rate of return analysis become applicable. The application of human capital theory to education has been directed at explaining preference for college majors, the relationship between earnings and productivity, and dropout rates.

Applied to education, production theory addresses the following key issues in an organization: First, are the organizational resources being used in a way that maximizes outputs and second, do differences in amounts, types, and organization of educational resources account for differences in educational outcomes? Production theory can also be used to find the least cost approach for achieving a desired outcome or to find which combination of resources maximizes some social criterion or outcome. In this context, an analytical technique called linear programming (discussed in Chapter 7), in which a linear objective function is maximized or minimized subject to resource constraints, becomes a subset of production theory.

The basic concept of production theory, which will also be developed in Chapter 5 on microeconomic theory, is utilized to examine how education is produced and to determine the link between inputs and outputs. Consequently, the input–output research paradigm described earlier is also applied in production function studies in education.

Table 1-2 summarizes how economists and psychologists view various aspects of research in education dealing with prediction, research designs, and research emphasis. Notice that while economists seek to find the underlying causal models that describe or simulate the system of cause and effect, psychologists are primarily interested in effects. While psychologists work primarily with experimental designs that are static and dichotomous (significant-nonsignificant improvement), economists often work with longitudinal data or at least data that are continuous and have some amount of generalizability. Economists are seriously concerned with marginal effects. For example, an extra dollar placed into teacher salary has what effect upon pupil performance? Moreover, the theoretical emphasis of the research is markedly different between these two disciplines: Economists are concerned about productivity, efficiency, effectiveness, and cost; psychologists are concerned about processes, techniques, and theories of learning.

The tools that both disciplines bring to bear in studying the phenomenon of education are also quite different. The economists are oriented toward mathematical modeling and estimating parameters in complex interactive systems, such as measuring relationships. Psychologists have developed a whole set of methodologies for measuring changes in performance and have developed analytical methodologies for insuring that the assumptions of the experiment are met and for assessing whether gains are statistically significant.

It is interesting to note that the discipline of psychology probably dominates policy making at the local school organization level, while economics probably (at least by examining the discipline backgrounds of directors of state and federal agencies) dominates policy making at the federal or state level.

The trend is, of course, toward an amalgamation of methodologies from both disciplines—the measurement of change from

Table 1-2. Comparison Psychological–Econometric Perspectives in Educational Research[a]

	Psychology		Economics
Objectives	Objectives of measurement and changes in measures—basic research		Objectives of finding underlying causal structures and mathematical models of the system—policy oriented research
Prediction or principal concern	IC	Achievement (individual centered)	HC Future earnings (human capital)
	LC	Treatment (learning centered)	PF Outputs or resource allocation to maximize outputs (production functions)
	ATI	Interaction of treatment with students (aptitude treatment interaction)	
Type of data	Work with principally static data and dichotomous interpretation of results		Work with principally continuous data and dynamic interpretation of results with marginal analysis
Research designs and methods	IC	Correlation–regression	HC Multivariate–growth formula analysis
	LC	Experimental–quasi-experimental designs analysis of variance—analysis of covariance	PF Linear programming Multivariate methods and causal models
	ATI	Regression–experimental	Path analysis—two stage least squares
Research or policy emphasis		Gains in achievement	Gains in productivity
	IC	Individual assignment	HC Investment assessment
	LC	Group assessment	PF Productive process of efficiency assessment
	ATI	Individual with group assignment	

[a]IC, Individual-Centered; LC, Learning-Centered; ATI, Aptitude Treatment Interaction; HC, Human Capital; PF, Production Functions.

psychology and the measurement of relationships from economics—into a single area of inquiry. One result of this amalgamation of research efforts from these two perspectives is to examine rate of change in output or learning to rate of change of treatment intensity. Such marginal analysis would be extremely useful for educational policy makers. Presently, the economists can examine and model the factors that produce learning, but they cannot provide the policy maker with instructional strategies. The psychologists, on the other hand, can provide the policy maker with elements of the instructional environment that produce learning, but they cannot provide any insight into marginal cost (how much extra learning for an extra dollar placed in the treatment), threshold C (minimum level of intensity for the treatment), or generalizability to different populations because the structural model to produce learning is unknown.

1-4 TAXONOMY FOR THE APPLICATION OF QUANTITATIVE ANALYSIS IN EDUCATION

If research methods in education have become more quantitatively oriented, so have methods of policy analysis in education. The policy analyst is at the interface between the research world and the real world. He has to interpret research findings and formulate policy in the real world organization. His principal purpose is not to perform basic research but to inquire and discover those practices that will make his organization more effective, hence insuring its survival. In educational organizations, such as school districts, the task of studying the phenomenon of education and presenting findings for the formulation of policy is given to the school administrator. This implies that school administrators must have certain quantitative analysis skills in order to discharge their duties.

It is important for policy analysts to understand the differences between the various tools and techniques of quantitative analysis and the types of educational problems they address. Table 1-3 illustrates the types of problems facing policy analysts and the techniques available for solving them.

The polar extremes of the types of tasks are labeled tactical

Table 1-3. Types of Problems Handled by Quantitative Analysis

Tactical policy problems	Strategic policy problems
Objectives, constraints, and criteria predetermined	Objectives, constraints, and criteria subject to challenge
Concerned with the question—How?	Concerned with the questions—What? and Why?
Typical tools:	Typical tools:
Operations research	Cost-effectiveness analysis
Operations analysis	Cost-benefit analysis
Cost-effectiveness analysis	PPBS (program planning and budgeting system)
Cost-benefit analysis	Systems analysis
	Policy analysis
Mathematical orientation	Social science and philosophical orientation
Technician plays major role	Technician plays supportive role

policy problems and strategic policy problems. For a school district policy maker, tactical policy problems might include items such as school bus routing; repair, replacement, and maintenance decisions regarding equipment; and student scheduling. At the other end of the continuum under strategic policy problems, the policy analyst might have to be involved in wage–salary negotiations, integration policies, curriculum issues, and the establishment of goals for the school organization.

In general, there are two major types of analysis that will influence the decisions of the policy maker. First, there is descriptive analysis that attempts to describe the state of the system and gives no prescription for decision making. Second, normative analysis is decision related and attempts to evaluate alternative courses of action and delineate criteria for evaluation of the system. Normative analysis can itself be viewed in two parts: first, input tradeoff analysis where operational control is desired (asks how well a system is mixing its inputs) and has as its main goals efficiency and management; second, the highest level of analysis, output tradeoff analysis (attempts to ask how well a system is mixing outputs) and has as its main goals system effectiveness and organizational planning and policy. Essentially, input tradeoff normative analysis focuses on the means of a productive process while output tradeoff normative analysis focuses on the results of a productive process.

The three types of analysis (see Table 1-4) can be compared with administrative functions in an educational organization. Notice the transitions in type of budget in Table 1-4 from line

Table 1-4.   Comparisons of Types of Analysis

	Descriptive analysis	Input tradeoff analysis	Output tradeoff analysis
Principal purpose	Control	Management	Planning
Unit of analysis	Function and objects of expenditures	Resources	Programs
Principal goal	Cost control	Efficiency	Effectiveness
Type of budget	Traditional line item	Performance budget	Program budget
Applicable tools and techniques	Cost accounting	Operations research	Systems analysis PPBS
Economic	Cost analysis	Production theory	Utility
Principal orientation	Job functions	Departments	Organization
Question	What?	How?	Why?

Table 1-5. Quantitative Techniques in Educational Policy

	Techniques covered in this book
I. Descriptive analysis Answers questions related to description of the system or measurement of change within a system—no criterion of effectiveness except for significant–nonsignificant change	Traditional statistical analysis and inference
II. A. Normative analysis (output tradeoff) Challenges organizational goals and effectiveness criteria Answers questions related to organizational effectiveness and policy problems	Human capital Multivariate analysis Delphi techniques
B. Normative analysis (input tradeoff) Answers questions related to organizational efficiency Achieves organizational goal at least cost or some other well defined criterion of effectiveness	Linear programming PERT (Program Evaluation and Review Techniques) Production theory Lorenz analysis

item to performance and program budgeting in American education clearly paralleled societal concerns for control (1940s–1950s), efficiency (1960s), and effectiveness (1970s).

Thus, while descriptive analysis might describe or ask the question "What?" about a reading program in terms of costs, facilities, and personnel, input normative analysis asks the question "How can these inputs be mixed to maximize reading scores?" Output normative analysis asks questions related to the goals of society, and if these goals are reflected in the reading program; it attempts to establish why even have a reading program.

The techniques discussed here on quantitative analysis for policy making in education can also be classifed into this framework as in Table 1-5 with the types of problems (tactical, planning, and policy) and the types of analysis (descriptive-normative).

1-5 SUMMARY

The remaining discussion will focus on the future of quantitative analysis specifically applied to policy related problems particularly at the school district level. The discussion, however, is applicable to a policy maker at any educational institution.

The application of quantitative analysis methods in the schools is by no means a simple and straightforward process. Both practical and theoretical problems must be confronted. Practical problems include the complexity and confusion associated with quantitative analysis and the fact that its promise often exceeds its results. Also, quantitative analysis is often biased toward quantifiable data. Finally, this kind of analysis is often expensive, making it more readily available to the wealthier educational organizations than to the poorer ones.

The theoretical issues center around the question, "Can the schools be viewed as factories?" Production theory is far more developed than educational theory. Educators know very little about what produces educational outcomes (the physics of learning remains a mystery). Moreover, much difficulty exists in defining and identifying both the inputs and the outputs of the educational process. While these practical and theoretical issues exist, the trend toward greater utilization of quantitative analysis by school administrators continues.

In 1967, the chairman of the AERA Committee on Educational Organization, Administration, and Finance observed: "There seems to be a growing tendency to assume that administrative procedures, instructional approaches, schools, and fiscal structures must be analyzed as systems or systems components" (Erickson 1967, p. 376). This trend has been projected into the present decade:

> School systems will see the advent of new staff specializations in the next five to ten years. . . . The new unit . . . may include computer and data processing experts, systems analysts, and operations researchers . . . . Problems that can be submitted to quantitative analysis will be increasingly solved using OR techniques . . . . Application of the systems approach will place greater emphasis on planning, thoughtful analysis, and increased information requirements (Culbertson et al. 1969, pp. 185-186).

Unfortunately, the problems associated with the limitations of quantitative analysis will continue to be evident in the 1970s.

> There will be improper adaptation of models developed elsewhere to educational situations, an overemphasis on the gathering of quantitative data through crude testing devices, and overemphasis on economic efficiency. It would also seem likely that because of the complexities involved in comprehensive analysis and lack of adequate data concerning

educational outputs that extensive use of formal methods of analysis will be somewhat limited during the next five to ten years. There will be a quantitative increase in the use of the techniques, but formal analysis will be directed at new programs, middle-range programs with similar objectives, programs where information is available or can be obtained at minimum cost, and programs where there is a clear relationship between input and output. However, even within these limitations a number of new trends associated with the use of management technologies may emerge that will affect educational organization and administration (Culbertson et al. 1969, p. 182).

It appears that as educational policy analysts become more proficient in the application of quantitative analysis, the scope and effectiveness of these tools and techniques are dramatically increased. A primary limitation of educational quantitative analysis in the past has been that studies were often conducted by those who were either insufficiently trained or not acquainted with quantitative analysis. It appears that the bridge between quantitative analysis and educational problems is becoming increasingly narrower. This closer relationship should result in analyses of higher quality that, in turn, should generate increased confidence in the applicability of these tools and techniques.

It is only natural to conclude this introductory chapter with some personal thoughts concerning the trends toward quantitative analysis in educational policy formation. It is my opinion that the trend should continue toward quantitative analysis of the phenomena of education with, unfortunately, cognitive outputs such as reading and mathematics being the principal outputs for evaluation. This prognosis is based upon the following observations.

First, education is an extremely expensive public service item in state budgets. It will naturally come under closer fiscal scrutiny for purposes of control or, more specifically, accountability (linking educational performance with cost). Education is now such a highly politicized institution and vulnerable to criticism from political forces that the defense of educational institutions will be derived principally from the analysis of outputs—again, this usually implies quantification.

Second, the enormous centripetal pull toward centralization and bureaucratization of the research and evaluation components of systems of education is propelling research in education toward greater use of quantitative analysis. The Central Planning Office of the University of California, state departments of education (who publish and compare reading scores by district much to the delight of some superintendents and despair of others), and federal governmental agencies, such as the National Institute of Education, are only a few examples of this centralization of data, analysis, and policy formation for controlling the direction of education and, more importantly, establishing its priorities and incentives.

Thus, an interesting contradiction emerges in terms of the organization of education. On the one hand, schools are moving toward greater decentralization, more local control and autonomy over inputs and minor, routine matters, and on the other hand, toward greater standardization of outputs as centralized data and research organizations, such as those mentioned previously, begin to exert greater control over school policies.

Third, if we examine the academic background of the directors and top echelon staff members of these centralized research organizations, we will find that they usually have strong quantitative orientation in psychology, economics, and sociology. These are important institutions as far as education is concerned since they pose major direct challenges, set the tempo, and call the tune for future practices in educational research. More importantly, however, institutions such as these will be the largest source of employment for college graduates, especially those with quantitative backgrounds.

Finally, education has dramatically changed in the way courts now view educational policies and practices. The legal concept of "reasonableness," which is amenable to soft analysis, impression, feeling, and other qualitative methodologies, has given way to the modern legal concept of "close scrutiny." This latter criterion can only be satisfied by dynamic analytical methodologies (usually quantitative) that must be able to withstand rigorous cross-examination in a court of law. Education is a fundamental right that affects a person's entire life. All practices, therefore, have to be evaluated to the best of our abilities and as scientifically as possible—again, this usually implies some sort of quantification.

The implications of these trends are obvious for those contemplating a career in educational policy or research: Develop a repertoire of broad-based analytical, quantitatively based skills of inquiry. The technical foundation is extremely important if rapid movement into policy-making positons and in school districts is desired, since more traditional advancement through administrative ranks will be seriously curtailed by future declining enrollments and funds. It is hoped that the remaining chapters of this book can provide part of this technical foundation.

Univariate and Bivariate Analysis: Review of Elementary Statistics for Analysis of Educational Policy Issues

2-1 INTRODUCTION

The purpose of this chapter is to present as concisely as possible the multitude of standard statistical techniques associated with univariate and bivariate analysis. Since many of these concepts, such as t tests and F tests, will be used in later discussions on multivariate analysis, it is essential that a general understanding be achieved. The reader is strongly advised to read more comprehensive texts, such as Popham (1976), if this review presented here is not sufficient in detail because of lack of statistics background.

2-2 TYPES OF DATA

The quantitative analysis of data typically forms the basis for educational planning and policy. Educational data is classified into four general types: nominal, ordinal, interval, ratio.

Unordered, categorical data, such as sex or marital status, are called nominal data. Categories of these data merely name types (male/female, married/single/divorced/widowed, etc.)—thus, the name "nominal." The numerical codes we attach to each category (1 = single, 2 = married, 3 = divorced, etc.) have absolutely no comparative value, i.e., they do not have any ordering into better or worse, but merely signify specific, discrete attributes.

The second type of data, ordinal data, are also categorical in nature but differ from nominal data in that they have a rank order and can be placed on a scale allowing a judgment of "more" or "less" (but not how much more or how much less). For example, level of education (with categories such as elementary, secondary, college graduate) is rank ordered data; a college education is worth more or has a greater numerical value than a secondary education. A "strongly agree" response on a questionnaire item is more emphatic than an "agree" response. Thus, the numerical codes used for the categories of ordinal data have comparative value: if 1 is elementary education and 2 is secondary education, a code of 2 would be considered of higher value than a code of 1.

Interval and ratio data actually quantify the comparison between categories and are based upon some constant unit of distance or equal intervals; these two types of data are often discussed together as "equal-interval data." Interval scales are used in psychological measurement (scores on a test), while ratio scales dominate in physical measurements, such as height and weight. Ratio data differ from interval data by having an absolute zero point in addition to equal intervals; the ratio of any two points on ratio scales measuring the same trait or phenomenon will be the same regardless of the unit of measurement used. For example, weight is measured on a ratio scale where zero actually means an absence of weight; and the ratio of the weights of two objects will be the same whether the objects are measured in grams or pounds. Thus, if 454 grams or 1 pound is the weight of object A and 908 grams or 2 pounds is the weight of object B, then the ratio of B to A is 2 regardless of the unit of measure. On the other hand, Centigrade or Fahrenheit temperature measurements are interval scales because $0°$ is an arbitrary point on each scale (and does not mean absence of heat); the ratio of two points on one scale would not be the same as the ratio of two equivalent temperatures on the other scale. For example, the ratio of $0°C$ and $100°C$ is not the same as the ratio between $32°F$ and $212°F$. Physical measurements of objects, phenomena, or people are often examples of ratio data;

however, few psychological measurements can be classified as ratio scales. Most psychological measurements are presumed to be interval scales because the zero points are arbitrarily set, and the intervals on the scale are assumed to be constant. Thus, a difference of 10 points is regarded as being the same whether the scores were 20 and 30 or 70 and 80 (i.e., a given interval has the same meaning or value anywhere in the range).

The structure of a ratio scale is undistorted under "scalar" transformations such as $x' = ax$ ($a > 0$); thus if $y = 3x$ then $y' = 3x'$ (one measurement is three times the other in both cases). For example, one can transform inches (x) into feet (x') by the formula $x' = 1/12x$.

The structure of the interval scale is undistorted under "linear" transformations $x' = ax + b$, ($a > 0$). Thus to convert the temperature in °Fahrenheit (x) to Centigrade (x') involves the transformation $x' = 5/9$ ($x - 32$). Note that in the linear transformation the y-intercept or b term determines where the arbitrary zero point is located.

Interval and ratio data can also be classified as discrete (no fractional parts) or continuous (fractional parts allowed). For example, number of children in a family is an integer (whole number) and is considered discrete data, while a person's weight can take any value within a range and can be considered continuous data.

2-3 DISPLAY OF DATA

Since data form an essential part of quantitative analysis, methods for displaying data should be carefully chosen by the policy analyst to convey the maximum amount of information. If it is desired to examine changes in frequencies and to convey these changes over specified intervals, one might use a polygon line graph (continuous change) or a histogram (discrete change). (See Figures 2-1 and 2-2.) Figure 2-3 depicts a horizontal bar graph that is useful for conveying progress in a "competition" or race to raise money, register voters, and so on.

Another means of presenting data, where the central focus is percentage allocations of some total value, is a circle graph. In this type of data presentation (usually for allocation of budgets), the percentages refer to the central angles of a circle (25% = 90°, 50% = 180°, etc.) and the "pieces of pie" are a direct visualization of how the whole is divided.

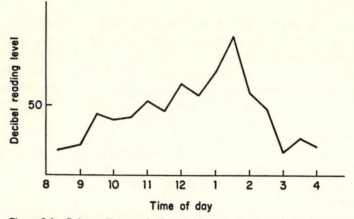

Figure 2-1. Polygon line graph: Comparing noise levels at a given school site at various times of the school day.

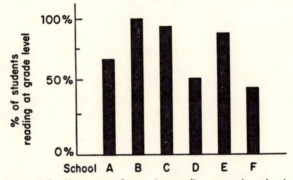

Figure 2-2. Histogram: Comparing reading scores by school site.

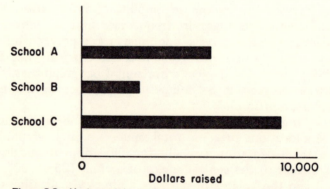

Figure 2-3. Horizontal bar graph: Comparison of school sites in terms of fund raising.

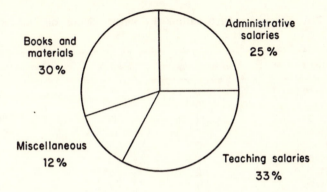

Figure 2-4. Circle graph: Allocation of a budget for a Title III program.

The beneficial feature of circle graphs is that by knowing the value of the whole (e.g., as in Figure 2-4, knowing the total budget for the Title III program), we can directly compare the value of each category or component. Thus, from Figure 2-4 if the total budget is $1,500,000.00, then administrative salaries (25%) = $375,000.00, teaching salaries (33%) = $495,000.00, miscellaneous (12%) = $180,000.00, and books and materials (30%) = $450,000.000. To find the central angle for any category in a circle graph, multiply 360° times the proportion of the whole amount consumed by the category.

$$\text{Miscellaneous} = (360°) \times \frac{180,000}{1,500,000} = 43.2°$$

Another useful data presentation mode that will be discussed extensively in Chapter 8 is the Ogive graph of cumulative frequency or probability distribution. Graphs of this type plot intervals versus cumulative percent and allow the analyst to view instantly where the majority of the distribution is located. Using the formula

$$P_j = \frac{N_j}{N} \times 100$$

where N_j is the number in interval or category j and N is the total, the percentage is calculated for each interval and a running total of percentages recorded. For example, suppose the number of students in Table 2-1 were determined for each of the 10 percentile

Table 2-1. Frequency Distribution of Students' Scores on Standardized Tests

Percentile interval	Frequency	Percent	Cumulative percent
1–10	8	8	8
11–20	25	25	33
21–30	47	47	80
31–40	10	10	90
41–50	3	3	93
51–60	2	2	95
61–70	2	2	97
71–80	1	1	98
81–90	1	1	99
91–100	1	1	100
	N = 100		

intervals on a standardized test. By plotting the cumulative percentage against score interval, we derive an Ogive graph of the form shown in Figure 2-5. Thus, from Figure 2-5 it is easy to visualize that a great majority of students in this school are below the 50th percentile.

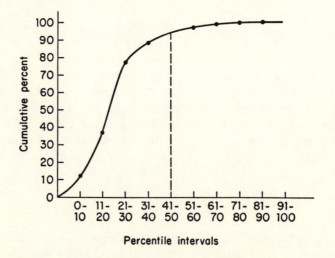

Figure 2-5. Graph of cumulative probability distribution.

2-4 SAMPLING PROCEDURES

As an educational analyst, one will probably find it necessary to collect data, using survey research methods, in order to gain insight into important educational policy problems. To accomplish this task, attention must first be directed toward rational and scientific sampling procedures. Samples are used when the populations being studied are very large and hence too time consuming and costly to survey in their entirety. More importantly, sampling is used because measurements can actually be made more accurately on smaller sample sizes. Thus errors which might be introduced or associated with collecting information in large samples is substantially reduced using sampling procedures.

The basic concept of sampling theory is to generalize information to an entire population from measurements taken from a small sample or subset of a population. For example, suppose we were interested in determining the average income for fathers of 5,000 students in a certain high school. Using sampling theory, we could use a small sample of students to make precise measurements of fathers' income, then generalize the results to the entire population of students at the high school.

To accomplish this end, the sample must be chosen in such a way that each individual in the total population being studied has an equal chance of being included in the sample used for the analysis. Suppose it is decided to generate a random sample of 200 students. First, each student (5,000) at the school is assigned an identification number. Then a four-digit field (either down the rows or across the columns) from a table of random numbers, as found in the appendix (pp. 257–262), is selected arbitrarily. The analyst then merely selects the next 200 random four-digit numbers (going across the columns or down the rows) ignoring all repeats and numbers greater than 5,000. Students with identification numbers the same as those chosen from the table of random numbers become the sample of 200 students to be used in the analysis. The researcher is then assured that the 200 students selected for the sample are random.

Suppose the school is half boys and half girls and the analyst wants to be sure the final random sample is 50% girls. This stratified type of random sample is derived by ignoring random numbers that result in the selection of a girl if the sample already has 100 girls. Such a procedure insures both randomness as well as the final percentage of boys to girls being exactly that found in the population. Stratified sampling is appropriate in situations where we know the population is composed of distinguishable levels or strata which can be accounted for as sampling is performed.

Another type of sampling procedure called systematic sampling is useful when we have serially ordered objects (such as school records listed alphabetically in a drawer), but the objects are randomly arranged with respect to the characteristic of interest. In this sampling procedure we randomly select the first object, then select the remaining objects at some specified interval (for example, every twentieth object) until we reach the required sample size.

In summary, a population is defined as the group or universe of individuals under investigation, while the subset of the population, a sample, is the portion of the population actually investigated. The procedure for deriving the sample must insure that each individual in the population has an equal chance of being selected for the sample. Random sampling procedures, using a table of random numbers, insure such required randomness.

Measurements or observations are made on each member of the sample with the hope that appropriate population parameters (mean, standard deviation) can be estimated. The effectiveness of the sampling procedure can be found using standard statistical tests. Many of these statistical tests are discussed in Sections 2-7 and 2-8.

2-5 DISTRIBUTIONS

One of the preliminary steps in social science research is to systematically investigate how certain data are distributed, in terms of frequency, for a given sample population.

Suppose the plot of the frequency distribution of scores for a certain aptitude test at a given school site looked like that in Figure 2-6. Such a distribution would be called negatively skewed since the direction of the tail or extension in the distribution is downward or toward the low scores. The reverse situation, with the tail of the distribution extending outward as shown in Figure 2-7, is called positively skewed. Thus, for a negatively skewed distribution we would expect the highest frequency (i.e., most of the scores, individuals, etc.) to be toward the right end of the distribution or above the mean score (such as the distribution of scores on an easy examination, e.g., a qualifying test for

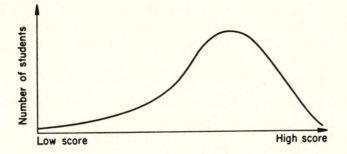

Figure 2-6. Negatively skewed distribution.

admittance to a program); and for a positively skewed distribution we would expect the highest frequency to be toward the left end of the distribution or below the mean score (such as the distribution of scores on a difficult test, e.g., achievement test).

There are other types of distributions that reflect certain behavior patterns of the indivduals in a sample. Suppose we were to plot the number of students turning in term papers at the required deadline period and days after the deadline. The plot for conforming behavior is J-shaped as in Figure 2-8. The J-type distribution is extremely difficult to deal with statistically because of its shape. Usually the distribution is broken into two groups, deadline and after deadline, and analyzed separately.

Another distribution that appears frequently in educational policy research is what is known as a bimodal distribution, where there are two "peaks" in the distribution. Suppose we were investigating the average achievement (grade point average—G.P.A.) of a high school that consists of 50% students from poor, culturally disadvantaged backgrounds and 50% from middle/upper class,

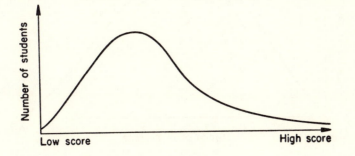

Figure 2-7. Positively skewed distribution.

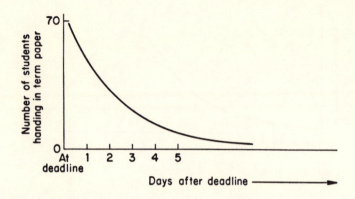

Figure 2-8. Graph of conformity distribution (J-shaped).

advantaged backgrounds. A frequency plot of average achievement for the total sample is shown in Figure 2-9. The slight depression in the middle of the distribution might be due to the fact that we are really dealing with two distributions or a bimodal distribution, one for each group being analyzed, as shown in Figure 2-10. While the foregoing illustrative distribution is symmetrical, bimodal distributions can be heavily asymmetrical. If, for example, in Figure 2-10 low SES (Socio Economic Status) children outnumbered high SES children 3 to 1, the resulting graph of the distribution might be too complex to analyze visually.

There are other distributions—beta + and beta − (similar to positively and negatively skewed distributions), gamma, chi square, F, binomial, t—all with special properties that relate frequency of

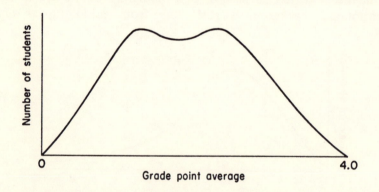

Figure 2-9. Graph of bimodal distribution of achievement.

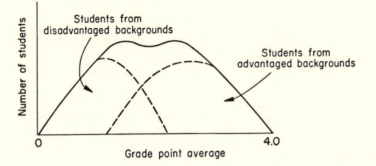

Figure 2-10. Composite graph of bimodal distribution of student achievement.

occurrence to some output measure or statistic such as a probability. Some of these distributions will be examined in greater detail in Sections 2-7 and 2-8 since many relate to statistical tests of significance.

Fortunately for social scientists, most phenomena studied tend to follow a distribution that is somewhat "normal" in shape; that is, in these distributions most observations are in the middle ranges with a few observations at either extreme. The binomial distribution, which describes dichotomous populations (that is, where some members possess a certain characteristic and the rest do not), approaches a normal shape when applied to populations larger than about 30. For example, suppose we had six coins, flipped them all at once, and recorded the number of heads. (See Figure 2-11.) Notice that after a few tosses the distribution has a strange shape. After a large number of tosses, the distribution "fills" out and begins to take a normal shape.

The primary distribution of concern to policy analysts is the normal distribution, since it serves as the best approximation to the kinds of distributions frequently encountered in educational policy research. The formula for the normal distribution is defined as

$$F(x) = \frac{1}{\sigma(2\pi)^{\frac{1}{2}}} \, e^{-\frac{1}{2}[(x-\mu)/\sigma]^2}$$

where μ is the population mean and σ^2 is the population variance. The following facts are associated with the normal distribution:

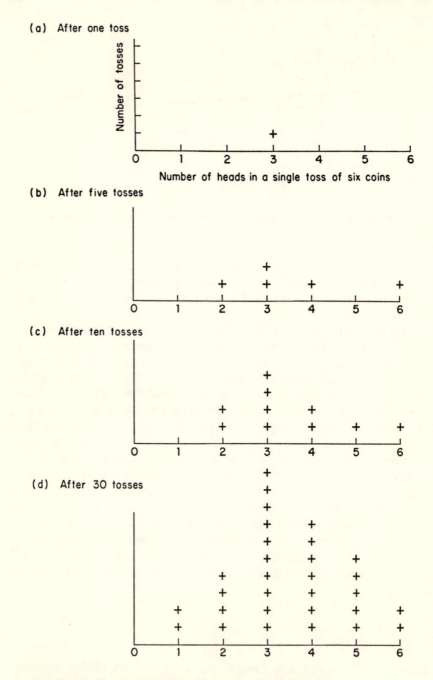

Figure 2-11. From binomial distribution to normal distribution.

1. completely determined by μ and σ (mean and standard deviation);
2. somewhat bell-shaped;
3. symmetric about μ (mean);
4. has a total area equal to 1;
5. extends indefinitely in both directions;
6. has mean, median, and mode equal to each ot'ier; **and**
7. lies above the x-axis.

A picture of the normal distribution is given in Figure 2-12.

There are four important statistics associated with a distribution. The first three are measures of central tendency, and the fourth is a measure of variability:

1. the mode, which is the point of highest probability or frequency in the distribution;
2. the median, which is the middle or point at which half the distribution is above and half the distribution is below;
3. the mean, which is the sum of the individual measurements divided by the total number of individual measurements; and
4. the variability or the scatter of scores about the mean of the distribution.

The mean $(\bar{x})$ is derived from the formula $x = \Sigma x/N$, where N is the sample size, and is truly the balance point of the distribution. It is sometimes called the center of gravity, or the main measure of central tendency. The most important properties of the mean are its stability as a measure of central tendency (since it is the balance point) and its usefulness in computing other measures of the distribution. The stability of the mean can be demonstrated by random sampling, say in a high school, 100 students and noting

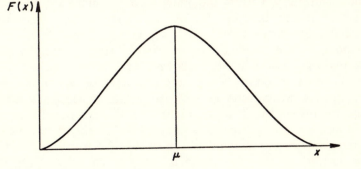

Figure 2-12. Normal distribution curve.

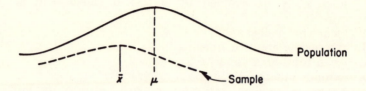

Figure 2-13. Population and sample distribution (normal).

the mean IQ (see Figure 2-13) where $\bar{x}$ (statistic) is the mean of the sample and μ (parameter) is the mean of the population. If we examined an infinite number of sample means $\bar{x}$ and found their mean $\mu_{\bar{x}}$, then

$$\mu_{\bar{x}} = \mu_x$$

In statistical analysis we cannot investigate an infinite set of samples. Instead we investigate one sample, use $\bar{x}$ as an estimate of the population mean μ_x, and then using formulas (to be discussed later) find the limits within which the true population mean probably lies.

One shortcoming in using the mean in educational policy is the implicit utility or value judgment of the measure. Suppose we were interested in the mean change in score as a result of some educational treatment. Using the mean as a basis for analysis would imply that one individual moving up ten units will exactly balance ten individuals moving down one unit. In many policy situations the fact that ten students went down in score is more important than one student moving up.

The median divides the distribution exactly in half; that is, it is the point midway within the range. To calculate the median, all measurements for the distribution are rank ordered from low to high. The measurement where half the measures are above and half are below is the median. It is useful when dealing with distributions that are markedly skewed or that are generally symmetrical but include a few extreme scores, or when performing measurements where one end of the scale of scores is not long enough to reveal the true variability of the sample. Thus, if the distribution is not perfectly symmetrical, it might be more appropriate to use the median as a measure of central tendency than the mean. Notice that the mean is sensitive to extreme changes in score for a few individuals, whereas the median is relatively stable in this situation.

The mode is the least stable of the central tendency measures since it only concerns itself with the point where the greatest frequency occurs. Its main use is to identify the point with greatest frequency or the most common score in a distribution. Figure 2-14 depicts where the mean, median, and mode can be placed relative to each other, in various types of distributions.

Variability (or deviation) in a sample distribution is described as

$$D_i = x_i - \overline{x}$$

where D_i is the variability, x_i is the observation, and $\overline{x}$ is the mean for distribution. The variance is then defined as the sum of average squared deviations from the mean

$$V = \frac{\sum\limits_{i=1}^{N} (x_i - \overline{x})^2}{N} = \frac{\sum\limits_{i=1}^{N} D_i^2}{N}$$

The statistic V is an estimate of the population paramater σ_x^2.

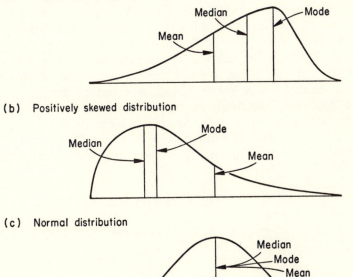

(a) Negatively skewed distribution

(b) Positively skewed distribution

(c) Normal distribution

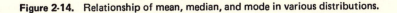

Figure 2-14. Relationship of mean, median, and mode in various distributions.

The standard deviation is the square root of the variance:

$$SD \text{ (or } S) = \sqrt{\frac{\Sigma (x_i - \bar{x})^2}{N}}$$

Many statisticians use the quantity $N - 1$ in place of N when estimating sample variance or standard deviation because $N - 1$ corresponds to the degrees of freedom in the calculation of the statistic (since one degree of freedom is taken because the mean is specified). The sample standard deviation is thus defined as

$$S = \sqrt{\frac{\Sigma(x_i - \bar{x})^2}{N - 1}}$$

At this point, the concept of degrees of freedom should be discussed. Suppose we had four scores (3, 4, 5, 6), and we were asked to tell what the first score was without having seen the above scores. Only a wild guess could be made and almost any number could be chosen. The same would occur if the first score were given, and we were asked for the second. In other words, each score has a complete freedom to vary. Suppose in this example that the mean of 4.5 and scores 3, 4, and 5 were given; then the only value possible for the fourth score is 6. Thus, if the mean is known, the missing score can be determined by our knowledge of the other three scores. One degree of freedom is used to calculate the mean, thus the standard deviation is estimated from $N - 1$ elements which are free to vary.

For large samples $N > 30$, the biased estimate $S = [\Sigma(x_i - \bar{x})^2 / N]^{1/2}$, and the unbiased estimate $S = [\Sigma(x_i - \bar{x})^2 /(N - 1)]^{1/2}$, are essentially the same. The sum of any set of deviation scores is zero. For example,

$$
\begin{array}{ccc}
 & 4 & D_i = (x_i - \bar{x}) = 0 \\
 & 5 & 1 \\
 & \underline{3} & \underline{-1} \\
\Sigma x_i = \text{total} = 12 & & \Sigma D_i = 0 \\
\bar{x} = 4 &
\end{array}
$$

This is one reason why the deviations are squared first and the standardized measure of the variance of a sample distribution is

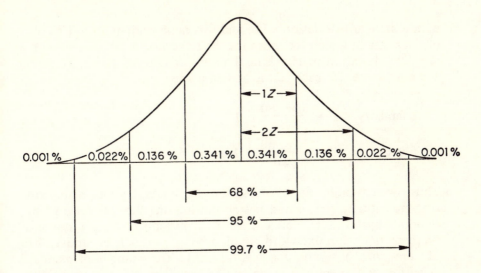

Figure 2-15. Percent of distribution at various standard deviations from the mean.

defined as the square root of the variance or

$$S = \left[\sum_{i=1}^{N} \frac{(x_i - \bar{x})^2}{N - 1} \right]^{\frac{1}{2}}$$

The standard deviation or standard measure of variation is useful in finding the percentages of the total distribution within certain standard deviations. Figure 2-15 records the percentage of the normal distribution found within certain standard deviations of the mean. Section 2-6 expands upon these standard characteristics of the normal distribution to develop the concept of statistical confidence.

2-6 STATISTICAL CONFIDENCE

Knowing the mean and standard deviation of a distribution, an individual score can be judged in terms of performance relative to a reference group (remember all we need is a mean and standard deviation to completely describe a normal distribution) by converting the observed score to a standard score using the formula $Z = (X_i - \mu)/\sigma_x$. For example, suppose a student scored 85 on a chemistry test in which the mean for the reference group was 80 with a standard deviation of 5, and this same student scored 75 on a physics test in which the mean for the reference group was 60 with a standard deviation of 10. Using the formula defined above, we derive standard scores for each test as shown below:

chemistry $\quad Z = \dfrac{85 - 80}{5} = 1$

physics $\quad\quad Z = \dfrac{75 - 60}{10} = 1.5$

Thus, even though the absolute score for chemistry was higher, the student actually performed better, considering the reference group, on the physics test. Notice that Z scores are nothing more than standard deviation units and are distributed normally around a mean of zero with a standard deviation of 1. The number of standard deviation units from the mean can be transformed into a probability value. A Z score of 1.96 is associated with a probability of 0.05 and means that only 2.5% of the distribution is higher than this value. This directly follows from the characteristics of the normal distribution described in Figure 2-15.

A statistic that provides the researcher with an estimation of the confidence that the sample mean represents the population mean is called the standard error of the mean. It should be clear that as

$$N \to \infty$$

then

$$\bar{x} \to \mu_x$$

where N is the sample size, $\bar{x}$ is the sample mean, and μ_x is the population mean. Thus, knowing the size and variability of the sample, we can estimate the standard deviation of a hypothetical distribution of sample means.

The standard error of the mean gives the researcher an indication of the confidence in examining how the sample mean differs from the population mean. A small standard error indicates the sample statistic is a reliable estimate of the corresponding population parameter.

$$SE_{\bar{x}} = \left(\frac{S_x^2}{N}\right)^{1/2} \quad \text{or} \quad \frac{S}{N^{1/2}}$$

where $SE_{\bar{x}}$ is the standard error of the mean and S_x^2 is the variance. The researcher should notice intuitively that the error in the measurement of the mean is directly dependent upon the variance of the distribution and inversely dependent on the sample size.

$$SE_{\bar{x}} \propto S_x^2$$

$$SE_{\bar{x}} \propto 1/N$$

Thus, if a researcher had a sample of ten students with a variance of 27, the same standard error of the mean would result as when the variance was 270 but the sample size was 100 or when the variance was 5.4 and the sample size was 2.

Suppose a standard error of the mean was calcuated to be 0.1 from the formula

$$SE_{\bar{x}} = \left(\frac{S_x^2}{N}\right)^{\frac{1}{2}}$$

We ask the following question: Having obtained a sample mean of 15 with $SE_{\bar{x}} = 0.1$, how confident are we that the population mean lies between 14.8 and 15.2? Figure 2-16 describes the procedure for answering this question.

We want to know the probability that the sample mean lies between the confidence limits of 14.8 and 15.2. We notice from Figure 2-16b that the probability is approximately 0.025 or 25 out of 1,000, that the hypothetical population mean is greater than 15, and from Figure 2-16c that the probability is 0.025 and that the hypothetical population mean is less than 15. Thus, the probability is 0.05 that the hypothetical population mean lies outside the interval and 0.95 that this mean is within the interval. Since $SE_{\bar{x}}$ is the standard deviation of the hypothetical distribution of sample mean scores, we can convert the deviation score (0.2 in the previous illustration) to a standard Z score by dividing the deviation score by the standard deviation (S).

$$SE_{\bar{x}} = 0.1 \text{ or standard deviation of hypothetical sample means}$$

deviation score = 0.2

$$Z = \frac{\text{deviation score}}{S} = \frac{0.2}{0.1} = 2$$

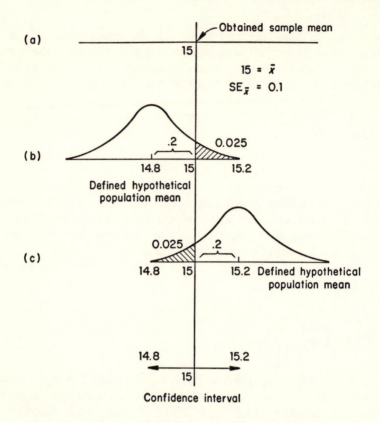

Figure 2-16. Determining confidence levels for a sample mean.

If we were to enter a "normal curve" table with a standard Z score of 2.00, we would see the area under the curve to be less than 0.025.

The standard error of the mean can be considered the standard deviation of a set of hypothetical means if the experiment were repeated· many times. The central notion is to obtain the best estimate of the population mean from a sample mean. If we performed the experiment hundreds of times, we would obtain hundreds of sample means, the distribution of which would have a mean and a standard deviation. The standard error of the mean is this standard deviation of hypothetical means.

2-7 DIFFERENCES BETWEEN MEANS

Often in educational policy analysis, it is important to know whether the means of two or more groups are statistically different from each other. In other words, are the samples being analyzed derived from different populations or are they merely samples from the same population? Using appropriate statistical analysis described below, it is possible to determine in probabilistic terms whether one or more populations are involved. The probability depends upon the size and direction of the observed differences between sample means and the variability of a hypothetical distribution of differences.

This type of analysis is the typical experimental design in education with treatment and control groups. For example, is the math achievement better for the group that has computer-aided instruction in math than for the group with traditional lecture instruction? The null hypothesis states that the difference between groups is not significant; that is, the observed difference is merely a chance difference resulting from ordinary sampling error. An arbitrary level of probability for the differences occurring at random or chance (called an alpha level, e.g., $P < 0.01$ or $P < 0.05$) is set, and the rejection or acceptance of this null hypothesis is then dependent upon this criterion. The alpha level informs us that the chance of the difference occurring at random is less than 1 out of 100 (or 5 out of 100, etc.).

Two Means: t Test

A t test is used to determine whether, in small samples, the differences in means between two distributions is statistically significant. For large sample sizes ($N > 30$) the t distribution approaches the normal distribution. t Ratios are derived from Z scores and have a distribution mean of zero. Therefore, t values are similar to Z scores, which relate standard deviation units to probabilities underneath the normal curve.

Notice that the distribution of t is determined by the number of degrees of freedom. The distribution of sample means is close to normal when $N \geq 30$. Below 30, the t distribution begins to flatten, making the use of Z unreliable. The value of t is determined by the degrees of freedom ($N - 1$) and the degree of confidence. The t distribution is often called Student's t because the individual who developed the test for small samples worked for a company which forbad publication of independent research. The individual therefore published his work and signed it "Student."

It is important to note that population(s) from which the sample(s) have been drawn should be normally distributed. In addition, if the researcher wants to be able to generalize the results of the t test to populations, then the samples must be randomly selected from the populations under consideration.

By using slightly different formulas for calculating t, t tests can be used to test for significance of a variety of statistics (testing either for differences between a pair of statistics or between a statistic and some given value):

1. statistical significance of a correlation coefficient r (Is the calculated r significantly different from zero?)

$$t = r\left(\frac{N-2}{1-r^2}\right)^{\frac{1}{2}}$$

where r is the correlation, N is the sample size, and $N - 2$ is the degrees of freedom;

2. difference between regression coefficients β_1 and β_2 (Is β_1 significantly different from β_2? A variation of this test can also be used to test whether a single coefficient is different from zero.)

$$t = \frac{\beta_1 - \beta_2}{S_\beta}$$

where $N - 1$ is the degrees of freedom and S_β is the standard deviation of the difference between betas;

3. difference between obtained and hypothetical ($\bar{x}_h$) means

$$t = \frac{\bar{x} - x_h}{SE_{\bar{x}}}$$

where $N - 1$ is the degrees of freedom and $SE_{\bar{x}}$ is the standard error of the mean;

4. difference between two independent means (typical in experimental designs)

$$t = \frac{\bar{x}_1 - \bar{x}_2}{\left(\dfrac{S_1^2}{N_1} + \dfrac{S_2^2}{N_2}\right)^{\frac{1}{2}}}$$

where N_1 and N_2 are the sample sizes, $(N_1 + N_2 - 2)$ is the degrees of freedom, and S_1^2 and S_2^2 are the variances of the two samples; and

5. differences between correlated means

$$t = \frac{\bar{x}_1 - \bar{x}_2}{SE_{\bar{x}_1 - \bar{x}_2}}$$

where $(N_1 + N_2 - 2)$ is the degrees of freedom, N_1 and N_2 are the sizes of the samples, and $SE_{\bar{x}_1 - \bar{x}_2}$ is the standard error of the difference scores.

Table 2-2 illustrates how a t test is used to examine differences in means for two populations. In this case the two groups are labeled superior and inferior teachers, and we need to examine whether teachers rated as "superior" teachers by raters achieve a different score on the Minnesota Teacher Attitude Inventory (MTAI) than a group of teachers rated "inferior."

The equation in item 4 is used to calculate the t statistic. In order to determine significance, the researcher must compare the calculated t value to values in a t table (see the appendix, Table 4, p. 266) using the desired probability or alpha level and the appropriate degrees of dreedom. For example, the tabled t value corresponding to an alpha level of 0.01 (column of table) and degrees of freedom $N_1 + N_2 - 2 = 142$ (row of table) is approximately 2.6.* Since in Table 2-2 the calculated $t = 2.81$ is greater than the tabled value 2.6, we can conclude that the sample of superior teachers do achieve different MTAI scores than the inferior teachers; that is, there is only one chance out of 100 that the difference between the groups could have occurred by chance.

Comparisons of Two or More Means

Sometimes behavioral research requires experimental designs comparing more than two groups. A sample t test could be used to assess the difference between two of the groups in this situation, but the overall probability of significance lowers considerably if

---

*Usually the columns of t tables correspond to probability levels for "one-tailed" tests, where the researcher is testing for a specific kind of difference between groups (i.e., *A is greater than B*); thus, when testing to see of two groups are merely *different from* each other (a "two-tailed" test), the researchers must use the column corresponding to half the desired probability level. (In a few tables, columns are labeled with both two-tailed and one-tailed probability levels; the researcher can then merely select the desired one.)

Table 2-2. Example of *t* Test: A Comparison of MTAI Scores for Superior and Inferior Teachers[a,b]

	Number	SD	Mean	t
Superior	72	40.6	23.6	
				2.81[c]
Inferior	72	38.8	5.3	

[a]*Source:* Popham and Trimble (1960). Reproduced with permission of the author and publisher.
[b]Superior and inferior teachers as determined by school principle.
[c]$P < 0.01$.

tests are also performed on other pairs of groups (e.g., groups 1-2, 1-3, and 2-3). Suppose the level of significance for each pair of groups 1-2, 1-3, and 2-3, is 0.95 using a *t* test; that is, group 1 is different from group 2 with 95% probability and so on. Then the probability of all three groups being statistically different from each other is only $(0.95)^3$ or 0.86.* A technique appropriate for analysis of multimean problems is called analysis of variance (ANOVA).

Analysis of variance differs from *t* test analysis in that the initial ratio is not the ratio of a difference in means to its standard error but the ratio of two estimates of the population variance—one estimate from the means of the categories or groups being studied and the other from individual scores within the categories. In other words, we would like to see if the variation between groups being studied is significantly higher than the variation between individuals within the groups. The distribution that this ratio follows is an *F* distribution, and the ratio itself is called an *F* ratio:

$$F = \frac{S_B^2}{S_W^2}$$

where $S_B{}^2$ is the variance between groups and $S_W{}^2$ is the variance

---

*In addition to labor saved by not taking a series of *t* tests for multimean experimental designs, the statistics based upon all the data have less error and are more stable than data which is only based upon part of the data. Of course as mentioned above with so many comparisons there is a higher probability that some will be statistically significant by chance. The 0.05 chance level with one comparison changes to .14 with three comparisons.

within groups. The numerator estimates the population variance from the variability of each of the category or group means, while the denominator estimates the population variance from the variability of individual scores within those categories. The result is a ratio of two estimates for the same population variance. The null hypothesis is that the two estimates are the same and that the ratio is one. In order to demonstrate significance, it must be shown that the ratio is different from one or specifically that the variance estimated from group means is greater than the variance estimated from individual scores. F Ratios larger than one can be evaluated by means of F tables that give the probability that any group differences could occur entirely by chance. (See the appendix for F tables, pp. 268–269.)

Thus, to test for the significant difference between the sample means, we compare the between-sample variation and the within-sample variation. The larger the first compared to the second, the more likely it is that the samples come from different populations.

The set of relations in analysis of variance is summarized as follows

Sample

	1	2	3 $\cdots m$
	X_{11}	X_{21}	$X_{31}\cdots X_{m1}$
	X_{12}	X_{22}	$X_{32}\ldots X_{m2}$
Observations	$\cdot$	$\cdot$	$\cdot$
	$\cdot$	$\cdot$	$\cdot$
	$\cdot$	$\cdot$	$\cdot$
	X_{1n}	X_{2n}	X_{3n} X_{mn}

where m is the number of groups and n is the number of cases. Consider

$$T_j = \sum_{i=1}^{n} X_{ij}$$

We first find the between-group variance

$$S_B^2 = \frac{1}{(m-1)(n)} \left[\Sigma T_j^2 - \frac{(\Sigma T_j)^2}{m} \right]$$

then the within-group variance

$$S_W^2 = \frac{1}{m(n-1)} \left[\Sigma X_{ij}^2 - \frac{\Sigma T_j^2}{n} \right]$$

We finally calculate the F ratio

$$F = \frac{S_B^2}{S_W^2}$$

The calculated F ratio is compared to the value found in an F table using the appropriate degrees of freedom and the desired probability level. If the calculated value is greater than the tabled value, the researcher can conclude that the groups differ significantly.

Analysis of variance results are usually presented in a table such as that in Table 2-3.

Figure 2-17 shows an analysis of variance situation where there is no difference among the three samples (left) ABC and one where there is a difference among the three samples $A'B'C'$. Note the similarities in the four distributions in the left-hand illustration in Figure 2-17. The last distribution was obtained by treating all measures as though they formed one total group rather than three separate groups. The means, ranges, and variances are identical; only the density of the distribution changes. We should expect that these samples were drawn from the same population. The situation is reversed with the right-hand illustration $A'B'C'$. Here the means and the variances are different, even though the arithmetic average for the means and variances are the same as those on the left-hand side. Essentially the variance of the pooled group is larger than the average variance for the three separate groups.

For cases where the null hypothesis is tenable, relatively little

Table 2-3. Simple Analysis of Variance of Final Achievement Performance of Five Groups of Students Taught by Different Instructional Variables[a]

Source of variation	Degrees of freedom	Sum-of-squares	Mean square	F
Between-groups	4	19.72	4.93	0.873
Within-groups	45	254.30	5.65	
Total	49	274.02		

[a]*Source:* From *Educational Statistics: Use and Interpretation* by W. James Popham. Copyright © 1967 by W. James Popham. By permission of Harper & Row, Publishers, Inc.

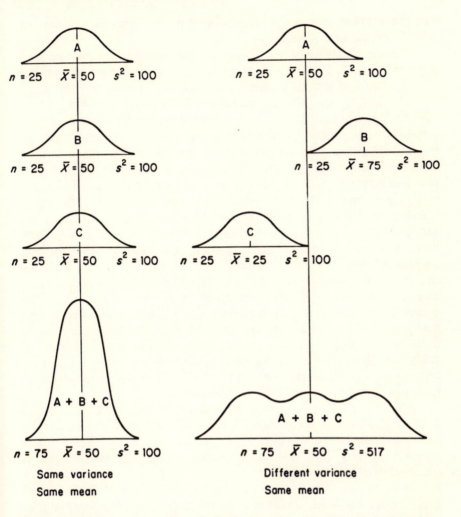

$n = 25$ $\bar{X} = 50$ $s^2 = 100$ $n = 25$ $\bar{X} = 50$ $s^2 = 100$

$n = 25$ $\bar{X} = 50$ $s^2 = 100$ $n = 25$ $\bar{X} = 75$ $s^2 = 100$

$n = 25$ $\bar{X} = 50$ $s^2 = 100$ $n = 25$ $\bar{X} = 25$ $s^2 = 100$

$n = 75$ $\bar{X} = 50$ $s^2 = 100$ $n = 75$ $\bar{X} = 50$ $s^2 = 517$

Same variance   Different variance
Same mean   Same mean

Figure 2-17. Graphical representation of analysis of variance—three separate samples and one pooled sample. *Source:* From *Educational Statistics: Use and Interpretation* by W. James Popham. Copyright © 1967 by W. James Popham. By permission of Harper & Row, Publishers, Inc.

difference between means will exist, and the average variance for the separate groups involved will be approximately equal to the variance of the pooled group. In cases where the null hypothesis is untenable, differences between means of the separate groups will be of greater magnitude so the variance of the pooled group will be considerably larger than the average variance of the separate groups. The statistical test is then to determine, using an F ratio, how great the difference between the variance of the pooled group and the average variance of the subgroups needs to be in order to reject the null hypothesis.

One-way analysis of variance with two groups and a *t* test give identical results. Both are dependent upon the random assignment of individuals to groups to eliminate bias due to unequal inputs.

In one-way analysis of variance, the analyst is interested in discovering whether there is a relationship between one output variable, such as test performance, and another variable, such as method of instruction represented by the groupings. When two or more variables affect the output variable, a more complex form of the analysis of variance model is required. This model for investigating one output variable and two or more influencing variables is known as multiple classification analysis of variance. For example, suppose we were interested in examining how treatment and teacher sex influence performance. A two-way analysis of variance could be used as is shown in Figure 2-18. We can now investigate main effects, treatment and teacher sex, as well as interaction effects, treatment with teacher sex. It is the mathematics involved in calculating these interaction effects that make multiple classification analysis of variance more complex as more intervening variables are considered. The basic theory of analyzing the variance of separate groups as well as total groups, only now with interaction effects considered, is still appropriate to multiple classification analysis of variance.

It is important to note that in analysis of variance it is assumed that each group is composed of randomly assigned students. The random assignment of individuals to groups is critical to the removal of any bias due to different inputs. In addition, it is assumed that the groups are normally distributed and that the variances within the groups are not substantially different from each other; however, violations of normality and homogeneity of

	Experimental treatment	Control treatment
Male teachers	Output measures	
Female teachers		

Figure 2-18. Two-way analysis of variance.

variance are not usually critical. In order to generalize the results, all subjects must have been randomly selected from the population.

To end a discussion on hypothesis testing, it is appropriate to discuss type I and type II errors. We may reject the null hypothesis when, in fact, the null hypothesis is true (type I error); or we may accept the null hypothesis when, in fact, it is false and some other hypothesis is true (type II error). If we increase the alpha level (level for accepting or rejecting the null hypothesis), we decrease the risk of type II error while increasing the risk of type I error. Decreasing the alpha level decreases type I error but increases type II error. To decrease the risk of making both types of error, we can increase the sample size thereby increasing the amount of information available upon which to base a decision.

2-8 SIGNIFICANCE OF FREQUENCY DIFFERENCES— CHI SQUARE

The chi square (χ^2) methodology is another tool used in a wide variety of situations by the policy analyst. The analyst often has data that is nominal in form in that the data can only be identified by group or class. For example, group members can only be identified as male or female; in some elections, voters may cast only Yes or No ballots. Consequently, the analyst collecting and displaying the data uses a contingency table type of format. (See Figure 2-19.) In contrast to some other methodologies, chi square is a tool for gauging the significance of the difference between sets of data frequency counts rather than an assessment of the relationship or the association. In chi square methodology, there are only two sets of data—"expected" and "observed"—even though there may be several categories in each set to be analyzed.

One set of data is considered expected because the analyst has drawn the frequency count from a defensible base, perhaps from theory or a clearly documented population, or from calculations based on marginal proportions (as in the example used in this section). Another set of frequency counts is called the observed data. Generally it is gathered by the analyst; occasionally, the second set may be existent and ready for testing. Whatever the source, given an expected set and an observed set, the analyst is ready for a mathematical assessment of the statistical significance of the difference between the two sets—a chi square test.

Broadly speaking, the analyst is asking, "Is the difference between the frequency counts of sufficient size that it could not

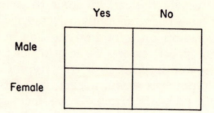

Figure 2-19. Contingency table.

have occurred by chance alone?" If Yes, the analyst must examine
the data in greater detail in a search for the reasons. Note that chi
square only tests for the statistical significance of the difference;
further searches for reasons must go beyond this method of
analysis.

Suppose we were interested in examining the voting in a bond
issue tax override election in a school district. A question that
might immediately come to mind is, "Did the men vote differently
than the women?" Data from a questionnaire asking how people
voted, when compiled and displayed, appear in Figure 2-20. Notice
that the data display in Figure 2-20 gives the frequency by which
Yes and No votes were cast for males and females. This is as
elemental and as explicit a display as the data permit; all other
data displays and any analysis require calculation and conversion.

By summing the number of males voting (row subtotal), we
find 100; for females we find 200. Likewise by summing the
number of votes cast Yes (column subtotal) we get 175; the
number of votes cast No was 125. The grand total of all votes cast
was 300. By inspection, males can be said to have voted equally

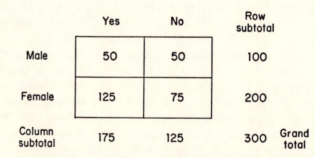

Figure 2-20. Vote on tax override—observed voting frequencies for males and females voting Yes and No.

Yes and No on the tax override—50 to 50 or 1:1. The voting of females was 125 to 75 or 5:3 for the Yes/No distribution. There appears to be a heavy skew for females to vote Yes. So the answer to our question is, "Yes, men and women voted differently." While this finding is an interesting descriptive statement, it does little to substantiate whether or not the observed differences could have occurred by chance alone. Before we can answer the question of occurrence by chance, other questions must be asked and steps must be taken.

Another question that could be raised is, "Did females and males vote differently from that which was expected?" A statement that logically explains the assumptions of the researcher in deriving the expected frequencies follows. The researcher or policy analyst can reasonably expect, in the absence of conflicting information, that females and males vote alike in an election; if not numerically equal, then in equal proportions. In algebraic notation the analyst writes $H:P_f = P_m$, where P_f is the proportion of females voting Yes and P_m is the proportion of males voting Yes; and this is the basis of our expected voting pattern. Having stated the assumption as an hypothesis, what is now needed is a way to express it quantitatively.

Previously, we added row subtotals and column subtotals calculating a grand total; these figures provide a base for determining the expected voting pattern. The expected pattern must be calculated for each cell (any single unit of frequency count). For example, in Figure 2-20, the cell having a frequency count of 75 is for females voting No.

The general procedure for calculating the expected frequency for a given cell follows: First, determine the proportion which the row subtotal is of the grand total—row subtotal divided by grand total. For example, if calculating the expected frequency count for the males/Yes cell, we are determining the proportion which male votes are of the overall total vote.

Second, multiply this derived figure by the Yes column subtotal. Having determined the portion of the total vote that is male, this total is used to calculate the portion of the total Yes vote that can be attributed to males if an assumption of equal proportion is applicable. The calculations appear thus

$$\frac{\text{Row subtotal}}{\text{Grand total}} \times \text{Column subtotal} = \text{Expected frequency}$$

$$\frac{100}{300} \times 175 = 58.3$$

or about 58 males can be expected to vote Yes. The same procedure is followed for each of the other cells

males expected to vote No: (100/300) × 125 = 41.7 or 42
females expected to vote Yes: (200/300) × 175 = 116.7 or 117
females expected to vote No: (200/300) × 125 = 83.3 or 83

Drawing on the calculations that have been made, a table can now be constructed giving both observed and expected voting frequencies.

Figure 2-21 presents a substantially different view of voting behavior than was presented in Figure 2-20. The difference can be accounted for by the calculations that adjusted the disproportionate male/female voter turnout. Consequently, when we view Figure 2-21, we observe that males were expected to vote with greater frequency for a tax override than actually occurred; females voted at a frequency higher than expected. Still, we cannot, on the basis of this data alone, responsibly answer the question, "Are the differences between observed voting and expected voting statistically significant, that is, are the differences so great as to rule out the probability that the differences occurred by chance alone?"

At this point, the chi square methodology can be applied to calculate a statistic from which the analyst can give a more definite answer concerning the relationship between sex and voting behavior. The data from Figure 2-21 is substituted into the chi square formula and calculations are carried out to give the chi square statistic:

	Voting Yes		Voting No	
	Observed	Expected	Observed	Expected
Male	50	58	50	42
Female	125	117	75	83

Figure 2-21. Vote on tax override—observed and expected voting frequencies for males and females voting Yes and No.

$$\chi^2 = \sum_{i=1}^{c} \frac{(\text{Observed frequency} - \text{Expected frequency})^2}{\text{Expected frequency}}$$

where c is the number of cells. Verbally, the chi square statistic is the sum of the following treatment of the frequencies in all cells: for each cell, subtract the expected frequency from the observed frequency and square the remainder; the product of the squaring is divided by the expected frequency. Arithmetically, the chi square statistic is calculated, in the current example,* in this manner:

$$\chi^2 = \frac{(50 - 58)^2}{58} + \frac{(50-42)^2}{42} + \frac{(125 - 117)^2}{117} + \frac{(75 - 83)^2}{83}$$

$$\chi^2 = \frac{(-8)^2}{58} + \frac{(8)^2}{42} + \frac{(8)^2}{117} + \frac{(-8)^2}{83}$$

$$\chi^2 = \frac{64}{58} + \frac{64}{42} + \frac{64}{117} + \frac{64}{83}$$

$$\chi^2 = 1.10 + 1.52 + 0.55 + 0.77$$

$$\chi^2 = 3.94$$

To answer the question, "Are the voting differences statistically significant?" the analyst needs only to interpret the chi square statistic. To aid in the interpretation of the chi square statistic, probability tables have been developed and can be found in the appendix. The arrangement of the probability tables allows for a range of significance levels, such as 0.5, 0.3, 0.2, 0.1, 0.05, and 0.01, and for a range of degrees of freedom from one to 25 or more. An explanation of how we determine the number of degrees of freedom for any chi square problem is necessary. The key lies in the number of cells.

We have noted that the contingency table (Figure 2-20) developed for this example is arranged in rows and columns. Figure 2-20 has two rows and two columns:

---

*Note: To keep the example simple, Figure 2-20 has only four cells, which is referred to as a 2 X 2 table. To be mathematically correct, an adjustment, the Yates correction for continuity, is required when the cell arrangement is 2 X 2 or smaller. "To use this correction, a value of 0.5 is subtracted from the absolute value (irrespective of algebraic sign) of the numerator contribution of each cell. . . ." (Popham and Sirotnick 1973, p. 285).

1. count the number of cells in the top row (NR), and from this number, subtract the number one;
2. count the number of cells in the left column (NC), and from this number, subtract the number one;
3. multiply the remaining number of rows by the remaining number of columns; and
4. the product is the number of degrees of freedom.

Mathematically, the formula and calculations are

$$df = (NR - 1) \times (NC - 1)$$

$$df = (2 - 1) \times (2 - 1)$$

$$df = 1 \times 1$$

$$df = 1$$

where df is the degrees of freedom. Interpretation of the results of the calculations of the chi square statistic and the determination of the degrees of freedom is straightforward:

1. locate a table containing the distribution of the probabilities for the chi square statistic;
2. along the left-hand side, the first column contains the degrees of freedom in ascending numerical order—in our example, $df = 1$;
3. along the top row are the significance levels in numerically diminishing, significance-ascending order; in our example consider the desired level to be 0.05, $P \leqslant 0.05$;
4. in the cell in the probability table that corresponds to $df = 1$ and $P \leqslant 0.05$, the number is 3.841;
5. to be significant at the 0.05 level, the calculated chi square statistic must be numerically larger than 3.841; if it is equal to or less than 3.841, it cannot be considered statistically significant;* and
6. our calculated chi square statistic is 3.94, which is greater than 3.841 and statistically significant!

But what does this mean? By being statistically significant, our chi square statistic permits us to report that our result, or one

---

*Note that if the contingency table is one in which one or both variables are nominal, the chi square statistic is used to test the hypothesis that the cell frequencies occurred at chance. If both variables are ordinal, the table may be examined for association using a gamma statistic (a nonparametric measure of association).

more extremely unbalanced, could occur only five times out of 100 by chance alone. Therefore, we conclude that men and women voted significantly different; the sex of the voter made a significant difference in the vote cast.

2-9 MEASURES OF ASSOCIATION AND CAUSALITY

Both in basic educational research and in policy-oriented research, the relationships between variables must be established before more sophisticated methodologies are employed. A standardized index of relationship or association between variables is the coefficient of correlation. While the analyst might define contingency tables with finer categories and analyze the association using chi square or gamma, with continuous (ratio and interval) data correlation is used. Correlation is a number that when close to zero indicates a lower degree of association and when larger indicates a higher degree of relationship between two variables. The index, which is really a standardized scale, ranges from -1, indicating perfect negative association, through zero, indicating no association, to $+1$, indicating perfect positive association.

Correlation can be used by the analyst to understand the nature and degree of an association between pairs of variables such as:

1. pupil intelligence and achievement or
2. student reading ability and student performance in mathematics.

Thus, correlation coefficients are standardized measures of association that consist of two information parts, magnitude and direction. At the extremes of correlation, we have perfect $r = +1$ where every individual is precisely the same distance (in standard deviations) above or below the mean for measure X as he is in the same direction for measure Y; we also have perfect $r = -1$ where every individual is precisely the same distance above the mean on measure X as below the mean on measure Y. Mathematically, this can be seen as follows:

$$r = \frac{\sum_{i=1}^{n} x_i y_i}{\left[\left(\sum_{i=1}^{n} x_i^2\right)\left(\sum_{i=1}^{n} y_i^2\right)\right]^{1/2}}$$

where x_i is the distance from $\overline{X}$ or $(X_i - \overline{X})$ and y_i is the distance from $\overline{Y}$ or $(Y_i - \overline{Y})$. If $x = y$, then

$$r = \frac{\Sigma x_i^2}{[(\Sigma x_i)^2 (\Sigma x_i)^2]^{\frac{1}{2}}} = \frac{\Sigma x_i^2}{[(\Sigma x_i^2)^2]^{\frac{1}{2}}} = \frac{\Sigma x_i^2}{\Sigma x_i^2} = 1$$

If $x = -y$ then

$$r = \frac{\Sigma - x_i^2}{[(\Sigma x_i)^2 (\Sigma x_i)^2]^{\frac{1}{2}}} = \frac{-\Sigma x_i^2}{\Sigma x_i^2} = -1$$

This equation can be written as

$$r = \frac{\Sigma (X_i - \overline{X})(Y_i - \overline{Y})}{[\Sigma (X_i - \overline{X})^2 \Sigma (Y_i - \overline{Y})^2]^{\frac{1}{2}}}$$

which is the formula version most commonly used by statisticians for the Pearson r where both variables are continuous.* The Pearson r is also termed product moment because the product XY in the numerator of the foregoing equation is important in determining the strength of the association. To illustrate a basic feature of correlation, consider the following problem (Table 2-4) where (1) data describing pupil intelligence and achievement are ordered and (2) where the data are placed at random. Thus, it can be seen from Table 2-4 that when X and Y are placed in direct association, the product XY is maximal and minimal when the data are placed at random. A plot or scattergram of pairs of variables is another way to illustrate the concept of correlation (Figure 2-22).

It should be stressed that causality is not considered in correlation analysis. Correlation is a symmetric or reflexive statistic (the association between the variable pair 1 and 2 is the same as

---

*There are other types of correlation coefficients in addition to the Pearson r product moment correlation. These are the phi coefficients, which are a measure of association between two dichotomous categorical variables, and the biserial, which is the measure of association between a dichotomous and a continuous variable. The point biserial and tetrachoric coefficients concern measures of association where one or two respectively of the continuous variables are artificially reduced to two categories. While each of the above coefficients are determined using different equations, the index generated for the measure of association still varies between -1 to $+1$.

Table 2-4. Illustration of Product Moment Correlation

	Ordered			Random	
IQ (X)	G.P.A. (Y)	XY	IQ (X)	G.P.A. (Y)	XY
160	4.0	640	160	3.2	512
140	3.7	518	140	3.7	518
120	3.2	384	120	3.0	360
110	3.0	330	110	3.2	352
$\Sigma X = 530$ $\bar{X} = 132.5$	$\Sigma Y = 13.9$ $\bar{Y} = 3.48$	$\Sigma XY = 1872$	$\Sigma X = 530$ $\bar{X} = 132.5$	$\Sigma Y = 13.1$ $\bar{Y} = 3.28$	$\Sigma XY = 1742$

between 2 and 1); it cannot deal effectively with policy oriented questions except for showing that an association exists between two variables. For example, suppose the correlation between the amount of dollars spent per pupil in a school district and reading scores is 0.75. This is a relatively high correlation indicating that districts spending larger amounts of money per pupil generally have higher reading scores (or districts with higher reading scores are usually those spending more money per pupil). The policy question might be "How much increase in reading scores would result for each additional dollar of district expenditure?" While correlation may show that an association exists between reading scores and expenditure levels, the predictive causal model, namely how does expenditure predict reading, is left undefined.

Because correlation summarizes a quantity of data on a standardized scale from -1 to $+1$, a great deal of information is lost to the policy analyst. For example, all three graphs in Figure 2-23 have the same correlation coefficient ($r = 0.65$) or measure of association, yet a scattergram of the data indicates three very different relationships.

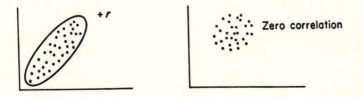

Figure 2-22. A scattergram approach to correlation. The narrower the cigar, the more strength of association between variables.

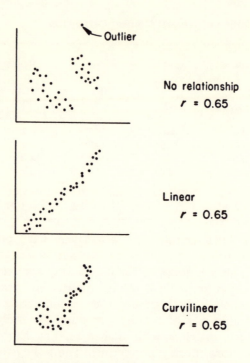

Figure 2-23. Different data scattergrams with same correlation.

Correlations between several pairs of variables are often written in matrix form as shown in Figure 2-24.

Suppose that there is a perfect correlation between IQ and achievement. Knowing a pupil's IQ would allow us to estimate his achievement with perfect accuracy. Thus, knowing one variable would allow us to explain 100% of the variation in the other variable. If the correlation between the two variables is zero, then knowing the value of one variable will not estimate any particular value for the other. We could do no better statistically than to use the mean value as the estimate for this second variable. Suppose the correlation between these two variables is 0.5. Just knowing IQ would allow less than a perfect prediction of achievement, but it would at least allow better than just using the mean value of achievement. If we square the correlation coefficient, thus $r = 0.5$, $r^2 = 0.25$, then we derive a quantitative measure for the amount of variation in one variable that can be explained by the other. Thus, 25% of the error in our estimate of a student's achievement is reduced by knowing the student's IQ.

Another way of quantitatively stating the above is to visualize a situation where the standard deviation for the measures of student achievement is 10. Knowing that the correlation between IQ and achievement is 0.5, we can reduce this error by using our knowledge of the student's IQ. In fact, in this hypothetical example the standard deviation of the difference between actual and predicted values (residual) for student achievement is now 7.5; that is, the standard deviation of the residuals (also called standard error) is reduced by 25%.

If the variables being analyzed can be assumed to be normally distributed, then additional interpretive information can be supplied along with the correlation coefficient. The statistical significance of a correlation coefficient can be found using

$$t = r \left(\frac{N-2}{1-r^2} \right)^{\frac{1}{2}}$$

and examining the t statistic with $n - 2$ degrees of freedom.

From measurements on a number of variables, correlation analysis measures the strength of association between pairs of variables. Degree of association runs from +1.0 (perfect) through

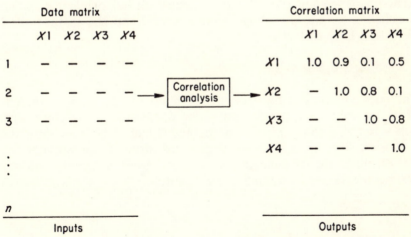

Data matrix						Correlation matrix			
	$X1$	$X2$	$X3$	$X4$			$X1$	$X2$	$X3$	$X4$

Data matrix	Correlation matrix
	$X1$ $X2$ $X3$ $X4$		$X1$ $X2$ $X3$ $X4$
1	— — — —	$X1$	1.0 0.9 0.1 0.5
2	— — — — → Correlation analysis →	$X2$	— 1.0 0.8 0.1
3	— — — —	$X3$	— — 1.0 -0.8
⋮		$X4$	— — — 1.0
n			

Inputs	Outputs
Repeated measures on a set of variables $X1$, $X2$, $X3$, and $X4$.	Correlations, a high 0.9 for $X1$ and $X2$, a low 0.1 for $X2$ and $X4$.

Figure 2-24. Inputs and outputs of correlation analysis.

0.0 (no correlation) to −1.0 (perfect inverse association). Policy analysts search for high correlations (actually, either high direct or high inverse) in order to eliminate superfluous data and to provide a better clue to which policy variables are important for understanding the problem. Correlation is considered the preliminary part of the analysis.

Before causation can be established, policy analysts must establish a reliable or statistically significant relationship between the variables (correlation). However, there is no reason to assume that one level of a variable causes a level of another variable merely on the basis of two events occurring together or their possible association. For example, using correlation, we can establish whether a relationship exists between expenditure per pupil and reading achievement in the school. However, if we propose that per pupil expenditures *cause* or result in reading achievement, we must use regression or least-squares analysis where causality based on theoretical insights, is first specified by the policy analyst. Once again, causality as defined a priori by the researcher, distinguishes correlation from a technique described below—regression.

Simple Linear Model

Sometimes two variables are linked by a linear causal relationship as defined by the policy analyst. A linear equation that relates y (called a dependent variable) to x (called an independent variable) is called a *simple linear regression equation* and the mathematical definition is given by

$$y = \beta_0 + \beta_1 x + \epsilon$$

The coefficients β_0 (the y intercept value) and β_1 (the coefficient of x) are called the parameters of the linear model, the unknowns; and ϵ is the amount by which any individual y deviates from the regression line. It is assumed that ϵ has mean 0 and variance σ^2. To estimate the parameters β_0 and β_1 from a sample the experimenter desires to minimize the quantity

$$S = \sum_{i=1}^{n} (y_i - \beta_0 - \beta_1 x_i)^2$$

The solutions obtained from the foregoing equation, β_0 and β_1, are given by the estimates b_0 and b_1

$$b_0 = \bar{y} - b_1 \bar{x}$$

and

$$b_1 = \frac{\sum\limits_{i=1}^{n} (x_i - \bar{x}) y_i}{\sum\limits_{i=1}^{n} (x_i - \bar{x})^2}$$

The estimate b_0 is called the constant or y-intercept and b_1 corresponds to the slope of the regression line.

Of course, we could pair the x and y values for each individual on a graph, then, using the "eyeball" method, draw a straight line. While this method of curve fitting is useful because it is so simple, we have no assurance that the line is the "best" line of fit. More importantly, we have no statistical information to examine the significance or reliability of the fit. The general linear model is discussed in greater detail in Chapter 3.

It is interesting to compare and contrast correlation and regression analyses. In correlation analysis x_1 and x_2 are observed in pairs with no causal specification such as x_1 predicts x_2. For example, in regression analysis we might take children of fixed ages and observe their height (i.e., control for age) but in correlation analysis we observe the height and weight for each child and develop a standardized index of their association.

Thus, while correlation analysis might show the degree to which variables are related and the direction of an association, regression analysis shows precisely how variables are related. In regression analysis, the entire mathematical function (slope and intercept) is estimated, but simple correlation analysis yields only the index of correlation, that is, a single estimate regardless of whether x causes y or vice versa or whether both or neither affect each other. Since educational policy analysts deal primarily with cause–effect relationships, they are likely to find regression to be of importance. The mathematical relationship between correlation and simple linear regression is that the correlation coefficient (r) is the slope (b) of the regression line when x and y are expressed in standard units.

Note that regression and correlation analyses answer different questions (formulas for prediction, measure of association) for the policy analyst, and data may be summarized by the same

(a) Similar regression equation but different correlation

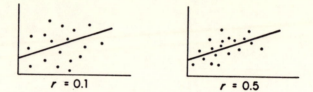

(b) Similar correlation but different regression equation

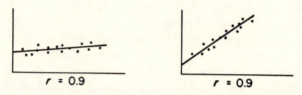

Figure 2-25. Graphical illustration of relationships with similar regressions but different correlations and similar correlations but different regressions.

predictive relationship, even though the correlations are different. Figure 2-25 shows regression lines and correlation coefficients for a set of points.

2-10 SUMMARY

While many statistical techniques presented in this chapter show how we shall establish significant (e.g., probability of event occurring by chance less than 5 out of 100) relationships or differences, it is important for the policy analyst to recognize other factors such as the size of the gain and the cost incurred to the educational institution to achieve this gain.

Notice in the formula

$$SE_{\bar{x}} = \frac{S}{N^{1/2}}$$

that by merely increasing sample size, we shall always derive a smaller standard error. In essence, if the sample sizes are large enough, almost any difference between groups will be statistically significant. The same fact holds for testing the statistical significance of a correlation coefficient, since its formula is

$$t = r \left(\frac{N-2}{1-r^2} \right)^{\frac{1}{2}}$$

which is also dependent on sample size.

The multivariate techniques presented in later chapters will be able to extend the policy analyst's research design to additional factors such as cost, as well as address the problem of quantity of gain and statistical significance. Table 2-5 summarizes the methods of analysis presented in this chapter and how these statistical tools can be used in different educational policy research situations.

For purposes of review, a list of hypothetical situations facing the educational policy analyst in a school district that can be investigated using the techniques indicated in the parenthesis follows:

1. A situation exists where it is necessary to establish the relationship between student reading score and family income in a single statistic (association—correlation).

2. A situation exists where the exact mathematical relationship predicting reading from family income must be established (regression).

3. A set of 50 randomly selected students are put in an experimental group and another 50 in a control group. We want to see if the experimental group did statistically better (*t* test or one-way analysis of variance).

4. We have a set of data concerning how people (parents and nonparents) vote (Yes or No) in a school bond issue and are interested in showing that parents support bond issues more than nonparents (chi square).

5. A situation exists where we need 200 students from a school of 1,000 students to perform an experiment (random number table—random sampling).

6. A situation exists where a sample is needed where the proportion of Blacks to Whites approximates the actual school percentages (stratified random sample).

7. A situation exists where it is necessary to compare whether a school did better in reading or math—scores are 84 in reading, 90 in math. The population statistics for reading are mean = 75, *SD* = 10; for math are mean = 82, *SD* = 16 (standard scores).

8. The mean IQ of a random sample of students is measured, and it is necessary to ascertain whether the observed mean is close to the true mean of the population (standard error of mean).

Examining the major objective for each type of statistical procedure, we have the following:

Table 2-5. Summary of Elementary Methods of Statistical Analysis

Statistic	Principal use	Usual input	Assumptions	Typical design
Chi square	Analysis of significant differences in cross tabulations of categorical variables or frequencies	Contingency table based upon nominal data		Is there a significant difference between men and women who vote Republican or Democrat?
				R D
				M 25 1
				W 16 6
Correlation	A measure of association between two variables	x and y scores for individuals—ordinal, ratio or interval data	No causality Normally distributed variables	Is there a relationship between IQ and achievement?
Regression	Examines a causal relationship between a dependent (y) and and independent (x) variable	x and y scores are fit into the model, $y = a + bx$ (interval or ratio data in most cases)	Causality Normally distributed variables	How does IQ predict GPA?
t test	Finds, for the same group or different groups (up to two), if the difference in mean scores is significant	Scores for groups 1 and 2	Normally distributed population sample drawn at random	Was there a significant difference between pre- and post-test scores?
Analysis of variance	Determines if there are significant differences in mean scores from multiple groups—experimental and control groups	Scores for different groups	Group members randomly assigned to experimental and control groups	Was there a significant difference in output scores between experimental and control groups?

1. *Chi square*—to examine whether there is a difference between the distribution of a sample (two or more response categories) and some other hypothetical or known distribution.

2. *Analysis of variance*—to examine whether differences between sample means are greater than would be expected by chance given the hypothesis that the samples come from the same population.

3. *t test*—to state the probability that the population mean will fall in some specified confidence interval around the sample mean and to examine whether two sample means are from different populations.

4. *Correlation*—to examine, without causality, whether there is a relationship or association between two variables.

5. *Regression*—to examine with an a priori defined causal model the exact mathematical relationship between a dependent and an independent variable.

Multiple Linear Regression: Issues Related to Educational Problems of Prediction

3-1 INTRODUCTION

Multiple linear regression is the most widely used method of multivariate analysis, and its frequent use makes it an indispensable technique for the researcher or policy analyst. Regression analysis attempts to find an exact mathematical formula to describe or model an input-output process; the formula is then used for *prediction* in similar situations. Regression procedures are also used for explanation of processes (finding the relative importance of variables), situations, or combinations of both explanation and prediction.

Regression analysis first requires the specification of the general nature of the mathematical relationship. The most commonly used model in social science is the multivariate linear model with a single output variable being made a linear function of a set of input variables. As mentioned in Chapter 2, the simplest linear model is written

$$y = a + bx$$

where y is the output variable under consideration, x is the input variable,* and a and b are parameters (quantities to be estimated from the data). A more complex multivariate linear model is the following

$$y = a + b_1 x_1 + b_2 x_2 + \cdots + b_n x_n$$

Other models, such as polynomial models

$$y = a + b_1 x + b_2 x^2 + \ldots + b_n x^n$$

or exponential models

$$y = ae^x$$

or logarithmic models

$$y = a \log x$$

are used less frequently. Most of the discussion in this chapter will focus on the multivariate linear model, where the dependent (or output) variable y is considered to be determined by a set of independent (or input) variables $x_1, x_2, \cdots x_n$. For example, a researcher proposes that reading achievement is determined by IQ, age, and SES.

A second requirement of regression analysis is that the analyst have quantified data for each variable being considered in the model.

Ordinary multiple regression analysis attempts to estimate from the given data the exact parameters of the mathematical relationship between a "dependent" variable and a set of "independent" variables. These parameters are the constant a, and the regression coefficients $b_1, b_2, \ldots b_n$ in the multiple (multivariate) linear regression equation

$$y = a + b_1 x_1 + b_2 x_2 + \cdots + b_n x_n$$

*Note that in some texts a distinction is made between X and Y as variables in raw data form and x and y as variables in deviation score form (i.e., $x = X - \overline{X}$, $y = Y - \overline{Y}$). However, in this text no such distinction is made. Variables are referred to both as X or Y and x or y in raw data form.

For example, regression analysis transforms a general causal linear model of the form*

$$y = a + b_1 x_1 + b_2 x_2$$

into an exact mathematical equation

$$y = 1.6 + 8.2x_1 + 3x_2$$

The parameters of the multiple regression model (estimated from the given data) in this example are the constant or y intercept value 1.6 (point where the line, plane, or hyperplane crosses the y axis) and the regression coefficients 8.2 and 3; the dependent or criterion variable is y; and the independent or explanatory variables are x_1 and x_2. Note, the researcher must a priori define the general causal model in terms of its dependent variable and independent variable or variables.

The dependent variable in a regression model is usually a continuous variable normally distributed with a mean and variance. While regression analysis is typically applied to interval or ratio data, nominal variables showing only two categories can also be used as independent variables. Again, before using regression analysis, the analyst must have some theoretical justification or confidence that the input–output relationship to be studied can be captured by the type or model (linear, polynomial, etc.) proposed and that the direction of causality is appropriate (the dependent variable is specified).

Thus, in its simplest form regression (1) finds a formula that relates two quantities (y to x) and (2) gives a prediction of a new y value corresponding to a given x value. In addition to formulas and predictions, regression analysis also supplies numerical values of statistical confidence or reliability for the model itself and for the independent variables used in the model. The general design of regression analysis can be more clearly understood by means of Figure 3-1.

The statistical problems involved in regression analysis entail (1) obtaining the "best" estimates for the unknown regression

---

*Note that the coefficients for the independent variables $x_1, x_2, \ldots, x_n$ are sometimes represented with the letter a as in Chapter 7. However, in this chapter, the letter b ($b_1, b_2, \ldots b_n$) is used to indicate the regression coefficient, and the letter a represents the constant.

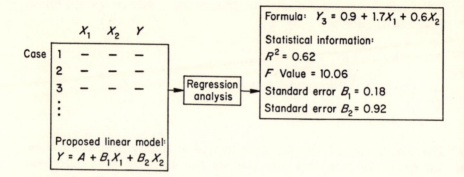

Figure 3-1. General design of regression analysis.

parameters (coefficients and constant or intercept), (2) systematically testing the statistical significance of the parameters, and (3) determining the adequacy of the assumed linear model for the data analyzed. Correlation analysis, as previously explained, is also a method for analyzing relationships between variables. The difference between a two-variable correlation and a two-variable regression stems primarily from the researcher's conception of the independent variables. The correlation model assumes a bivariate normal distribution; that is, both variables are random and may be interchanged without affecting the results. In a regression model, the independent variables are treated as fixed, and the distribution of the dependent variable at each value of the independent variable is random.

We can also describe the difference between multiple regression and correlation in terms of a "one-way-ness" or symmetry. Correlation is the study of the linear relationship between two variables; because either variable can be considered dependent, the relationship can be termed symmetric. Multiple linear regression, on the other hand, is the study of the "one-way" linear relationship between a dependent variable, which must be specified in advance, and a set of independent variables (statistically controlling for any interrelationships between the independent variables).

3-2 GRAPHIC REPRESENTATION OF REGRESSION

Graphs are used to illustrate simple relationships between variables. For example, the general equation $y = a + bx$ expresses the linear relationship between y and x. The graphic representation for this

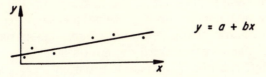

Figure 3-2. Linear relationship between two variables.

equation is shown in Figure 3-2. The constant a is the y-intercept, and b is the slope of the line (i.e., the unit change in y for each increment of x).

Regression analysis selects the particular line (or surface or hyperplane) that best fits the set of data points (see Figure 3-3). The criterion "best" means that this particular line, of all lines that could have been chosen, best satisfies the requirement of "least squares." That is, when the vertical or y-direction deviations (or residuals) of each point from the line are squared and summed, the summed value for this calculated line is less than for any other possible line for this set of points. (This selection technique is often referred to as the least-squares method, based on the sum-of-squares.)

Simple linear regression expresses the linear relationship between two variables (one dependent and one independent). When one dependent variable is determined by several independent variables, multiple linear regression analysis is used to determine the parameters for the regression model. When x and y are nonlinearly related, polynomial regression is used to find an equation of the form

$$y = a + b_1 x + b_2 x^2 + \cdots + b_n x^n$$

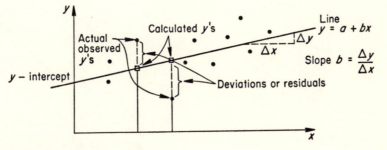

Figure 3-3. Concept of regression.

which best represents the curvilinear relationship. Figures 3-4a and 3-4b show a line and a curve in two-dimensional space; Figures 3-4c and 3-4d show how a line and a curve are transformed to a plane and a surface when a third dimension is added.

Technically, the linear regression equation locates a hyperplane in the m-dimensions from which projections are made to the criterion or dependent variable axis. That is, projections are made from the data points to the fitted hyperplane such that: (1) in variable space the projections are parallel to the criterion axis, or (2) in sample space the projection from the criterion vector to the hyperplane is perpendicular to the hyperplane. The complete test space in the analysis is m-dimensional, with $m - 1$ predictors (independent variables) plus the criterion (dependent variable).

(a) Straight line   **(b)** Curve

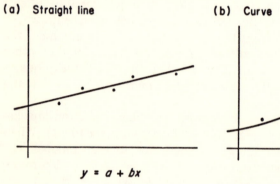

$$y = a + bx$$

$$y = a + bx^2$$

(c) Plane   **(d)** Surface

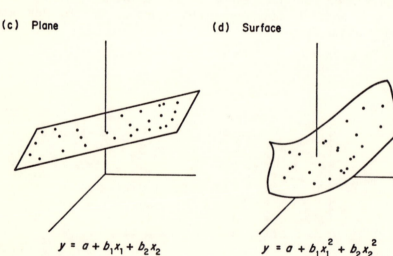

$$y = a + b_1x_1 + b_2x_2$$

$$y = a + b_1x_1^2 + b_2x_2^2$$

Figure 3-4. Illustration of various types of regression.

Thus, it is necessary to have *at least* m measurements or observations for each of the m variables ($m - 1$ independent variables plus one dependent variable); for example:

1. At least two data points (observations) are needed for a straight line (two dimensions)

$$y = a + bx$$

with each coordinate (x, y) requiring data for two variables (one dependent plus one independent);

2. At least three data points are needed for a plane (three dimensions)

$$y = a + b_1 x_1 + b_2 x_2$$

with each coordinate (x_1, x_2, y) requiring measures on three variables (two dependent variables plus one independent variable);

3. At least m data points are required for an m-dimensional hyperplane

$$y = a + \sum_{i=1}^{m-1} b_i x_i$$

with each coordinate having measures on m variables ($x_1, x_2, \ldots, x_{m-1}, y$)

Figure 3-5 illustrates the step-by-step procedure of regression analysis and how this technique summarizes data, fits a linear equation to the hyperplane, and is ultimately used in prediction.

For many observations on variables y and x, where the hypothesized relationship is nonlinear, polynomial regression finds an equation of the form

$$y = a + b_1 x + b_2 x^2 + \ldots + b_k x^k$$

Other types of nonlinear relations between one dependent and one independent variable are given in Figures 3-6 and 3-7.

3-3 MATHEMATICAL ASPECTS OF REGRESSION*

In order to illustrate a mathematical procedure for estimating the coefficients in a regression model, a simple two-dimensional

---

*Asterisks following headings indicate a fuller mathematical exposition of the topic which can be skipped by most readers without losing the principle objectives of each chapter. Subsequent asterisks following headings mean the same thing.

(a) Step I : Graph of data

Data

y	x_1	x_2
—	—	—
—	—	—
—	—	—
—	:	—
—	—	—
—	—	—

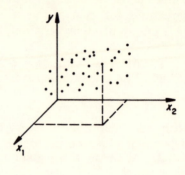

Proposed general equation or model

$y = a + b_1 x_1 + b_2 x_2$

(b) Step II : Graph of regression fit

Fitting regression plane to point gives

$y = 6.1 - 2(x_1) + .5(x_2)$

$b_1 = -2$

$b_2 = .5$

$a = 6.1$

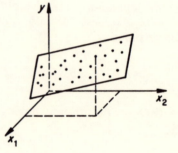

(c) Step III : Graph of prediction

If $x_1 = 10$ and $x_2 = 8$, then

$y = 6.1 - 2(10) + .5(8)$

$= 5.1$

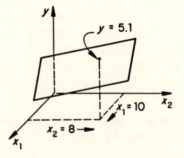

Figure 3-5. Multiple regression example.

(two-variable) model will be considered. The estimation procedure explained below is called the least-squares method. As previously mentioned, this method is based on the criterion that the estimated line minimizes the sum of the squared deviations of the observed points from the line.

A set of points exist in an x-y plane. A straight line of the form $y = a + bx$ is fitted such that the sum-of-squares of the deviations of the observed points from the line are minimized as shown in Figure 3-8. The goal then is to find the parameters a and b in order to minimize D

$$D = d_1^2 + d_2^2 + d_3^2 + d_4^2 + d_5^2 + d_6^2$$

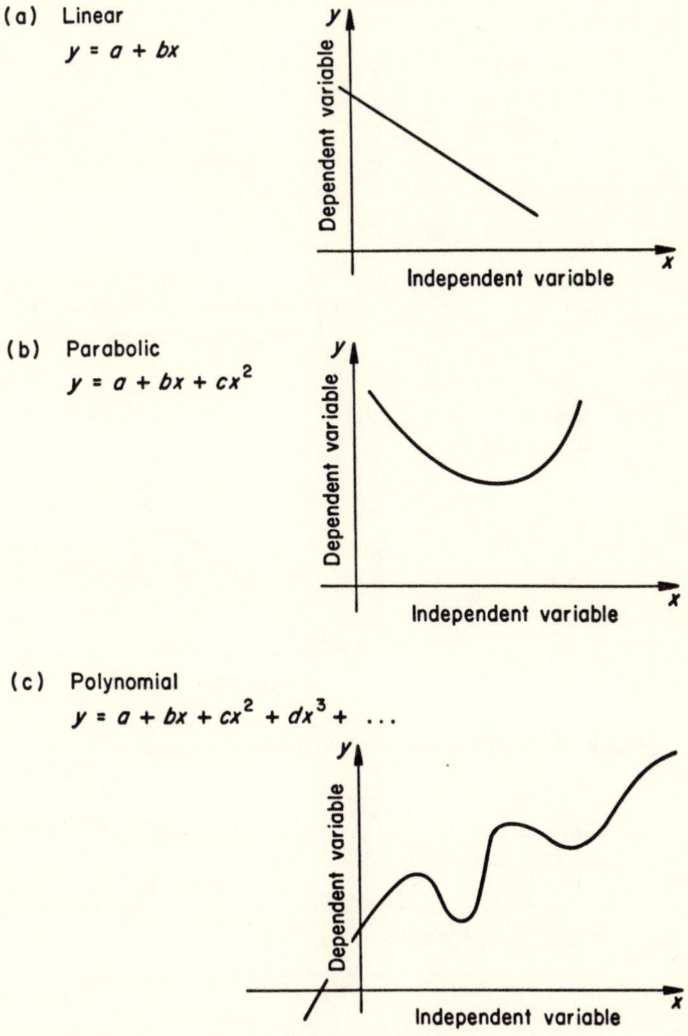

(a) Linear

   $y = a + bx$

(b) Parabolic

   $y = a + bx + cx^2$

(c) Polynomial

   $y = a + bx + cx^2 + dx^3 + \ldots$

Figure 3-6. Various functional relationships in education.

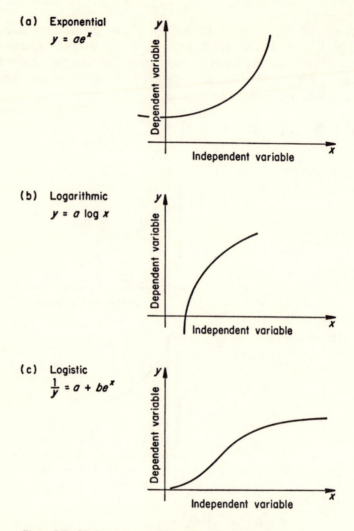

(a) Exponential

$y = ae^x$

Dependent variable

Independent variable

(b) Logarithmic

$y = a \log x$

Dependent variable

Independent variable

(c) Logistic

$\frac{1}{y} = a + be^x$

Dependent variable

Independent variable

Figure 3-7. Various exponential relationships in education.

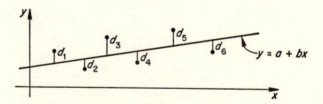

$y = a + bx$

Figure 3-8. Deviations from regression line.

or expressed mathematically, we wish to minimize D

$$D = \Sigma (y_o - \hat{y})^2$$

where y_o = observed y and $\hat{y}$ = calculated y or the y value on the fitted regression line. Since

$$\hat{y} = a + bx$$
$$D = \Sigma(y_o - \hat{y})^2$$
$$D = \Sigma[y_o - (a + bx)]^2$$
$$D = \Sigma[y_o - a - bx]^2$$

Written in this way, the expression for D involves two parameters, a and b, and two sets of known quantities (the data points), $x_1, x_2, \ldots, x_n$ and $y_1, y_2, \ldots, y_n$. Expressing D more precisely, we have

$$D = \sum_{i=1}^{n} (y_i - a - bx_i)^2$$

In order to find a and b to make D a minimum value, set the partial derivatives equal to zero

$$\frac{\partial D}{\partial a} = 0 \qquad \frac{\partial D}{\partial b} = 0$$

Since

$$D = \Sigma (y_i - a - bx_i)(y_i - a - bx_i)$$
$$= \Sigma (y_i^2 - 2ay_i + a^2 - 2bx_iy_i + 2abx_i + b^2x_i^2)$$
$$\frac{\partial D}{\partial a} = \Sigma (2y_i - 2a - 2bx_i)$$
$$0 = \Sigma (2y_i - 2a - 2bx_i)$$
$$0 = \Sigma y_i - an - b\Sigma x_i$$

Similarly

$$\frac{\partial D}{\partial b} = \Sigma (-2x_iy_i + 2ax_i + 2bx_i^2)$$
$$0 = \Sigma (-2x_iy_i + 2ax_i + 2bx_i^2)$$
$$0 = -\Sigma x_iy_i + a\Sigma x_i + b\Sigma x_i^2$$

With these two equations

$$0 = \Sigma y_i - a_n - b\Sigma x_i$$
$$0 = -\Sigma x_i y_i + a\Sigma x_i + b\Sigma x_i^2$$

We can solve for a and b by supplying values for n, Σy_i, Σx_i, $\Sigma x_i y_i$, and Σx_i^2. This yields the numerical values of the two parameters a and b, which minimize D (the sum-of-squares). The algebraic derivation for a is as follows

$$0 = \Sigma y_i - an - b\Sigma x_i$$
$$an = \Sigma y_i - b\Sigma x_i$$
$$a = \frac{\Sigma y_i}{n} - \frac{b\Sigma x_i}{n} \quad \text{or} \quad a = \bar{y} - b\bar{x}$$

The derivation for b is as follows

$$0 = -\Sigma x_i y_i + a\Sigma x_i + b\Sigma x_i^2$$
$$b\Sigma x_i^2 = \Sigma x_i y_i - a\Sigma x_i$$
$$b\Sigma x_i^2 = \Sigma x_i y_i - (\bar{y} - b\bar{x})\Sigma x_i$$
$$b\Sigma x_i^2 - b\bar{x}\Sigma x_i = \Sigma x_i y_i - \bar{y}\Sigma x_i$$
$$b(\Sigma x_i^2 - \bar{x}\Sigma x_i) = \Sigma x_i y_i - \bar{y}\Sigma x_i$$
$$b = \frac{\Sigma x_i y_i - \bar{y}\Sigma x_i}{\Sigma x_i^2 - \bar{x}\Sigma x_i} \quad \text{or}$$
$$b = \frac{n\Sigma x_i y_i - \Sigma y_i \Sigma x_i}{n\Sigma x_i^2 - (\Sigma x_i)^2}$$

3-4 ASSUMPTIONS UNDERLYING REGRESSION ANALYSIS*

The IBM document on regression analysis (1969) warns that the assumptions implicit in regression must be checked before the results can be considered trustworthy or reliable. Dei Rossi and Sumner (1969) refer to "classical linear regression assumptions" as encompassing the conditions under which the least-square estimators produce minimum variance and unbiased results. From Chapter 2 we remember that variance is a statistical measure of the scatter or spread of a set of values around the average value. If the values are $x_1, x_2, \ldots, x_n$ and the average or mean value is $\bar{x}$, then the variance is

$$\frac{\sum_{i=1}^{n} (x_i - \bar{x})^2}{n-1}$$

The classical assumptions of regression analysis concern the population distribution of the residuals or error terms, e_i. The notion of error is discussed in the following pages and precedes a list of the classical assumptions and descriptions of violation of these assumptions.

To statistically explain 100% of the variation in the dependent variable about its mean value (a perfect predicting model) would require the use of an infinitely large number of explanatory variables in the regression model.* A more feasible approach to the problem is to represent the dependent variable (y) not as an exact function of the independent variable, but as a stochastic or statistical function

$$y_i = f(x_{i1}, x_{i2}, \ldots, x_{ij}, \ldots, x_{in}) + u_i$$

The two terms on the right-hand side of the equation show that variation in y is partitioned into two components:

1. One associated with the independent variables

$$(x_1, x_2, \ldots, x_n)$$

2. Another associated with a stochastic component or error term u_i, which is the residual resulting from the omission of some explanatory variables. This residual value results from inaccuracies in the data or from the basic unpredictable element of randomness in human responses which can only be characterized by the inclusion of a random variable term.

In more concrete terms, the error e is often considered to be the "residual" or distance that separates an original observation y (for a particular x) from the calculated value $\hat{y}$ (for the same x). See (Figure 3-9). The e_i correspond to the $d_1, d_2, \ldots$ in Figure 3-8 that are minimized in the least-squares estimation procedure.

Mathematically, for a particular x

$$y = \hat{y} + e$$

---

*Obviously if the number of cases equaled the number of variables, we would have a set of simultaneous equations with a unique solution.

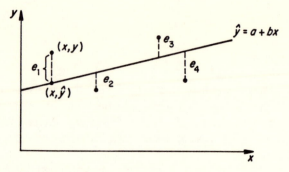

Figure 3-9. Residual or error.

Because $\hat{y}$ is calculated from the estimated regression line ($\hat{y} = a + bx$), we can substitute $a + bx$ into the above expression giving

$$y = a + bx + e$$

To allow for all data points, this equation is usually written

$$y_i = a + bx_i + e_i \ (i = 1, 2, \ldots, n)$$

The assumptions of classical linear regression, given in terms of the errors e_i, follow:

1. The e_i have the same variance; that is, the variance is constant for all values of x;

2. The e_i are independently distributed; that is, there is no serial correlation among the e_i; and

3. The e_i are normally distributed with the mean at zero.

These conditions are met in the example in Figure 3-10. The

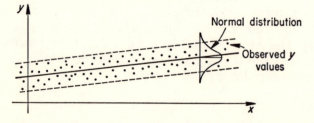

Figure 3-10. Equal variance error band and normal distribution of error.

(a) Unequal variance error band

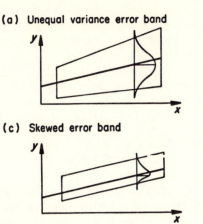

(b) Correlated error band

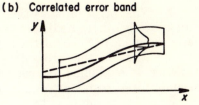

(c) Skewed error band

Figure 3-11. Violation of assumptions.

parallel lines define a band of equal variance, and the normal distribution of observed y values indicate that the data points are normally distributed about the underlying straight line, clustering near the line and falling off symetrically on either side of the line.

In Figure 3-11a the error variance (or σ_e^2) is *not* constant over all values of x. For the case shown, the first basic regression assumption is violated, and the variance is proportional to x. This type of residual plot is referred to as heteroscedasticity. The second basic assumption of regression is violated in Figure 3-11b. The e_i in this figure are not independent but are positively correlated in a curvilinear relationship. The third basic assumption, that the e_i are normally distributed with zero mean, is violated by the skewed distribution shown in Figure 3-11c.

3-5 OUTPUTS OF REGRESSION ANALYSIS

The principal interpretable outputs found in most computer software packages on regression analysis include:

1. How much variation in the distribution of the dependent variable is "explained" by the set of independent variables? (multiple R^2 or coefficient of determination)

2. What is the exact mathematical relationship between each independent variable and the dependent variable? Stated differently, all other variables used in the model held constant, what is the relationship between the dependent variable and a given independent variable? (regression coefficient)

3. What is the statistical significance of each independent variable (all other predictive variables are held constant when these tests are made) (*t* test of the regression coefficient)?

4. What is the ordinal rank of importance and how much variance is explained by each independent variable in the model? (standardized regression coefficients, beta weights)

5. How accurate is the model in prediction? (standard error of the estimate)

6. Does the model explain a significant amount of variation—the ratio of explained to unexplained variance? (*F* test)

The multiple R^2 or coefficient of determination gives the percent ($R^2 \times 100$) of the total variation about the mean of the dependent variable that is explained or predicted by the independent variables used in the model. The value R^2 varies from 0 to 1.00 and is derived from the analysis of variance table (sum-of-squares due to regression divided by the total sum-of-squares). Note as R^2 approaches 1, the linear fit becomes perfect and all of the variation is explained.*

The sum-of-squares about the mean for the dependent variable can be broken in two parts—total sum-of-squares (SST) and sum-of-squares due to error (SSE). The total variation sum-of-squares is defined as

$$\Sigma(Y_i - \overline{Y})^2 = \text{SST}$$

where Y_i is the observed value and $\overline{Y}$ is the mean value. The sum-of-squares due to error or unaccounted variation is defined as

$$\Sigma(Y_i - \hat{Y}_i)^2 = \text{SSE}$$

where $\hat{Y}_i$ is the value of y predicted by the model. The sum-of-squares due to regression (SSR) is then the difference of the error sum-of-squares subtracted from the total sum-of-squares.

$$\text{SSR} = \text{SST} - \text{SSE}$$

In analysis of variance format this relationship is defined in Table 3-1. The following statistics are thus obtained:

---

*Note another method for describing the multiple correlation coefficient or multiple R is that it is identical to an ordinary correlation coefficient between the predicted and observed Y's.

Table 3-1. Analysis of Variance for the Regression[a]

Source of variation	Degrees of freedom	Sum-of-squares
Regression with k independent variables	k	SSR = SST − SSE
Error	$n - k - 1$	SSE = $\Sigma(Y_i - \hat{Y})^2$
Total	$n - 1$	SST = $\Sigma(Y_i - \overline{Y})^2$

[a]Where k = number of independent variables and n = sample size.

$$\text{Mean square} = \frac{\text{Sum-of-squares}}{\text{Degrees of freedom}}$$

$$F \text{ Ratio} = \frac{\text{Mean square (regression)}}{\text{Mean square (error)}} \quad \text{or}$$

$$= \frac{\text{Explained variation}}{\text{Unexplained variation}}$$

$$R^2 = \frac{\text{SSR}}{\text{SST}}$$

As depicted in Figure 3-12, the total variation of y about its mean is partitioned into two parts: the variation explained by the regression model and the unexplained residual variation. The ratio of these two sources of variation, or the F ratio, is used to explain the significance of the linear fit with k and $n - k - 1$ degrees of freedom (where n = sample size, k = number of independent variables). The F statistic is then examined using an F table at desired levels of significance, 0.05 or 0.01, to test the null

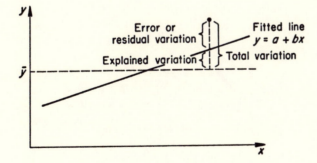

Figure 3-12. Graph of analysis of variance in regression.

hypothesis that the amount of variation explained by the model has occurred by chance.

Another extremely important output of regression analysis is the measures for statistical significance of the regression coefficients. For the model $y = a + bx$, the statistical significance of b, or the slope of the regression line, is of important interest. Notice in Figure 3-13 that the dotted lines all have the same intercept but different slopes. Hence different slopes yield totally different relationships between dependent and independent variables. We would like to test the hypothesis that the slope or regression coefficient is statistically different from zero. In short, we are basically interested in two aspects of the slope: the sign and magnitude and the statistical significance of that magnitude. The t statistic, which is standard output in most computer programs on regression, provides insight concerning the error associated with each of the regression coefficients. The null hypothesis that the regression coefficient is not statistically different from zero is examined by comparing the t statistic as found in the computer output with the t value from a t table (see the appendix) with $n - 2$ degrees of freedom at the desired level of statistical significance (usually 0.05 or 0.01 levels). If the calculated t value is larger than the value from the table, then the null hypothesis is rejected; that is, the slope can be considered significantly different from zero. If the calculated t value is smaller than the tabled value, then the null hypothesis cannot be rejected; that is, the slope cannot be considered substantially different from zero.

The raw regression coefficients, of course, cannot be used to rank order variables in terms of their statistical significance in predicting y. For example, a variable with a regression coefficient of 2 is not necessarily a stronger predictor than a variable with a

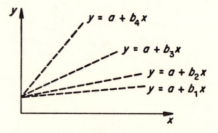

Figure 3-13. Graph of equation with different slope but same intercept.

regression coefficient of 0.2. This is because the ranges of possible values for each of the independent variables can differ widely. Fathers' income might have values in the thousands range, while racial balance might be in the hundredths range. The key interpretive element in the regression coefficient is the sign. A positive coefficient, other things being equal, means that the larger the value of the independent variable, the larger the value of the dependent variable. Another interpretive output is that the value of each regression coefficient tells how much the dependent variable changes in value for a unit change in the independent variable, with other independent variables held constant. Thus in the equation

$$y = 2.3x_1 + 7.2x_2 - 3.4x_3 + 10$$

y increases by 2.3 units for each change in x_1, with x_2 and x_3 held constant.

A systematic procedure for comparing apples and oranges (raw regression coefficients) is to standardize them. The standardized regression coefficient is called a beta weight. The beta weights combine both the error and magnitude of the regression coefficients by scaling each of the variables in terms of their standard deviations. The formula for converting a raw regression coefficient b to a standardized regression coefficient B is*

---

*The derivation of the formula follows: With suitable translation of axes, the regression equation $y = a + bx$ becomes

$$y = bx$$

with a y-intercept of zero. Thus,

$$b = y/x$$

Now consider the first equation where x and y are given in standardized form

$$y' = Bx'$$

where $y' = y/S_y$, $x' = x/S_x$, B is the standardized regression coefficient, S_y is the standard deviation of y, and S_x is the standard deviation of x. Thus,

$$B = y'/x' \text{ or}$$

$$B = \frac{y/S_y}{x/S_x} = \frac{y}{x}\left(\frac{S_x}{S_y}\right)$$

Using the second equation the above equation simplifies to

$$B = b\,(S_x/S_y)$$

$$B = (b)\left(\frac{S_x}{S_y}\right)$$

For example, a beta weight

$$y = 0.845x$$

means that for each increase of a standard deviation of x, y increases by 0.845 standard deviations. Note that in standardized or normalized regression models there is no regression constant or y-intercept value. This is because the normalization process requires that when all independent variables are at their mean value, the dependent variable is at its mean value. Since beta weights are in standardized units, they can ordinally be ranked in terms of their significance in predicting the level of the dependent variable.

The amount of variance accounted for by each predictor variable in the regression model is another output which has policy relevance. The total variance associated with the criterion variable c and the independent variable i is accomplished by taking the product of the beta weight B_i of variable i times the correlation between this variable and the criterion variable (r_{ic}). Thus, the total variance associated with variable i is

$$V_T = (B_i)(r_{ic})$$

If the predictor variables are intercorrelated, which is usually the case, some of the total variance is obviously shared with other predictor variables. To find the unique variance solely associated with the variable i, we have to square the beta weight. The unique variance associated with the variable i is

$$V_u = B_i^2$$

Thus, to find the total variance associated with i, we have to consider both the shared and unique variance explained; and to find only the shared variance associated with variable i, we use the formula for shared variance associated with the variable i, which is

---

Note that in the simple 2-variable model, the B corresponds to the regression coefficient b for variables measured in standard units and equals the correlation coefficient r.

$$V_s = V_T - V_u$$

$$V_s = (B_i)(r_{ic}) - (B_i)^2$$

Thus, there are several policy-relevant statistical outputs in a multiple linear regression model. The reliability of the model, presented by the multiple R^2, indicates how much variation in the dependent variable about its mean value is explained with the linear model. The significance of the model is presented by the F ratio statistic. This ratio indicates whether a statistically significant amount of variation in the dependent variable has been explained by the model. The accuracy of the model is presented by the standard error of the estimate; one standard error of the estimate shows that 68% of the time the value of the dependent variable will be within this range (estimate ± standard error).* The significance and confidence of the variables used in the model are found by the t values. The t value indicates the probability that the regression coefficient is statistically different from zero. Finally the importance of each of the independent variables in the model in terms of explaining variation of the dependent variable is indicated by the beta weights. Beta weights show how many standard deviation unit changes occur in the level of the dependent variable when the independent variable changes by one standard deviation; and the square of the beta weight shows the unique contribution of the variable in explaining variance.

3-6 EXAMPLE OF INTERPRETATION OF COMPUTER OUTPUTS OF LINEAR AND POLYNOMIAL REGRESSION

There are many standard computer programs available for performing regression analysis. In the BIOMED series, there is BMD01R for simple linear regression, BMD03R for multiple linear regression, and BMD05R for polynomial regression.

Problem 1—Linear Regression

The following is a description and interpretation of the output from BMD03R, which is a straightforward multiple linear regression analysis program. The first part of the output gives information about the independent variables (see Table 3-2). Column

---

*Thus, the standard error of the estimate is merely the standard deviation of the residuals or the observed minus calculated y's used in the model.

Table 3-2. Regression Output from BMD03R

Variable	Mean ($\bar{x}$)	Standard deviation (σ)	Correlation x versus y	Regression coefficient (b)	Standard error of regression coefficient	Computed t value
1	46.93	2.71	0.16	−0.00	0.09	−0.02
2	333.86	134.34	0.48	0.01	0.00	5.24
3	239.26	48.16	0.18	0.01	0.00	3.27
4	112.39	19.52	0.16	−0.10	0.04	−2.52
5	39.20	16.36	0.19	0.17	0.05	3.42

1 is the variable number, columns 2, 3, and 4 are the mean $\bar{x}$, standard deviation σ, and correlation between each independent variable and the dependent variable. Column 5 is the regression coefficient or b in the equation $y = a + bx$. This coefficient is *not* the standardized coefficient (called a beta weight) but rather the raw regression coefficient. (Beta weights allow us to compare variables in the model directly since all are standardized to standard deviation units.) Column 6 is the standard error of the regression coefficient, or the confidence the analyst can have in the regression coefficient. The smaller this value in relation to the coefficient, the greater the confidence that the regression coefficient did not occur by chance or is statistically different from zero. The last column gives the t values (regression coefficient divided by standard error) which can be evaluated with t tables at $n - k - 1$ degrees of freedom (k is the number of independent variables) and assigned a probability estimate of chance occurrence. The greater the absolute value of t, the higher the level of statistical significance or the less chance of occurrence of a regression coefficient.

	Dependent	Mean	Standard deviation
	6	2.73333	1.38701
Intercept			−0.35655
Multiple correlation			0.89210
Standard error of estimate			0.78165

Variable 6 is the dependent variable with a mean of 2.73 and a standard deviation of 1.39. The y-intercept, or a in $y = a + \sum_{i=1}^{5} b_i x_i$, is −0.357; therefore, if all the independent variables were set equal to zero, the equation of the line would cross the y-axis at −0.357.

There are options in the BIOMED series for suppressing the intercept and having the regression line intercept the origin. This feature is especially useful when the dependent variable y must equal zero when the independent variables are zero. Production functions and objective functions of linear programming models require this type of flexibility.

The multiple correlation of 0.89 reflects the goodness-of-fit of the line to the set of data. A value of zero implies poor fit, and a value of one reflects a perfect fit. The square of this number gives the researcher the percentage of variation in the dependent about its mean, which is explained by the independent variables used in the model. Thus, if R^2, called multiple R squared, is 0.74, then 74% of the variation of y about its mean value is explained or determined by the independent variables used in the regression model.

The standard error of the estimate 0.782 gives the researcher some notion of the accuracy of the regression model. The smaller the standard error, the greater the accuracy of the model in prediction. Sixty-eight percent of the time the actual value for the dependent variable will be within one standard error of the regression estimate ($y = \hat{y} \mp 1$ standard error) for the dependent variable.

Analysis of variance is a statistical technique for splitting the total variation in regression analysis into its various sources. Most computer regression programs use analysis of variance to test if the estimated regression line has explained a significant amount of the variance of the dependent variable. (See Table 3-3.) Following the analysis of variance format, the sum-of-squares about the dependent variable mean is split into two parts and calculated: the variation explained by (or attributable to) regression and the variation not explained by (or the deviation from) regression.

The total degrees of freedom available to the regression line are one less than the number of cases ($n - 1$); the degrees of freedom

Table 3-3. Analysis of Variance for the Regression

Source of variation	Degrees of freedom	Sum-of-squares	Mean square	F Value
Attributable to regression	5	21.43	4.28	7.01
Deviation from regression	9	5.49	0.61	
Total	14	26.93		

for the explained variation equal the number of independent variables (k), leaving the number of cases minus the total number of variables for the error variation caused by the deviation from the regression line ($n - k - 1$). Then the mean squares are found by dividing the sum-of-squares by the degrees of freedom. Finally, an F value is formed by the division of the mean squares attributable to regresssion by the mean squares attributable to the deviation from the regression or error. The F value follows an F distribution and is merely the ratio of the variance explained by regression model to the unexplained variance or error. With 5 and 9 degrees of freedom, the calculated F value is compared to values in an F table, and an associated probability of its chance occurrence is noted. The calculated value must exceed the table value at the related degree of probability. This probability now gives the researcher information as to the significance of his regression line in terms of explaining variance.

The relative importance of each variable can now be determined using the equation for calculating beta weights from raw regression coefficients

$$B_j = b_j \frac{\sum_{i=1}^{n} (x_{ji} - \bar{x}_j)^2}{\Sigma (y_i - \bar{y})^2} \quad \text{or} \quad b_j \frac{S_{x_j}}{S_y}$$

The larger the B_j, the more the influence on y is attributed to variable x_j.

Finally, we compare the y value estimated from the calculated regression equation with the actual y value and calculate the residuals. The residuals as shown in Table 3-4 should be normally distributed about the mean of zero.

Summary of Output—Problem 1

In this problem a multiple regression analysis was performed on five variables. A line of the form

$$y = a - 0.00265x_1 + 0.01124x_2 + 0.0179x_3 - 0.1028x_3$$
$$- 0.1028x_4 + 0.1714x_5$$

was calculated, describing the relationship with unstandardized regression coefficients between the five variables in question and a given dependent variable.

Table 3-4. Table of Residuals

Case no.	y Value	y Estimate	Residual
1	3.0	2.5	2.5
2	1.0	1.9	−0.9
3	2.0	4.0	−2.0
4	3.0	0.2	2.8
5	4.0	8.6	−4.6
6	4.0	0.2	3.8
7	3.0	6.7	−3.7
8	4.0	2.0	2.0
9	1.0	−3.3	4.3
10	0.0	0.6	−0.6
11	1.0	−2.4	3.4
12	4.0	7.8	−3.8
13	3.0	6.8	−3.8
14	4.0	1.6	2.4
15	4.0	5.8	−1.8

Problem 2—Polynomial Regression

The polynomial regression program BMD05R fits an equation of the form

$$y = a + b_1 x + b_2 x^2 + b_3 x^3 + \cdots + b_n x^n$$

to a set of data. There is only one dependent and one independent variable. This particular computer program fits successively higher-order equations to the set of data and prints an analysis of variance for each degree equation. Finally, when the program has reached its specified limit (degree of the equation), a final summary analysis of variance and a list of residuals with a plot of observed versus predicted y values are printed. Table 3-5 gives the results for a model with one independnet variable raised to degree one. For the straight line $y = 8.47x + 2.59$, the analysis of variance in Table 3-6 is performed. The calculated F value of 548 with 1 and 13 degrees of freedom is statistically significant at the 0.01 level.

The computer program now repeats the same calculations with higher-order terms. Thus, for a second degree equation, the results in Table 3-7 are obtained. The analysis of variance for this second degree polynomial is seen in Table 3-8. For a third degree, then the following results in Table 3-9 are obtained, and the analysis of variance is shown in Table 3-10. For a fourth degree, the following

Table 3-5.   Regression—One Independent Variable[a]

x Mean	8.0
y Mean	70.3
Intercept (a value)	2.5
Regression coefficient	8.4
Standard error of regression coefficient	0.3
Correlation coefficient	0.9
$y = 8.47x + 2.59$	

[a]x Mean is the mean of the independent variable; y mean is the mean of the dependent variable; a value is the y-intercept; the regression coefficient is coefficient of the independent variable; and the standard error is the confidence in the regression coefficient.

Table 3-6.   Analysis of Variance for Simple Linear Regression

Source of variation	Degrees of freedom	Sum-of-squares	Mean square	F value
Due to regression	1	20077.24	20077.24	548.22
Deviation about regression	13	476.08	36.62	
Total	14	20553.33		

Table 3-7.   Polynomial Regression of Degree 2[a]

Intercept (a value)	5.5
Regression coefficients	
7.4 0.06	
Standard error of regression coefficient	
1.58 0.09	

[a]$y = 5.57 + 7.41x + 0.065x^2$.

Table 3-8.   Analysis of Variance for 2 Degree Polynomial

Source of variation	Degrees of freedom	Sum-of-squares	Mean square	F value
Due to regression	2	20095.17	10047.58	263.16
Deviation about regression	12	458.15	38.17	
Total	14	20553.32		

Table 3-9. Polynomial Regression of Degree 3[a]

Intercept (a value)	24.99
Regression coefficients	
−5.16 1.96	−0.07
Standard error of regression coefficient	
2.11 0.30	0.01

[a] $y = 25 - 5.17x + 1.97x^2 - 0.08x^3$.

results in Table 3-11 are obtained, and the analysis of variance is shown in Table 3-12.

The fourth degree equation is the highest-order equation fitted to the data in this example because this value was specified to the computer program. Usually polynomial regression programs automatically terminate when no more variance to a certain tolerance specified by the user can be explained. When the program reaches the final equation, a summary analysis of variance is obtained as in Table 3-13. In addition, a list of residuals with the highest-order equation fitted to the data is shown in Table 3-14.

Finally, a graph of the observed and predicted values can be requested; an example is given in Figure 3-14.

Summary of Output—Problem 2

The goal of this problem was to find the best nonlinear equation to relate two variables over many observations. The fitting of a nonlinear function for this problem produced, using polynomial regression techniques, the resulting equation

$$y = 27.47486 - 7.57648x + 2.59782x^2 - 0.13901x^3 + 0.00187x^4$$

to describe the relationship between x and y.

Table 3-10. Analysis of Variance for 3 Degree Polynomial

Source of variation	Degrees of freedom	Sum-of-squares	Mean square	F value
Due to regression	3	20455.69	6818.56	768.19
Deviation about regression	11	97.63	8.87	
Total	14	20553.33		

Table 3-11. Polynomial Regression of Degree 4[a]

Intercept (a value)			27.47
Regression coefficients			
−7.57 2.59 0.13 0.00			
Standard error of regression coefficient			
5.06 1.23 0.11 0.00			

$$^{a}y = 27.47 - 7.58x + 2.59x^2 - 0.139x^3 + 0.002x^4$$

Table 3-12. Analysis of Variance for 4 Degree Polynomial

Source of variation	Degrees of freedom	Sum-of-squares	Mean square	F value
Due to regression	4	20458.33	5114.58	538.41
Deviation about regression	10	94.99	9.49	
Total	14	20553.33		

Table 3-13. Final Analysis of Variance for 4 Degree Polynomial

Source of variation	Degrees of freedom	Sum-of-squares	Mean square
Linear term—accounts for most of the variance; it is a near-linear relationship	1	20077.24	20077.24
Quadratic term	1	17.92	17.92
Cubic term	1	360.51	360.51
Quartic term	1	2.64	2.64
Deviation about regression	10	94.99	9.49
Total	14	20553.33	

Table 3-14. Table of Residuals

Number	x Value	y Value	y Predicted	Residual
1	1.0	20.0	22.3	−2.3
2	2.0	25.0	21.6	3.3
3	3.0	26.0	24.5	1.4
4	4.0	30.0	30.3	−0.3
5	5.0	35.0	38.3	−3.3
6	6.0	49.0	47.9	1.0
7	7.0	58.0	58.5	−0.5
8	8.0	65.0	69.5	−4.5
9	9.0	86.0	80.6	5.3
10	10.0	92.0	91.1	0.8
11	11.0	102.0	100.7	1.2
12	12.0	109.0	109.1	−0.1
13	13.0	113.0	115.8	−2.8
14	14.0	120.0	120.7	−0.7
15	15.0	125.0	123.5	1.4

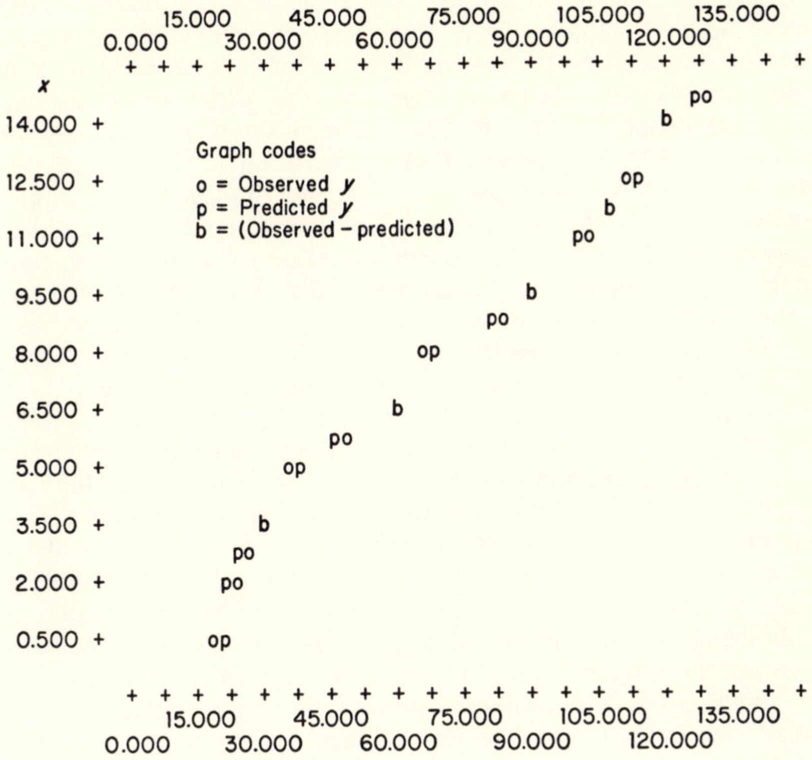

```
             15.000      45.000      75.000      105.000     135.000
      0.000      30.000      60.000      90.000      120.000
       +  +  +  +  +  +  +  +  +  +  +  +  +  +  +  +  +  +  +  +
  x                                                        po
14.000 +                                                b
              Graph codes
12.500 +      o = Observed y                         op
              p = Predicted y                          b
11.000 +      b = (Observed − predicted)            po

 9.500 +                                    b
                                         po
 8.000 +                          op

 6.500 +                    b
                         po
 5.000 +               op

 3.500 +            b
                  po
 2.000 +          po

 0.500 +          op

       +  +  +  +  +  +  +  +  +  +  +  +  +  +  +  +  +  +  +  +
             15.000      45.000      75.000      105.000     135.000
      0.000      30.000      60.000      90.000      120.000
```

Figure 3-14. Graph of the observed and predicted values.

3-7 APPLICATION OF REGRESSION ANALYSIS
TO PROBLEMS IN EDUCATIONAL
POLICY AND PLANNING

Since multiple regression analysis is one of the most commonly used analytical techniques in educational policy and planning, a comprehensive review of applications would be prohibitive. To present a flavor of the wide range of applications and the type of interpretive information reported, a few studies are described below.

The reward structure in a public high school was investigated utilizing multiple regression (Spuck 1974). In this study eight categories of rewards (independent variables) available to teachers in high schools and teacher behaviors (dependent variables) of absenteeism, recruitment, and retention (behaviors assumed to be necessary to but not sufficient for organizational effectiveness) were examined using multiple linear regression analysis. The purpose was to identify linear combinations of reward variables that were significantly related to each of the three organizational behavioral variables. Two intrinsic reward variables combined to account for 43% of the variation in recruitment ($N = 28$; $R^2 = 0.43$, the multiple correlation coefficient, indicates how much variation in y is "explained" by the two independent variables; regression coefficients giving the relationship of each independent variable to the dependent variable were 0.38 and 0.42, respectively; F, the ratio of explained variation to unexplained variation, was 9.35 with degrees of freedom of 2 and 25. This was significant at the 0.001 level of indicating that the model did, in fact, explain a significant amount of the variation). For absenteeism, four variables combined to account for 35% of the variance ($N = 28$; $R^2 = 0.35$; regression coefficients were 0.3574, -0.4976, and -0.5510; $F (4,23) = 3.05$, $P \leqslant 0.04$). For turnover or retention four variables combined to account for 38% of the variance ($N = 28$; $R^2 = 0.38$; regression coefficients were 0.5618, 0.5975, 0.4628, 0.3308; $F (4,23) = 3.61$; $P \leqslant 0.02$). This body of data was interpreted as emphasizing the importance of intrinsic motivators in professional organizations (i.e., independent variables accounting for variance in the above dependent variables were all intrinsic motivators) and suggest basic differences in motivational patterns between professional and production oriented organizations.

In another application, regression analysis was used to study public school effectiveness and equality of opportunity (Walberg and Rasher 1974). In this study, some of the findings of the Coleman study and others on the research of school effects were re-examined by considering additional variables such as scores from the Selective Service Test. The rate of failures on this test in a school was the dependent variable, while independent variables included such areas as adult education, per capita income, homicide rate, library books, symphony orchestras, urban index, newspaper subscriptions, public school enrollment, pupil/teacher ratio, and per pupil expenditures. Walberg and Rasher felt that conclusions could be drawn from the results because of the completeness of the data, the extensiveness of the socioeconomic and environmental control variables, and the confirmatory cross-validation of the results.

The three educational input measures that were found significantly associated with high rates of test failure in this study include high pupil/teacher ratios, low rates of pupil expenditures in the public schools, and low rates of age-eligible children enrolled in public schools. A significant regression weight for public school enrollment suggests that higher percentages of age-eligible children in public schools are associated with fewer test failures. Higher levels of educational expenditures and smaller pupil/teacher ratios in the public schools are related to lower rates of the Selective Service Test failure.

These results agree with local surveys of more refined indicators of educational environments and resources that show educational expenditures, teacher education, experience, salary, instructional techniques, subject matter content, and sociopsychological properties of classroom groups are also associated with test performance. Thus, one implication drawn from the Coleman report, that variations in inputs in education make little difference for test performance and equality of opportunity, may be scientifically and socially unsound according to the authors.

3-8 LIMITATIONS OF REGRESSION ANALYSIS

Many authors caution, and rightly so, that too often the researcher applies statistical techniques, in this case regression, without carefully thinking through the problem and deciding upon the objective of the study. The researcher frequently is guilty of violating the rules and assumptions underlying regression techniques. These violations are discussed by Brandt (1970), Dei Rossi and Sumner (1969), Kelly et al. (1969), and Gordon (1968). If any of the assumptions presented in Section 3-4 are violated, then the ordinary least-squares regression method may calculate a line that does not properly fit the data.

In addition, Crow et al. (1960, p. 148) points out that a statistically significant regression relation of y on x (and similarly for more than one independent variable) is no indication that the independent variable x actually causes the observed change in the dependent variable y, since both may be caused to vary by an ignored third variable. For example, if the order is not random during the experiment (as when the successive x values are chosen in descending order), a change in y may reflect not the influence of x, but that of some hidden variable that changes steadily during the experiment. Crow et al. (1960) also indicates that a regression-derived prediction is no longer valid if the situation has changed since the data were taken, for example, regression is based upon past relationships and has built into its framework an implicit assumption that the past predicts the future.

Also, in a regression analysis the assumption is made that the mean of y is a linear function of the x's (more generally, a function of given form). If the resulting equation is used for predicting beyond the range of x's for which this assumption holds true, errors not accounted for in the confidence intervals for the regression will occur. For this reason, extrapolation is inadvisable.

Finally, another important limitation in regression analysis, typically called the "regression fallacy," occurs when we attempt formulation of predictive models that are based upon data which themselves have a great deal of variation. For example, suppose we developed a predictive model based upon data dealing with educational achievement. We would find that high scoring students would have generally lower scores and the low scoring students generally higher scores (that is, each group would drift closer to the overall mean) than we would predict from the model. This regression to the mean forms one of the most important controversies in using regression analysis for predicting educational outcomes.

3-9 FURTHER CONSIDERATIONS IN REGRESSION

Almost all referenced documents in this chapter contain application and interpretation of regression analysis examples. The IBM document on regression analysis (1966) is particularly outstanding in this regard. Tintner (1970) describes several regression applications and also presents a lengthy discussion on weighted regression. Pederson (1967) describes how regression was used to create and interpret models of urban residential development in Denmark.

Some researchers prefer to use a variation on regression analysis that mathematically provides the best prediction with the fewest number of independent variables. To find the best subset of variables to use in a regression model, we could run all combinations of independent variables. This would require, however, $2^p - 1$ separate regression equations (where p is the number of independent variables). Thus, if we had ten variables in the regression model, we would generate 1,023 separate regression equations. Obviously a systematic procedure for finding this best subset of independent variables had to be developed. The procedure known as stepwise regression analysis selects the best subset according to the following criteria. The first step selects the single variable that best predicts y. The second and subsequent steps each find the variable that best predicts y given the variables already entered in the regression model. In regression steps either a variable is entered in order to best improve the total prediction given all variables entered from previous steps or a variable is removed from a set of predictors if its predictive ability falls below a given level specified by the researcher. The stepwise procedure is terminated when the prediction of y does not improve. Stated differently, the variable added to the model makes the greatest reduction in the error sum-of-squares and is the variable that has the highest partial correlation with the dependent variable adjusted for the variables which have already been added. (Partial correlation finds the linear association between two variables after removing the linear effect of a set of other variables.)

Specifically, the stepwise procedure is as follows. First, a simple correlation and F-to-enter are calculated for all variables. If the calculated F value is above the F-to-include value specified in the computer program, then the variable is considered for inclusion. The variable having the largest F or correlation is included first in the regression model. On the second and subsequent steps, the variable having the largest F-to-enter or largest squared partial correlation with the dependent variable, which is statistically controlled for all independent variables already entered, is then selected for inclusion. At each step if any of the F-to-remove values for the variables are less than the prescribed deletion level specified by the analyst to the computer program, then that variable is replaced by a variable with the largest F-to-enter.

Thus, the stepwise technique selects for inclusion into the regression equation the variable that makes the greatest single contribution to the explanation of the variance.* There is a danger, however, that the variable combination selected by the program may not explain as much variation as another combination whose members did not make a significant contribution to the goodness-of-fit when considered singly. The prudent analyst is, therefore, cautioned to be thoroughly acquainted with the interpretation associated with the program's computational procedure of

---

*Backward stepping is another procedure in basic multiple regression analysis where we wish to identify important predictor variables. In this technique all variables are entered into the equation in a regular forward manner, then variables that contribute least to prediction are removed one at a time.

including the rejecting of variables. Only then will he be able to avoid this danger by judicious manual forcing and deleting of variables.

In a very short but appropriate paper on abuses of stepwise multiple linear regression analysis, Brandt (1970) demonstrates how merely having more variables in a regression model insures significant F values. The logic of his argument is that if a researcher had five variables he felt might be related to the dependent variable and three others that were collected because they are easily quantified, the probability that all eight variables are not statistically significant at the 0.05 level is $(0.95)^8 = 0.66$; that is, the probability of rejecting the null hypothesis is as high as 0.34 or 1 out of 3. If the eight variables are considered two at a time (28 pairs) then the probability of nonsignificance at the 0.05 level for 2 out of eight variables is $(0.95)^{28}$ or 0.22. Hence when using regression, the number of observations, the number of independent variables included, and, most importantly, the number of variables originally examined are critical to determining the statistical significance of the model. Experiments or "fishing expeditions" with stepwise regression should be avoided. Hypotheses should be constructed and tested in the classical sense—one time experiment consistent with the theory—and the computer should not be allowed to crunch numbers and generate its own theory (unless, of course, the purpose of the experiment is to suggest new theory).

Independent variables used in regression analysis are sometimes shown (by means of scattergrams or plots of the independent variable against the dependent variable) to be highly nonlinear. In this situation transformations of the independent variable are sometimes required. Thus, if a variable follows a general $y = x^2$ type of plot, the appropriate transformation would require taking the square root of the variable before placing the variable in the regression model. This procedure is usually accomplished by means of transgeneration statements found in most computer software packages. If higher-order exponentials are observed in the relationship, then logarithmic transformations can be used to insure a linear relation between dependent and independent variables.

Distributions such as t or F and statistical operations such as correlation and regression belong to a form of statistics called parametric statistics. These parametric statistics must be measured on an interval or ratio scale, and the population of values are usually normally distributed about the mean. However, sometimes social science research deals with ordinal or nominal types of data instead of interval or ratios. Nonparametric statistical tests have the characteristic that they depend upon fewer assumptions than parametric statistics and may be used with nominal or ordinal data and with ratio or interval data which are not normally distributed. Nonparametric tests, however, such as chi square or gamma, require more data (larger sample sizes) to achieve the same level of statistical confidence. More importantly, nonparametric tests typically cannot examine the effect of two or more independent variables on a dependent variable. Fortunately, multiple regression is relatively insensitive to nonexcessive violations of the assumption of normally distributed variables. (Regression is said to be "robust" with respect to violations of normality.) For example, family income, skewed to the right, is a frequently used nonnormally distributed variable in social science.

The regression model permits the use of artificial or "dummy" variables when dealing with categorical (nominal) data. Suppose we had sex of the subject as variable in a regression model. We could code this variable as one or Yes if the subject was male and zero or No (i.e., "not male") if the subject was female. We would then have a variable with only two possible values (called a binary variable) that would follow a binomial distribution. The binomial distribution, however, approaches a normal distribution when sample size is larger than 30; therefore, dummy or artificial variables fit into the regression assumption of almost normally distributed independent variables. This subject was discussed with the coin tossing experiment in Chapter 2. If we had a variable such as racial or ethnic identification and had categories such as White, Black, Mexican American, or other, we could convert this one variable to three dummy variables with a Yes/No response to each category. A White subject would be coded 100, a Black 010, a Mexican American 001, and someone fitting the "other" category (Asian-American, American Indian, etc.) would be coded 000. In order to go from m categories or classifications, we must have $m - 1$ dummy (Yes/No) variables. We cannot have m dummy variables because we must have at least one degree of freedom. If not, we would have perfect intercorrelations, since knowing $m - 1$ categories would predetermine the final category.

The reason these artificial or dummy variables are coded 0, 1 is to eliminate the possibility of comparison of values or intervals (e.g., that no one value is a certain number of times greater than another value) as can be done with interval or ratio measurements. The regression coefficients for the $m - 1$ dummy variables formed from the categories of an original independent variable would describe the change in the dependent variable corresponding to the particular nominal characteristic represented by the dummy variable (or the relevant category of the original independent variable—for example, the change in grade point average if the person is male (assuming 1/0 for male/female). The only disadvantage of dummy variables is that the number of variables in the regression model increases, hence might lead to lower confidence in predictions from the model or result in having to collect more data.

Often in regression analysis, the independent variables may be related to each other as well as to the dependent variable. A situation of very strong interrelationships (correlations) among independent variables is termed multicollinearity. Such a situation usually leads to larger standard errors, thus weakening the reliability of the coefficients, while increasing R^2. The regression coefficients themselves are not affected except in the case of very strong (almost perfect) multicollinearity that prevents the calculation of coefficients in most computer programs. But the confidence we can have in a prediction made by the model regression equation is lessened.

To guard against the problem of multicollinearity, the analyst should use as few independent variables as possible in the model by including only those that are deemed necessary by the theory. In addition, by constructing and inspecting a matrix of correlations between independent variables, the analyst may be able to isolate relationships that are strong enough to cause multicollinearity problems. The solution of the problem is at the discretion of the analyst. In some cases, a multicollinearity-causing variable could be eliminated from the model. But in other situations the theory may not allow the omission of any variables and the analyst must then make any decision based upon the application of the model.

Finally, most statisticians utilize scatter plots of observed and predicted values of the dependent variable and scatter plots of residuals and independent variables in their analysis. These plots are useful in detecting lack of linearity, heteroscedasticity (lack of constant variance), unusual outliers, unusual subpopulations, and so on. Scatter plots and analysis of residuals can be of important policy relevance when performing a deviant case analysis, e.g., an identification of extreme outliers or deviations from the regression line. Most regression analysis computer programs calculate the ratios of residuals to standard errors of the estimate for the regression line. High absolute ratios indicate that these cases have other factors or variables not considered by the model which make them unique. In-depth studies can then be directed at these "deviant cases" to try to find why they outperform or underperform so much more than expected.

3-10 SUMMARY

Regression analysis is a powerful analytical tool that, used effectively, can assist in educational policy and planning problems of prediction or problems related to significance of variables in prediction.

There are three major precautions in using regression in educational policy analysis. First, as previously mentioned, correlation does not usually imply causation; causation, however, usually implies correlation since one can disprove a research hypothesis using correlation, but we cannot prove a research hypothesis. Second, interpolation of data in regression is much safer than extrapolation. Using regression analysis, we can predict levels of variables that are within the range of the values used for the variables in construction of the model. Most importantly, multicollinearity (where there is high correlation between independent variables), while increasing the multiple R^2, might play havoc with the reliability of the regression coefficients.

Of course, in addition, the proposed regression model (e.g., linear) must be appropriate to the theorized relationship, and there must be some conceptual foundation for selecting the dependent and independent variables. For a list of multiple linear regression applications to input-output relationships in schooling, the reader is directed to Educational Applications of Regression Analysis in the bibliography (see pp. 277-280).

Chapter 4

Discriminant Analysis: Issues Related to Educational Problems of Classification

4-1 INTRODUCTION

Many situations facing educational planners and policy analysts involve developing predictive formulas for assigning or classifying individuals to appropriate groups for special educational treatments. Multiple discriminant analysis is an analytical technique used for answering questions related to the validity and dimensionality of any a priori defined system of classification. This multivariate technique also defines the predictive relationship between variables used for appropriate assignment of new individuals into groups.

While in linear regression analysis we are primarily concerned with predicting the value of the dependent variable from a given set of independent variables, in discriminant analysis we are concerned with developing a linear equation to distinguish two or more a priori defined groups from each other, that is, to develop a mathematically precise discriminating function based upon a set of variables or attributes. The multivariate techniques of regression and discriminant analysis are compared in Table 4-1.

In discriminant analysis, we are specifically interested in finding the linear composite of variables that "best" discriminates between groups. Here the criterion of "best" is defined as the specific weighting of the variables so that the ratio of the variation between groups (between-groups sum-of-squares of the linear function) to the variation within groups (the within-groups sum-of-squares) has a larger value than that for any other possible linear function of the same variables (i.e., the ratio is maximized). The ratio itself is called the discriminant criterion, and this optimum linear combination of the variables is called the discriminant function. Figure 4-1 illustrates discriminant functions resulting in good and bad discrimination.

A simple example can be used to illustrate the basic theory of two-group discriminant analysis. Suppose nine individuals are categorized into two known groups (Group 1 and Group 2) such as dropout and nondropout from an instructional program; and each individual has characteristics X_1, X_2, X_3 such as age, IQ, and father's income. Discriminant analysis is used to compute the weight attached to each variable so that the ratio of the variation between the two groups to the variation within each group is a maximum. Schematically, we begin with three observations in discriminant analysis on each of nine individuals classified into two a priori defined groups (four in Group 1 and five in Group 2 in Table 4-2).

Discriminant analysis is then performed as in Figure 4-2. To yield the coefficients of the linear function and a composite index or score F_1

Table 4-1. Regression and Discriminant Analysis

Multivariate technique	Number of dependent variables	Number of independent variables	Purpose
Simple two-group discriminant analysis	One—variable which dichotomizes individuals into groups	Many	To develop linear equations to discriminate between groups
Regression	One	Many	To predict the level of the dependent variable from a set of independent variables

(a) Example of moderately good discrimination

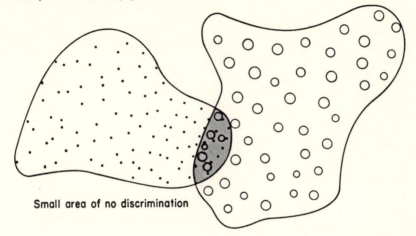

Small area of no discrimination

(b) Example of bad discrimination

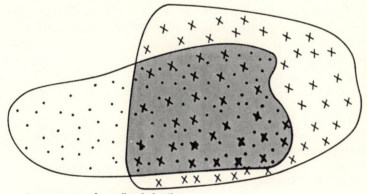

Large area of no discrimination

Figure 4-1. Discriminant functions resulting in good and bad discrimination.

$$F_1 = 2.6 + 1.1 \, (X_1) + 0.9 \, (X_2) - 7.0 \, (X_3)$$

where 1.1, 0.9, and −7.0 are the discriminant function coefficients. The number of variables in discriminant analysis must be less than the smallest number of observations in any one group. Another important point concerning the use of discriminant analysis is that it is not a technique for establishing or discovering groups (as is

Table 4-2. Data for Sample Discriminant Analysis Problem

		Characteristics (variables)		
		X_1	X_2	X_3
Group 1	Case 1	—	—	—
	Case 2	—	—	—
	Case 3	—	—	—
	Case 4	—	—	—
Group 2	Case 1	—	—	—
	Case 2	—	—	—
	Case 3	—	—	—
	Case 4	—	—	—
	Case 5	—	—	—

the case for factor or cluster analysis); instead, it begins with a priori defined or recognized groups. The principle objective of discriminant analysis is then to classify new individuals into appropriate groups on the basis of certain characteristics. Also, the ratio of between-groups sum-of-squares to within-groups sum-of-squares is similar to the criterion for analysis of variance. (See Chapter 2.) In discriminant analysis, however, we want to find the one unique linear composite of variables that maximizes this ratio.

In general, the assumptions of discriminant analysis are:

1. the groups being studied are distinct and identifiable;

2. each observation in each group can be described by a set of m variables; and

3. the m variables are assumed to have a multivariate normal distribution in each population.

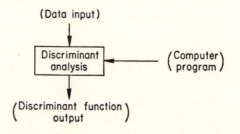

Figure 4-2. Discriminant analysis procedure.

Stated differently, the principal objective of discriminant analysis is to find the weights to be attached to each variable in the linear model in order to minimize the probability of incorrect classifications. Thus, if we had two groups, Group 1 and Group 2, we should like to minimize the probability of an individual being classified in Group 2 given that he is a priori defined to be in Group 1 [written $P(2|1)$] and the probability of an individual being classified in Group 1 given that he is a priori defined to be in Group 2 [written $P(1|2)$]. In mathematical form, we desire

$$P(2|1) + P(1|2) = \text{minimum}$$

This area of misclassification is illustrated in Figure 4-3 by the shaded area.

That all subjects in a discriminant analysis situation must have equal treatments is a concept worth remembering. What distinguishes the performance of each group is then due totally to the attributes or variables being analyzed and not to the environment. In short, each person being studied in each group is assumed to have equal access to all resources; and only individual differences based upon the variables being measured by the discriminant analysis result in the person's classification into the defined groups. In using discriminant analysis for purposes of classification, therefore, we are interested in knowing how these individual measures should be weighted so that future individuals can be assigned to appropriate groups. It should be noted that discriminant analysis is also a useful adjunct to multivariate analysis of variance, in which

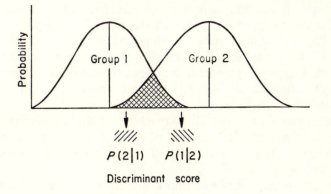

Figure 4-3. Probability of misclassification.

treatment differences may be all that distinguishes the subjects (other than idiosyncratic characteristics).

4-2 APPLICATION OF TWO-GROUP
DISCRIMINANT ANALYSIS

For two-group discriminant analysis any binary (two-category) variable, such as success–failure, or positive gain–negative gain, can be used as a dependent or classification variable. In fact, most computer algorithms utilize the least-squares techniques with dummy independent variables (coded 0,1) to represent each group, although the multiple linear regression model can solve only two-group discrimination problems. If three groups are indicated with only one dependent variable vector, such as 1 for Group 1, 2 for Group 2, and 3 for Group 3, a special ordered relationship is assumed. This violates the important assumption of discriminant analysis that all groups are considered equal, for example, one group does not have an inherent value greater than some other group.

For multiple-group discriminant analysis the computational procedure requires that each group membership be coded as a dummy variable (Yes/No or 1,0 binary-coded values are used to indicate group membership). We thus have a situation with not one variable as a dependent group variable, but a multiple set of dependent variables. A multivariate technique called canonical correlation analysis, which will be discussed in Section 4-3, is appropriate to problems dealing with multiple dependent and independent variables.

Two-group discriminant analysis involves less difficult mathematics than three or more group discriminant analysis. However, the multigroup multivariate discriminant analysis provides, in addition to formulas for the classification of new individuals into appropriate groups, powerful interpretive statistics concerning the factors or dimensions of the discrimination and the variables related to these dimensions. This analysis can be used to find the theoretical basis or underlying structure of the discrimination. The weights of the variables on each of these roots or factors show the relation between each variable and this hypothetical dimension of discrimination.

The following simple example illustrates the use of two-group discriminant analysis. Assume that the special program to be analyzed is an ordinary third grade elementary school program in some underdeveloped country. In underdeveloped countries, dropout rates at this grade level are extremely high, and they constitute one of the most serious and costly educational policy problems. Suppose each student is measured on each of the following four variables:

1. months of formal school,
2. months of formal schooling for father,
3. months of formal schooling for mother, and
4. average monthly family income.

The problem situation is that each student receives identical treatment in school, yet half of the students drop out of school by June. For policy purposes, we are interested in developing a linear discriminant function so that when next year's entering third grade class is measured on these variables, we are able to predict potential dropouts and provide these students with special enriched instructional programs (tutors, liaisons with parents, etc.).

Suppose each group (nondropouts and dropouts) is measured on the four variables; the average values are given in Table 4-3.

A two-group discriminant analysis is performed, and the following weighted function is derived to classify members into appropriate groups. The discriminant score function is given in Table 4-4. To determine the classification for a new individual with specific characteristics, we substitute that individual's characteristics into the following formula and record the score.

$$
\begin{aligned}
\text{Score} = \quad & (0.1) \times (\text{Value of characteristic 1}) \\
+ \; & (8.2) \times (\text{Value of characteristic 2}) \\
+ \; & (7.3) \times (\text{Value of characteristic 3}) \\
+ \; & (2.0) \times (\text{Value of characteristic 4})
\end{aligned}
$$

Table 4-3. Average Values for Characteristics by Group

Characteristic	Average	
	Nondropout group	Dropout group
Months of schooling	38	34
Months of father's schooling	88	40
Months of mother's schooling	97	48
Total family income (monthly)	$416	$339

Table 4-4. Weights Derived from
Discriminant Analysis

Characteristic	Weight
Months of schooling	.1
Months of father's schooling	8.2
Months of mother's schooling	7.3
Total family income	2.0

The scores for an average dropout and an average nondropout follow. The discriminant score for the average nondropout

Score =   (0.1) X (38)
         + (8.2) X (88)
         + (7.3) X (97)
         + (2.0) X (416)
       = 3.8 + 721.6 + 708.1 + 832.0
       = 2265.5

The discriminant score for the average dropout is:

Score =   (0.1) X (34)
         + (8.2) X (40)
         + (7.3) X (48)
         + (2.0) X (339)
       = 3.4 + 328.0 + 350.4 + 678.0
       = 1359.8

If we substitute the values for the variables for each individual into the above formula, we derive a mean discriminant score or index for each group as well as a measure of the variance (how much each individual deviated from the mean). Such an analysis would yield a bimodal distribution as depicted in Figure 4-4.

Each student entering the program in subsequent years could now be placed on a profile scale based upon these four characteristics, the extremes of this profile being potential dropout or potential nondropouts (Figure 4-5). A point between the two distributions or means on the profile scale can then be selected as a breaking point for assigning students to a particular group. A new student falling below the breaking point is provided with extra instructional resources in order to try to maintain his presence in

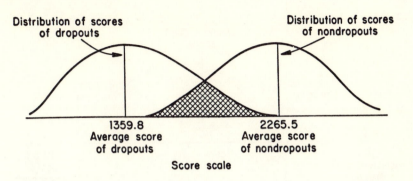

Figure 4-4. Distribution of scores about the means for dropout and nondropout groups.

the educational system. A breaking point analysis is described in Figure 4-6. In our illustrative problem we notice that, for discriminating purposes, months of father's education and months of mother's education are the important variables for membership in the dropout or nondropout groups of students. If the variables were standardized (standard deviation units) in this problem, we could determine the order of importance for each variable in prediction of membership into the dropout or nondropout group.

The cost of misclassifications can also be included in the analysis. Suppose the cost of a student classified as a nondropout but who drops out is $300 and the cost of a student classified as a dropout but who stays is $500. We could adjust the cutoff or selection into Group 1 or Group 2 on the basis of the combination of cost and probability of membership.

Before concluding our discussion of two-group discriminant analysis, a brief review of typical computer printouts resulting from this analysis might be useful. The printout is based upon BIOMED04M discriminant analysis for two groups, using a different data set than discussed previously. First, the names for each variable in each group and their difference are described (Table 4-5).

+		+
1359.8	Score scale	2265.5
Average score of potential dropout		Average score of potential nondropout

Figure 4-5. Profile scale showing average scores of dropouts and nondropouts.

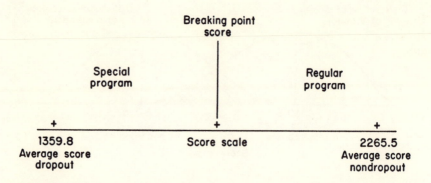

Figure 4-6. Profile scale showing breaking point score for assignment to groups.

Second, the coefficients of the discriminant score function are indicated along with a statistical test of the discrimination. The coefficients are the weights given to each variable such that the distribution of index scores for the two groups is maximally separated. The test of significance refers to the statistical significance of the differences in the means of these distributions and is given as the Mahalanobis D (distance between the groups) Square Statistic or its equivalent F statistic with the appropriate degrees of freedom indicated.

Discriminant function coefficients
   3.20869   −0.06243   −0.00128

Mahalanobis D Square Statistic*   10.83019
   $F(3,6) = 6.49811$

The degrees of freedom are R and $N_1 + N_2 - R - 1$, where N_1 is

*The Mahalanobis D Square Statistic tests the hypothesis that the distances between the means for the two distributions are zero.

Table 4-5. Variable Means by Group and Difference in Means

Variable	Mean 1	Mean 2	Difference
1	0.85	0.38	0.47
2	7.25	5.33	1.92
3	58.75	40.00	18.75

the sample size for Group 1, N_2 is the sample size for Group 2, and R is the number of variables. Finally, the distribution of the index scores themselves is analyzed using the formula

$$Z_j = \sum_i a_i x_{ij}$$

where a_i is the discriminant function coefficient, x_{ij} is the value of the discriminant variable i, and Z_j is the discriminant score index for person or observation j.

For each case from the original data, an index score is derived using the calculated weights. Mean, variance, and standard deviation measures are then calculated for the distribution of the index scores for Group 1 and Group 2 (remember the square root of the variance equals the standard deviation). The rank ordering of the index scores is then presented. Any misclassifications—those observations given to be in Group 1 and calculated to be in the distribution characterizing Group 2—are indicated in the last two columns in Table 4-6.

Finally, a summary correct–incorrect classification matrix is presented where an individual starting in an a priori defined group is classified in that group or possibly reclassified to another group based upon the discriminant score (see Table 4-7). Note in Table 4-7 that the diagonals represent correct classifications and the off diagonals, the incorrect classifications. A percentage of misclassifications to total classifications can then be calculated.

Table 4-6. Index Scores Calculated from Discriminant Function

Pop. no.	Sample size	Mean Z	Variance Z	SD Z
1	4	2.20	0.18	0.49
2	6	0.85	0.16	0.40

Rank	Group 1 values	Group 2 values	Group 1 item no.	Group 2 item no.
1	2.32		1	
2	2.39		2	
3	2.16		3	
4	1.63		4	
5		1.35		2
6		1.12		3
7		0.97		1
8		0.32		4
9		0.61		5
10		0.20		6

Table 4-7. Correct Classification Matrix

| Starting | Classified into | |
	Group 1	Group 2
Group 1	4	0
Group 2	0	6

There are generally two types of procedures for calculating the probability of group membership in two-group discriminant analysis. One procedure is where a discriminant function is calculated to serve as a way of finding an index of discrimination between groups. The best linear discriminant score function is based upon the criterion that the difference between mean indices for the two groups divided by a pooled standard deviation of the indices is maximized. This type of analysis is presented in Tables 4-5 to 4-7.

Another type of two-group discriminant analysis procedure calculates a set of linear functions (one function for each group). Group assignment is then based upon a multivariate normal distribution. The hypothesis tested is that the group means are the same. In essence, variables are weighted differently for each group so that the means between groups are equal. In this latter procedure, the individual is assigned to the group where the probability density is highest or where the computed linear function for each group results in the highest value.

Consider the comparison (Table 4-8) of two-group discriminant analysis with the corresponding features of regression analysis.

4-3 CANONICAL CORRELATION AND DISCRIMINANT ANALYSIS*

Before discussing multigroup discriminant analysis, it is important to provide a basic understanding of canonical correlation. This is important because (1) canonical correlation methods are used in performing multigroup discriminant analysis and (2) the interpretation of computer printouts for multigroup discriminant analysis is much easier with a fundamental understanding of canonical correlation. For an educational application of canonical correlation methods with interpretations see Wang (1970).

Canonical correlation is a general case of regression analysis that permits multiple dependent as well as independent variables. Mathematically, canonical correlation finds a_i and b_i such that the

Table 4-8. Comparison of Regression and Discriminant Analysis

Multiple linear regression	Two-group discriminant analysis
Purpose	
Educational problems in prediction—significance of variables	Educational problems of assignment or classification
Model	
$y = a_1 x_1 + a_2 x_2 + \cdots + a_n x_n + b$ a_i = regression coefficient $i = 1, \ldots, n$ x_i = independent variable y = dependent variable b = y-intercept	Develop an index Z where $Z = a_1 x_1 + a_2 x_2 + \cdots + a_n x_n$ Find the a_i such that the ratio of between-group variance to within-group variance is maximized
Rules	
Usually normally distributed dependent variable	A priori classification of groups
Low intercorrelation between independent variables	Measures all individuals on all discriminatory variables Dependent variable is a category or a classification
Basic Notion	
Try to explain variation about the mean of the dependent variable by means of a set of independent variables	Try to classify members into groups by means of a linear discriminant function

Given:	y	x_1	x_2	x_3		x_1	x_2	x_3
	–	–	–	–	Group 1	–	–	–
	–	–	–	–		–	–	–
	–	–	–	–		–	–	–
					Group 2	–	–	–
						–	–	–
						–	–	–

indices or scores resulting from $\Sigma a_i y_i$ and $\Sigma b_i x_i$ are maximally correlated

$$a_1 y_1 + a_2 y_2 + \cdots + a_p y_p = b_1 x_1 + b_2 y_2 + \cdots + b_q x_q$$

Before the development of canonical correlation, the researcher's available options in situations of multiple dependent and independent variables were limited. Variables could be examined in pairs. Unfortunately, even with a moderate number of variables in each set, there would be many relationships to be examined. Additionally, individual relationships may not describe the overall relationship between the two sets of variables. By combining some of the features of both factor analysis and multiple regression, canonical correlation enables the researcher to examine simultaneously the overall relationship between two sets of variables.

The basic idea of canonical correlation, as described above, is to find the linear combination of variables in each set in such a way that the resultant correlation between the two composite indices—known as canonical variates—is maximum. If there is no significant linear association between the two sets of variables, there will be no significant set of canonical variates. On the other hand, if there is significant linear association between the two sets of variables, we may further examine whether or not the relationship is completely accounted for by the first set of canonical variates. If the first set of canonical variates successfully accounts for the relationship between the two sets of variables, no additional significant canonical variates can be extracted. If, on the other hand, some linear relationship between the dependent and independent variable sets still remains unaccounted for by the first set of canonical variates, we can continue the process of finding new linear combinations that would best account for the residual relationships between the two sets. This process continues until no significant linear associations remain.

In multigroup discriminant analysis, dummy variables or artificial variables are placed on the left-hand side of the equation for Yes/No membership (1,0) for each group or classification. We then try to find the weights that should be assigned to each variable or attribute so that the resulting correlation with each group is a maximum. Thus, canonical correlation provides the researcher with a tool for assessing the relationship between two sets of variables where each set itself may be characterized by more than a single underlying dimension.

The method of canonical correlation may be relevant, for example, if the researcher wishes to study the relationship between a set of many environmental variables and a set of variables measuring intelligence, or a set of attribute variables and a set of group classification variables. In order to use this technique, the researcher must be able to assume that each set of variables can be given a theoretical meaning as a set. For discriminant analysis we can logically state that each of the attribute variables as a set should be maximally correlated with group membership.

The correlations between such linear combinations are called canonical correlations, and the meaning is equivalent to the simple product moment r. The only modification is that the independent and dependent variables are composite indices and not simple variables. By definition, the first canonical correlation is the largest, and the first set of canonical variates may be taken as the best predictive index representing the respective set of variables. The second canonical correlation, if it exists, is the second best, and so forth. Furthermore, each set of canonical variates is, by definition, orthogonal (or unrelated) to other canonical variates.

The principal computer output in canonical correlation is the set of canonical coefficients. There are two matrices of canonical coefficients, one for the set of dependent variables and the other for the set of independent variables. The designation of variables as independent or dependent has no special meaning here, except for identification. These coefficients may be interpreted as standardized regression weights or relative contributions of variables to the respective canonical variates. They may be expressed as:

$$
\begin{aligned}
D_1 &= A_{11}Y_1 + A_{12}Y_2 + \cdots + A_{1p}Y_p \\
D_2 &= A_{21}Y_1 + A_{22}Y_2 + \cdots + A_{2p}Y_p \\
&\;\;\vdots \\
D_n &= A_{n1}Y_1 + A_{n2}Y_2 + \cdots + A_{np}Y_p
\end{aligned}
\qquad
\begin{aligned}
I_1 &= B_{11}X_1 + B_{12}X_2 + \cdots + B_{1q}X_q \\
I_2 &= B_{21}X_1 + B_{22}X_2 + \cdots + B_{2q}X_q \\
&\;\;\vdots \\
I_n &= B_{n1}X_1 + B_{n2}X_2 + \cdots + B_{nq}X_q
\end{aligned}
$$

where $D_1, D_2 \ldots, D_n$ represent canonical variates for dependent variables, while $I_1, I_2, \ldots, I_n$ represent canonical variates for independent variables; A's and B.s are the respective canonical coefficients; and Y_i and X_i represent standardized dependent and independent variables, respectively.

It is from the canonical correlation model that the eigenvalue or root λ is extracted. Each root extracted accounts for a decreasing proportion of variance and chi square tests are used to examine the statistical significance of these roots. Another output of canonical correlation, therefore, is the proportion of variation in one canonical variate accounted for by the variation in the other canonical variate. The meaning of these statistics is equivalent to r^2 or the square of the canonical correlation between the given pair of canonical variates.

Finally, the Wilks' Λ tests the null hypothesis that after extracting the canonical variates preceding the given one, there is no significant linear association between the two sets of variables. For an actual test of significance, the chi square approximation is used for the sampling distribution of Λ. (See the appendix for chi square tables.) For instance, the first Λ may be used to test whether there is a set of significant canonical variates. The second Λ tests whether some significant linear relationship still remains after removing the first set of canonical variates, and so on. The chi square statistic in canonical correlation is equal to

$$\chi^2 = -[N - 1 - \tfrac{1}{2}(p + q + 1)]\ \log_e \Lambda$$

where N is the number of observations, p is the number of left-hand variables, q is the number of right-hand variables, s is the smaller of p and q, and $\Lambda = \Pi_{i=1+r}^{s}(1 - \lambda_i)$. The degrees of freedom are $(p - r)(q - r)$ where r is the number of roots previously extracted (thus if we are testing the third root, then r is 2).

In a three-variable right-hand side, four-variable left-hand side canonical correlation problem, we should like to find a_i's in the following model:

$$a_1 x_1 + a_2 x_2 + a_3 x_3 + a_4 x_4 = a_5 x_5 + a_6 x_6 + a_7 x_7$$
$$p = 4 \qquad\qquad q = 3$$

Figure 4-7 shows a typical computer output.

The interpretation of this output follows: Since we have four variables (LHS)p and three variables (RHS)q, we should expect the number of roots to be extracted to be the smaller of p or q. In this case, the maximum number of roots is q or 3.

The first root λ extracted is equal to 0.38, and the square root of this value is the canonical correlation or 0.62. The chi square for this eigenvalue is 53.57 and with 12 degrees of freedom $[(4 - 0)\ (3 - 0) = 12]$; the chi square statistic is significant at the 0.05 level. Associated with this canonical correlation is the left-hand linear function:

$$6.74x_1 + 0.58x_2 - 5.12x_3 - 0.69x_4$$

and the right-hand linear function:

$$0.809x_5 + 0.573x_6 + 0.126x_7$$

Using these coefficients and substituting the respective values of x_i, the right and left indices will be maximally correlated at a level of 0.62.

The second root is now extracted. Its canonical correlation, of

EIGENVALUE	LAMBDA	CANONICAL CORRELATION	CHI-SQUARE	DEGREES OF FREEDOM
0.380256	2.043151	0.616649	53.575369	12
0.096499	3.296767	0.310643	13.665905	6

CANONICAL CORRELATION   0.616649
COEFFICIENTS FOR LEFT-HAND VARIABLES
6.747534   0.583345   -5.120486   -0.697400
COEFFICIENTS FOR RIGHT-HAND VARIABLES
0.809287   0.573605   0.126618

CANONICAL CORRELATION   0.310643
COEFFICIENTS FOR LEFT-HAND   VARIABLES
-0.032357   -0.175203   0.156378   0.291643
COEFFICIENTS FOR RIGHT-HAND VARIABLES
-0.536383   0.750204   -0.179473

Figure 4-7. Typical computer output for canonical correlation.

course, is lower than the previous correlation. This canonical correlation is distributed according to a chi square distribution with $(4 - 1)(3 - 1) = 6$ degrees of freedom. The column Λ is associated with

$$\Lambda = \prod_{i=2}^{3} (1 - \lambda_i)$$

and is used in determining the chi square distribution. The chi square is not significant. For the left-hand side with the second root removed, we have

$$-0.08x_1 \quad -0.175x_2 + 0.156x_3 + 0.291x_4$$

and for the right-hand side

$$-0.63x_5 + 0.75x_6 \quad -0.18x_7$$

A third root can be extracted but is not reported because it is not significant. (Note that the linear functions associated with a nonsignificant root generally need not be reported.)

Many computer programs compute the loading or correlation of each right-side and left-side variable with the canonical variates. This type of information provides the researcher with the relationship or association of each variable with the underlying structure common to the variables.

To illustrate how canonical correlation is used in studying

multiple dependent and independent variables consider a study by
F. V. Waugh (1942) who applied canonical correlation to a
problem investigating the relationships between the characteristics
of wheat and flour.

The variables for wheat included:

x_1 = kernel texture

x_2 = test weight

x_3 = damaged kernels

x_4 = foreign materials

x_5 = protein content

The variables for flour included:

x_6 = wheat per barrel of flour

x_7 = ash in flour

x_8 = crude protein

x_9 = gluten

Theoretically these composite variables should be maximally correlated using the canonical model. Waugh found the canonical variate
for wheat was

$$U = 0.039x_1 + 0.238x_2 - 0.032x_3 - 1.18x_4 + 0.776x_5$$

for flour

$$V = -0.12x_6 - 13.12x_7 + 1.12x_8 + 0.059x_9$$

The canonical correlation between U and V is 0.91. This number
represents the highest-possible correlation between the linear combination of wheat and flour characteristics. U may be then used to
predict V and vice versa.

4-4 MULTIGROUP DISCRIMINANT ANALYSIS*

As previously mentioned, multiple discriminant analysis procedures
based on finding underlying dimensions (or factors) must be used
if there are more than two groups in the classification scheme. This
procedure determines the extent and manner in which two or more
previously defined groups or subjects may be differentiated by a
set of variables operating together. With two groups, of course, the
separation can be represented along with a single dimension, but
with more than two groups the differentation could be described
in terms of multiple independent dimensions although even here
there may be only one dimension. The maximum number of these

factors or dimensions will always be the smaller of the two numbers: the number of groups minus one or the number of variables used in the classification.

Educational policy analysts using multigroup discriminant analysis can study empirically the configuration of n-groups across multiple criteria in $n-1$-dimensional space. When concerned with three or more groups, the underlying structure may be unidimensional, bidimensional or, with more than three groups, multidimensional. While multiple discriminant analysis cannot be used as a substitute for theory in selecting the groups or attributes for study, the technique is of considerable value in supporting or refuting educational, psychological, sociological, or economic theory that predicts the grouping. For example, Rao (1952) was able to demonstrate that two dimensions were sufficient to discriminate among 12 Indian castes using nine anthropological characteristics. Rao and Slater (1949) were able to align five different groups of neurotics and a group of normal individuals on a single discriminant dimension using 13 personality variables.

Factor analysis and discriminant analysis are related—the former is used to create a classification, while discriminant analysis is used to validate a classification. For example, factor analysis is the appropriate technique to answer a question such as: Given several school districts measured on many socioeconomic indicators, how can we best classify or group these variables (R type factor analysis) or school districts (Q type factor analysis)? Stated differently, is there an underlying dimension or composite of variables common to two or more school districts? Discriminant analysis, on the other hand, is used for examining the statistical significance of an existing system of classification that is either implicitly or explicitly based upon several characteristics.

Thus, the critical difference is that in multiple discriminant analysis attempts are made to maximize the discriminations between already defined and existing groups, whereas in factor analysis attempts are made to extract the latent structure of a set of attributes from an overall random sample of individual observations in order to subdivide it according to the obtained clusters. In discriminant analysis after having chosen each group and selected attributes that theoretically should separate and position these groups in discriminant space, the hypothesized structure is tested by extracting the significant intergroup dimensions and measuring the distances between the groups. This type of spatial configuration based upon composite group attributes rather than individual characteristics with each group predefined is not achieved with other multivariate techniques.

The principal computer outputs to multigroup discriminant analysis include policy relevant interpretive measures of validity or statistical significance of classification, dimensions or structure of the classification, nature of classification itself, and finally the reliability of classification scheme.

The validity or statistical significance of the discrimination between groups is indicated by the magnitude of the F statistic. The level of significance of the F ratio represents the probability that the defined classification might have been produced by chance. If the null hypothesis is accepted (the differences between the groups is not significant), there are two possible reasons. First, the classification is in fact spurious, and the hypothesis of a valid discrimination has to be rejected; or second, there are too many variables in the analysis and a genuine classification of the data is being diluted by the small cumulative effects of a large number of insignificant variables. Stepwise multiple discriminant analysis is used to eliminate problems with variable selection, because variables are entered or deleted according to the amount of dispersion variance that is explained. A second analysis is usually performed with only those variables having statistically significant F ratios. Thus, two important tests of significance are printed in most discriminant analysis programs; these are the F test to determine the statistical significance of group discrimination and a table of univariate F tests to examine the statistical significance for each variable used in the classification scheme. A typical univariate F table is shown in Table 4-9.

Stepwise discriminant analysis is therefore analogous to stepwise

Table 4-9. Typical Univariate F Ratios in Discriminant Analysis[a]

Variable	F ratio
1	25.2
2	17.3
3	6.7

[a]Examines the statistical significance of each variable in the discriminant model with $(g-1)$ and $n - g - q + 1$ degrees of freedom. q equals number of variables entered, n equals number of cases, g equals number of groups.

Table 4-10. Computer Output (BIOMED07M) from Stepwise Discriminant Analysis

Step	Variable Enter	Variable Remove	F to[a] Enter	F to[a] Remove	Number of variables included
1	x_2		1117.3		1
2	x_3		117.2		2
3	x_1		3.1		3

[a]The degrees of freedom are q and $n - g - q + 1$.

linear regression where a subset of independent variables that best predict the dependent variable is sought. In regression analysis, an F statistic based upon the partial correlation is used as the criterion for a variable to enter. In discriminant analysis, the F statistic based upon an analysis of variance test is used. In either case, the terminology F-to-enter for variables not chosen and F-to-remove for chosen variables is used. Essentially, a one-way analysis of variance procedure blocked by group classification with measures in each variable is generated. The variable that has the largest F statistic is chosen for entry. On successive steps, the conditional distribution of each variable not entered, given the variables entered, is calculated and then submitted to a one-way analysis of variance. Again, the variable with the largest F is chosen to be included in the model.

The stepwise procedure terminates when no additional variables contribute significantly to the discrimination. The degrees of freedom associated with each F-to-enter depends upon the number of groups. For two groups, the degrees of freedom for F are then 1 and $N_1 + N_2 - N_I - 1$ where* N_1 is the population of Group 1, N_2 is the population of Group 2, and N_I is the total number of variables included. Programs such as BIOMED07M provide the summary output (a two-group, three-variable, 100-case sample) as in Table 4-10.

The exact test statistic for examining the hypothesis that the group means are equal is the U statistic. Due to the complexity of the distribution of U, however, an F approximation to U is

*The general case for determining degrees of freedom is based upon the following expression $(g - 1)$ by $n - g - q + 1$ where g = number of groups, n = number of cases, and q = number of variables entered.

provided in most computer software packages along with the appropriate degrees of freedom. The F test is exact whenever the number of discriminating variables is one or two regardless of the number of groups or whenever the number of groups is two regardless of the number of variables.

Note that statistical significance in discriminant analysis is extremely sensitive to group sample sizes in addition to the number of variables used in the classification. For given differences among group means, large samples *ceteris paribus* increase the likelihood that the equality of group means and dispersions will be rejected. For extremely large sample sizes, the nature of the statistical test is such that even very small differences among group means will be statistically significant. There are numerous statistics used to test for significance of the discrimination. These inter-related tests of significance include the Mahalanobis D Square Statistic, Hotelling's T^2, the F statistic, and Wilks' Λ. The statistics used in most computer software packages are the Mahalanobis D Square Statistic, which gives the distance between groups means and its significance, and the F statistic, which provides the statistical significance of the discrimination between groups. The validity of classification for discriminant analysis compares homogeneity within groups to heterogeneity between groups in a manner similar to analysis of variance.

The dimensions of the classification refer to the underlying structure to the discriminant analysis model. In a manner similar to factor analysis, discriminant analysis also has characteristic roots of a polynomial equation that reflects the total amount of discrimination explained by the factors.* Each root extracted from the equation explains a decreasing proportion of the dispersion variance and the sum of all roots equals $(K - 1)(p)$. The proportion of variance explained by each root is, therefore, the root divided by $(K - 1)(p)$, where K is the number of groups, and p is the number of variables. For example suppose we had a four-group, ten-variable discriminant analysis model. Thirty would then be the total variance and each root extracted would explain a certain portion of this variance. This is illustrated in Table 4-11.

---

*The characteristic root λ comes from the equation

$$(W^{-1}B - \lambda I)\, v = 0$$

where W is the within-group pooled dispersion, B is the between-group dispersion matrix, λ is the characteristic root or eigenvalue, v is the set of characteristics, and I is the identity matrix.

Table 4-11. Eigenvalues in Discriminant Analysis

Root number	Eigenvalue (root)	Percentage variance explained
1	20	0.66
2	10	0.33
3	0	0.00

Notice if the classification is compact and the research design is tight, then only a few roots have to be reported. Remember each root reflects a dimension of the classification and gives a quantitative index of how much variance in the discrimination is explained. As in canonical correlation, statistical tests, such as chi square, are usually provided by computer programs to test the level of significance of these roots. Significant roots are used in explaining the variation in the data that validates the classification and forms the basis for the underlying structure.

It is worth noting that these underlying dimensions are artificial constructs whose axis is mathematically oriented so that the ratio of between-group variance and within-group variance is maximized. In factor analysis, these factors can be rotated to make interpretation easier. In discriminant analysis, these factors cannot be rotated to more interpretable solutions although research in this area is underway.

Results of multigroup discriminant analysis might appear in a computer printout as follows. First, the eigenvalues (roots) and the associated cumulative proportion of total dispersion explained by the root are printed. The eigenvalues are related to the λ value in canonical correlation.

Eigenvalues
140.1   12.7   0.0003   0.00

Cumulative proportion
0.92   1.0   1.0

In this example, two factors (or dimensions) explain nearly all of the dispersion in the discrimination. One factor explains 92%, and the other factor explains 8%.

Canonical correlation is also used in multigroup discriminant analysis to show the discriminant dimensions and their relationship to the variables used in the discriminant analysis. The degree of association of these variables on these dimensions is indicated by the canonical coefficients. For example, if four dimensions or

Table 4-12. Canonical Variate or Dimension[a]

Variable	Dimensions			
	1	**2**	**3**	**4**
1	8.9	−0.79	0.33	−0.127
2	3.9	−0.33	−1.32	−0.348
3	−7.1	−0.92	0.66	−0.038
4	−0.04	0.49	−0.07	−0.005
5	−0.06	−0.02	0.125	0.289

[a]Notice these are the unscaled weights attached to each variable and they are interpreted as regression coefficients (the magnitude and sign of the weight show how each variable predicts the discriminant score). Some computer programs also report the scaled canonical variates that are similar to beta weights in regression and represent the unique amount of variation in the discriminant dimension that is explained by each variable. Thus, the scaled variates reflect the relative contribution of each variable toward differentiating among groups.

canonical variates are extracted, then the canonical coefficients or b_i for each canonical variate or dimension is reported (see Table 4-12).

Finally, group indices are found by substituting and then averaging for each group each individual's characteristics multiplied by the canonical coefficient (see Table 4-13). These values might be considered as the centroids for each discriminant dimension in reduced discriminant space.

With each canonical variate or dimension we have the canonical correlation between attributes, when weighted with the above canonical coefficients: 0.99; 0.96; 0.004; 0.002. The canonical coefficients or weights on the four scaled canonical variates (or dimensions) can be directly interpreted, depending upon the sign and magnitude of the weights attached to these dimensions, as being the pattern of variables that distinguished the two discriminant dimensions. Thus, for each variable or attribute, we have its measure of association with the underlying discriminant structure.

Table 4-13. Canonical Variates at Group Means

Group	Dimensions			
	1	**2**	**3**	**4**
1	7.8	3.88	−00	00
2	−14.5	0.54	−00	00
3	5.06	−3.32	00	00

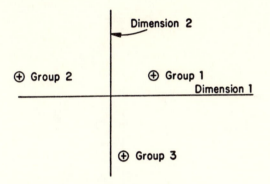

Figure 4-8. Graph of group centroids.

We can now picture the centroids for each group in reduced discriminant space and see how these centroids orient themselves with respect to each of the discriminant dimensions. In two dimensions, this is illustrated in Figure 4-8. The BIOMED computer printout also gives for two canonical variates the indices or values for each observation and for each group, as well as the mean or centroid values. Table 4-14 gives an example of this.

Finally, a plot of these values (Figure 4-9) gives the researcher some perspective concerning where these groups are located, relative to each other, in reduced discriminant space and more important the orientation of each case to both the centroid and

Table 4-14. Values for Each Observation and Each Group on Two Canonical Variates

Group 1	Mean coordinate $X = 7.8$ $Y = 3.88$ centroid for Group 1	
Case	x	y
1	8.1	3.7
2	7.2	4.6
3	8.1	3.3
Group 2	Mean coordinate $X = -14.5$ $Y = 0.54$ centroid for Group 2	
Case	x	y
1	−14.6	0.7
2	−13.2	1.7
3	−15.7	−0.82
Group 3	Mean coordinate $X = 5.06$ $Y = -3.3$ centroid for Group 3	
Case	x	y
1	4.8	−2.7
2	3.8	−2.3
3	6.2	−4.5

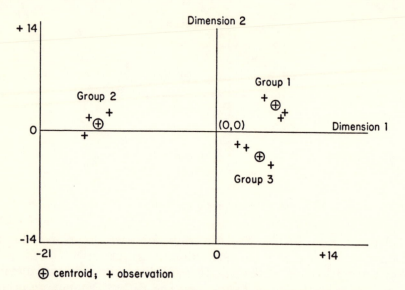

Figure 4-9. Graph of individual scores in discriminant space with centroid score.

the discriminant dimensions. Geometrically the plot of the canonical variables can be thought of plotting each case as a point and where each variable is a dimension (axis). Since we have two dimensions with computer printouts, we can only use the first two variables in the discriminant model. The cases are then projected onto a line for 2 groups, a plane for 3 groups, or hyperplane for four or more groups in discriminant space such that the groups are farthest apart. The x axis is the value for the first canonical variable of the classification function, the y axis is the second. The canonical variables evaluated at the group mean for each group (canonical variable coefficient times average group value for the variable) are also plotted. Such a visualization is useful for depicting how distinct the groups are from each other.

Some computer software programs calculate the loadings or correlations between each discriminatory variable and the computed discriminant score for each dimension upon which the discrimination is based. This information is valuable for understanding the nature of the relationship between the variable and the dimension of the classification. Table 4-15 illustrates this important interpretive output.

We can now discuss variables that are loaded or related to the

Table 4-15. Correlations or Loading of
Variables on Discriminant Factors

Variable	1	2
1	0.00	0.01
2	−0.09	0.04
3	0.37	0.13
4	0.46	−0.06
5	0.91	0.01
6	0.02	0.87

discriminant dimensions.* We can also plot the values on such dimensions as in Figure 4-10. The scale of each axis runs from −1.0 to 0.0 to +1.0. Variables 3, 4, and 5 are loaded on or positively correlated with Dimension 1, indicating that high or low scores on these variables are related to high or low scores (respectively) on the first discriminant function while a high or a low score on variable 6 is related to high and low scores on Dimension 2. Some computer programs present the intergroup distances in the form of a Mahalanobis D Square Statistic or its equivalent F ratio (Table 4-16). We can then say that Table 4-16 shows the spatial distances between Group 1 and Group 3 as approximately three times the distance between Group 1 and Group 2. Thus, in discriminant space, we have a quantitative distance measure between groups as measured on the variables used in the analysis.

The final feature of multivariate discriminant analysis is the assignment of individuals to their proper groups. First, a discriminant score function must be calculated for each group, an example of which is found in Table 4-17. A statistical technique called Bayesian analysis is then used in conjunction with the discriminant score function and prior probability of group assignment (usually specified to the computer program) to derive a posterior probability for each case being in each group. This is usually presented in table form such as in Table 4-18.

Finally, a summary table of correct and incorrect classifications

---

*The loading of each variable with the discriminant factor can be found by finding the correlation of the variable with the total discriminant scores obtained. The interpretation of these values is similar to that of the factor loadings in a factor analysis, that is, the correlation or association between the variable and the underlying discriminant dimension.

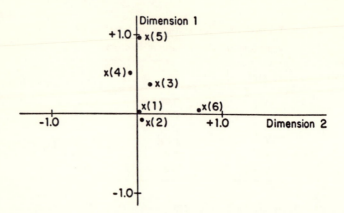

Figure 4-10. Plot of loadings on factors of discrimination.

are presented in Table 4-19. With discriminant analysis models powerful output statistics that can be used for the formulation of educational policy can be derived. Suppose we could estimate the probability (from the variables used in the discriminant analysis model) of a new student dropping out of school or of drug abuse or of success or failure in an educational program. Suppose we knew the costs associated with such outcomes. We could, using expected value theory, determine (multiplying the probability times the cost) the expected cost to the organization for incorrect classification.

We can also use the probability of group membership in a modified form $\ln [p/(1-p)]$ as a dependent variable in a multiple regression model. This transformed regression equation

$$\ln \left(\frac{p}{1-p}\right) = a_1 x_1 + a_2 x_2 + \cdots + a_n x_n + c$$

is called a logit model and can be used by policy analysts to see how the probability of group membership can be influenced by unit changes in the independent variables.

Table 4-16. Intergroup Distances

	Group 1	Group 2	Group 3
Group 1	—	1.1	3.0
Group 2	—	—	3.6
Group 3	—	—	—

Table 4-17. Discriminant Score Function

Variable	Group 1	Group 2	Group 3
1	−140.2	−343.5	−165.3
2	− 67.3	−155.9	− 76.5
3	120.6	270.8	146.7
4	0.4	−0.16	−3.0
5	150.0	357.2	179.2
Constant	142.2	−780.3	−230.6

Table 4-18. Summary Table of Correct and Incorrect Classifications

Group 1 Case	Group 1	Group 2	Group 3
1	1.0	0.0	0.0
2	0.8	0.2	0.0
3	0.09	0.05	0.05
4	0.6	0.3	0.1

Group 2 Case	Group 1	Group 2	Group 3
1	0.0	1.0	0.0
2	0.0	1.0	0.0
3	0.2	0.7	0.1
4	0.6[a]	0.4	0.0

Group 3 Case	Group 1	Group 2	Group 3
1	0.0	0.0	1.0
2	0.0	0.0	1.0
3	0.0	0.7[a]	0.3
4	0.0	0.2	0.8

[a]Note the misclassification.

Table 4-19. Classification Matrix

Group	1	2	3
1	4	0	0
2	1	3	0
3	0	1	3

Thus, the logit model coupled with discriminant analysis can be used to study change in the probability of group membership, such as a new student dropping out of school as a function of school resources. We might find that there is a 10% decrease in dropout probability for an additional $10.00 placed in the counseling program. Similar cost benefit analysis can then be performed on each of the resource allocation options. For an illustration of an educational policy application of logit analysis and regression see Bruno and Nelkin (1975).

4-5 ILLUSTRATIVE USE OF MULTIGROUP DISCRIMINANT ANALYSIS*

The following illustration of multigroup discriminant analysis concerns the classification of four groups of Israeli settlers (Rettig 1964). The four groups consisted of first generation (immigrant) *Kibbutz*, second generation (Israeli born) *Kibbutz*, first generation *Moshavah* and second generation *Moshavah*. The *Moshavah* are noncollective communities. The purpose of the study was to see whether there was an underlying structure that discriminated between these four groups on responses to a moral–ideological questionnaire consisting of 50 questions. There were 150 respondents in each group.

Table 4-20 presents the roots extracted, the variance explained by each, and the residual variance following each extraction. The two roots accounted for nearly 90% of the variance between groups, leaving approximately 10% for error. The first root absorbed 63% and the second root 26%. The weights of the first 9 of the 50 questionnaire items on the two canonical variates are listed in Table 4-21.

Table 4-20. Characteristic Roots (λ), Explained Variance, and Residual Variance Between Groups[a]

Order	λ	Explained variance (%)	Residual variance	df	p[b]
0	—	0	686.31	150	< 0.001
1	0.732	63.6	250.10	98	< 0.001
2	0.300	26.1	71.30	48	NS[c]

[a]*Source*: S. Rettig, "Multiple Discriminant Analysis, An Illustration," *American Sociological Association*, vol. 10, no. 6, 1964. Reproduced with permission of the author and publisher.

[b]Probability that the residual variance contains additional significant roots; the significance level is $P = 0.001$, based on a chi square test.

[c]NS = not significant.

Table 4-21.   Scaled Characteristic Vectors[a]

Item	$\overline{a}_1$	$\overline{a}_2$
1. Killing a person in defense of one's own life	−0.466	0.430
2. Kidnapping and holding a child for ransom	−0.469	3.306
3. Having sex relations while unmarried	1.274	−0.336
4. Forging a check	0.143	0.161
5. Habitually failing to keep promises	−0.100	1.256
6. Refusing aid to a person who was hurt in an accident	−0.352	−0.427
7. An industry maintaining working conditions for its workers known to be detrimental to their health	0.946	0.974
8. A doctor allowing a badly deformed baby to die when he could save its life but not cure its deformity	−0.469	0.310
9. A legislator, for a financial consideration, using his influence to secure the passage of a law known to be contrary to public interest	1.367	−0.217
10–50. (Left out due to space limitations)		

[a]*Source*: S. Rettig, "Multiple Discriminant Analysis, An Illustration," *American Sociological Association*, vol. 10, no. 6, 1964. Reproduced with permission of the author and publisher.

Figure 4-11 shows the composite mean score of each group across the 50 weighted judgments, in two-dimensional fashion. The first canonical variate $\overline{a}_1$ separates both generations of Israeli settlers according to type of community, collective versus non-collective. The collectivity effect alone accounts for approximately 64% of the total variance in ethical judgments between the groups. Inspection of the weights attached to each question on the

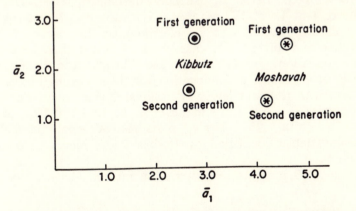

Figure 4-11. Mean values of four groups on two canonical variates. *Source*: S. Rettig, "Multiple Discriminant Analysis, An Illustration," *American Sociological Association*, vol. 10, no. 6, 1964. Reproduced with permission of the author and publisher.

questionnaire (the first nine of which are reported in Table 4-21) reveals that the collectivity dimension predominantly contrasts judgments that express on the one hand an anti-exploitative value orientation (*Kibbutz* highest on items 45 and 30—not shown) and on the other a value orientation focusing more on general social responsibility (e.g., *Moshavah* high on items 47 and 19—not shown).

The second canonical variate separates the first from the second generation, in both types of communities. The generational effect accounts for approximately 26% of the total between-group variance. The greatest contribution to this dimension is made by judgments relating to criminal or otherwise irresponsible behavior involving a strong economic motive (first generation high on items 2, 42, and 14—not shown) versus those less directly related to economic profit (second generation very high on item 28—not shown).

The intergroup distances are presented in Table 4-22. The socioethical distance between the two types of communities exceeds the distance between the two generations: Intergroup distances are smallest for the settlers in the same type of community and largest for any two groups differing in both community and generation. Groups that differ only in type of community show an intermediate distance. The four groups can therefore be positioned in two-dimensional, perpendicular space.

Another illustration of multivariate discriminant analysis is found in Asher and Shively (1969). Harbison and Myers* developed a composite index to distinguish countries in terms of four a priori defined levels of human resource development: Level I, underdeveloped; Level II, partially developed; Level III, semi-advanced; and Level IV, advanced. Harbison and Myers suggested that countries should also be classified on the basis of several qualitative and quantitative characteristics rather than ranked on a single dimension. In the Asher and Shively study discriminant analysis of economic and education variables was used to place 75 countries into the four levels of national development. There were 21 countries in Level I, 19 in Level II, 21 in Level III, and 14 in Level IV, (total, 75). Twelve measures of economic and educational variables identified by Harbison and Myers were used as predictors.

Table 4-23 presents the correlation matrix. Many of the values

---

*Harbison, F., and Myers, C. *Education, Manpower and Economic Growth*. New York: McGraw Hill, 1964.

Table 4-22. Intergroup Distances (Mahalanobis D Square Statistic)[a]

	First generation kibbutz	Second generation kibbutz	First generation moshavah
Second generation Kibbutz	1.108	—	—
First generation Moshavah	3.316	4.606	—
Second generation Moshavah	3.555	2.419	1.397

[a]Source: S. Rettig, "Multiple Discriminant Analysis, An Illustration," American Sociological Association, vol. 10. no. 6, 1964. Reproduced with permission of the author and publisher.

are lower than those reported by Harbison and Myers. This is presumably due to the different techniques for handling missing data. Discriminant analysis indicated that only two predictor variables were not significant at the 0.001 level: variable 9, percent in science and technology and variable 10, percent in humanities, law, and arts. There were three eigenvalues or dimensions significant at the 0.05 level. Table 4-24 summarizes these results (the correlation between the variables and the discriminant scores). Thus, the first dimension eigenvalue accounted for 85.40% of the total discriminating power, the second eigenvalue for 11.32%, and the

Table 4-23. Correlation Matrix of the 12 Social and Economic Variables[a,b]

	1	2	3	4	5	6	7	8	9	10	11	12
1.	—											
2.	−0.83	—										
3.	0.77	−0.80	—									
4.	0.73	−0.84	0.74	—								
5.	0.68	−0.79	0.83	0.73	—							
6.	0.74	−0.85	0.87	0.77	0.97	—						
7.	0.83	−0.84	0.80	0.73	0.70	0.81	—					
8.	0.85	−0.73	0.76	0.69	0.68	0.74	0.82	—				
9.	0.08	−0.12	0.09	0.05	0.17	0.17	0.13	0.07	—			
10.	−0.07	−0.07	−0.04	0.02	−0.15	−0.14	−0.10	−0.14	−0.30	—		
11.	0.36	−0.19	0.35	0.29	0.19	0.28	0.43	0.34	0.12	−0.15	—	
12.	−0.64	0.64	−0.50	−0.62	−0.55	−0.59	−0.66	−0.54	−0.27	0.13	−0.29	—

[a]Source: Asher and Shively (1969). Reproduced with permission of the author and publisher.
[b]$N = 75$.

Table 4-24. Vectors of $W^{-1}A$, as Columns (Factors)[a]

Row		I	II	III
l. root		9.03	1.20	0.35
percent trace		85.40	11.32	3.28
Vector				
1	Per capita GNP	0.00	−0.00	0.00
2	Percent in agriculture	−0.09	−0.01	0.06
3	Teachers, first and second level	−0.09	0.04	−0.03
4	Physicians per 10,000	0.04	0.13	−0.00
5	First level enrollment	−0.37	0.11	−0.16
6	First and second level enrollment	0.46	−0.06	0.17
7	Second level (adjusted) enrollment	0.04	0.04	0.04
8	Third level (adjusted) enrollment	0.21	0.00	−0.14
9	Percent in science and technology	−0.08	0.03	0.08
10	Percent in humanities, etc.	−0.03	0.01	0.01
11	Percent national income on education	0.70	−0.95	−0.84
12	Percent age 5–14	−0.29	0.23	0.46

[a]*Source*: Asher and Shively (1969). Reproduced with permission of the author and publisher.

third for 3.28%. Noting the values of the coefficients of the discriminant function, the predictors could be reduced to one major factor (discriminant function), with a second contributing somewhat to the accuracy of the grouping. The characteristics contributing to each factor can be inferred from Table 4-24. For example, we can learn that Factor I is high on variables 11 and 6, but low on variables 5 and 12. Thus, Factor I indicates that the allocation of resources should be weighted toward education, and this is the factor that primarily distinguishes the grouping of countries on economic development. This classification scheme was

Table 4-25. Correct Classification Matrix[a]

Row	1	2	3	4
1	19	2	0	0
2	3	15	1	0
3	0	4	16	1
4	0	0	0	14

[a]*Source*: Asher and Shively (1969). Reproduced with permission of the author and publisher.

fairly effective; 64 of the 75 countries were correctly classified, a success rate of 85.33% (Table 4-25).

In summary, the canonical correlation part of the multigroup discriminant analysis is used to find the underlying structure of the a priori classification. For example, if we had four groupings of students:

1. minority high achiever,
2. minority low achiever,
3. majority high achiever, and
4. majority low achiever

and gave an attitude questionnaire or measured these students on background socioeconomic variables, we might find variables from the questionnaire or background survey clustering (high canonical coefficients) to indicate that certain attitudes concerning achievement and minority identification form the underlying structure to the four classifications. Alternatively, we might find that there is no underlying structure, or we might find an additional structure such as economic class.

4-6 EDUCATIONAL APPLICATIONS OF DISCRIMINANT ANALYSIS

In an educational application of multigroup discriminant analysis, classroom status and teacher approval and disapproval were investigated (Herrmann 1972). The purpose of the analysis was:

1. to examine the interrelationships between the three status dimensions of acceptance, competence, and power;
2. to ascertain whether sex differences exist in the pattern of these relationships; and
3. to examine the relationship between teacher approval and disapproval and each of the three status systems.

In another application, discriminant analysis was used to find a composite of variables that discriminate between students of high and low ability (Simon and Ward 1973). The variables used in the discriminant function were intelligence scores, scores on the Junior-Senior High School Personality Questionnaire (H.S.P.Q.), and a drawing test on a specific theme. The latter two tests were measures of creativity. Information was sought on variables that would maximally disperse students into two groups. It was found that there was a significant difference between high- and low-ability groups on the drawing test measure of creativity. A significant difference between the high- and low-ability groups on the H.S.P.Q. measure of creativity was found. The mean difference between the two ability groups on the intelligence tests was significant. The discriminant analysis supported the view that the probability of membership in high- or low-ability groups forms correlates with scores on certain measures of creativity and intelligence tests.

Finally, another study employed discriminant analysis to examine college persistence, withdrawal, and academic dismissal (Bean and Covert 1973). In this application, it was hypothesized that measures of scholastic aptitude would discriminate between persisters and academic dismissals, whereas measures of personality would discriminate between persisters and withdrawals.

The measure of scholastic aptitude was the Scholastic Aptitude Test—Verbal (SAT-V) and Scholastic Aptitude Test—Mathematics (SAT-M). The personality measures were Runner Studies of Attitude Patterns College Form. The Runner scales were reduced to three component areas: independence, acquiescence, nonassertiveness. These areas accounted for 54% of the total variance. The three criterion groups were persisters, withdrawals, and academic dismissals. Five predictors (the three components of the Runner scale and the SAT-V and SAT-M) were used to predict membership in the three criterion groups through a discriminant analysis.

Results of the discriminant analysis for both sexes showed that the predictors discriminated significantly among the three criterion groups. For males the academic function (SAT-M and SAT-V) accounted for 89% of the variance, for females 77%. The personality function was significant only for females in the area of independence and nonassertiveness.

The hypothesis that academic aptitude measures discriminated between persisters and academic dismissals was supported for both males and females. The hypothesis that personality measures discriminated between persisters and withdrawals was supported for females only.

4-7 SUMMARY

Discriminant analysis can be used by the educational policy analyst for two principal policy relevant purposes: assignment or classification and finding hypothetical constructs or underlying structures which explain the a priori defined discrimination. Extensions of discriminant analysis methods such as the combining with regression analysis to yield a logit model insure the future potential of this sophisticated multivariate methodology for both theoretical and application studies in education. The vast interpretive output associated with multigroup discriminant analysis also offers the educational policy analyst an excellent methodological tool for performing basic research on problems related to the underlying discrimination between groups.

Foundations of Microeconomic Theory for Educational Policy Analysis

5-1 INTRODUCTION

Economists are assuming a larger role in educational research and have made substantial contributions in terms of both conceptualization of problems and methodologies. Probably the greatest methodological contribution of economists can be found in the applications of human capital and production function concepts to the study of education. Economists, as mentioned in Chapter 1, are primarily concerned with causal modeling and estimating parameters of the system under investigation rather than measuring specific aspects of the system. In education, this latter area is typical of the concerns of psychometrists. It is this transition from a focus on measurement to a focus on causal modeling that requires the policy analyst to develop a fundamental understanding of certain economic principles and concepts. The purpose of this chapter is to provide a capsule overview of microeconomic theory and to examine how it relates to problems in educational policy and planning. A comprehensive bibliography is provided at the end of this book.

5-2 PRODUCTION FUNCTIONS

The school administrator is principally concerned with transforming resources (teacher time, teacher quality, money, laboratory space, etc.) into outputs (student achievement). It is important, therefore, to study the transformation process (inputs to outputs) itself in order to insure better resource allocation. The transformation process is depicted in Figure 5-1.

In microeconomic theory this transformation system is known as the production process and the relationship between inputs and outputs is known as the production function. The production function itself contains three components as shown in Figure 5-2. Production functions are used in the following ways. First, they predict how decision makers will allocate resources. Second, they are useful for determining how the decision maker should allocate his resources. Finally, they are used as frames of reference for comparing alternative or more complex models of a physical system.

Thus we can distinguish the normative and positive or descriptive uses of production functions. The positive uses show how producer behavior is explained by postulating the particular production function. In the normative uses the producer is given information concerning which elements or variables in the production process are most important in producing a given output.

The production function is mathematically the means by which maximum output can be obtained from any given set of resources (output is a mathematical function of inputs)

$$\text{outputs} = f(x_1 \cdots x_m)$$

where x_i are the resources. In addition, the production function can be defined as the locus of all technically efficient combinations of resources whose output dominates all other outputs that might be achieved through the less effective use of given resources.

Production functions in industry are based upon the assumption that firms will always desire to maximize outputs for any given set of inputs, for example, firms are assumed to be technically efficient. To

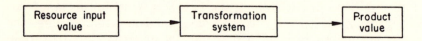

Figure 5-1. Production function process.

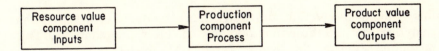

Figure 5-2. Production function components.

satisfy this important assumption of a production function, the industry or company must possess knowledge of its relevant production set and must also have discretion over the way its resource inputs are used. There must also be an incentive to apply its knowledge of the production function; that is, it has the desire and ability to combine inputs into maximizing output for any set of physical inputs.

The role of prices of inputs for determining the optimal or exact combination of inputs thus becomes a crucial factor for consideration in production functions. In addition, outputs also have an associated price. The application of production theory to education becomes even more complex since in education we do not have a "price" for educational outputs or at least these prices as well as the outputs themselves are difficult to measure.

In education we are also faced with problems of multiple outputs. For example, one production function might take the form required to maximize the number of graduates from a system. Another production function might relate system educational resource inputs to student scores on standardized examinations (as are found in the Coleman study). Education production functions might also examine outputs in terms of net future earnings of graduates.

Along with the problem of multiple outputs, school administrators have little discretion (especially in school districts with strong teacher unions and state-mandated instructional programs) for mixing inputs. Those inputs relevant to the production set, especially when the output is in the cognitive area, are not clearly known—essentially the physics of the learning process is still a mystery. While the assumptions of production function theory pose major limitations in terms of its applicability to the study of the phenomena of education, it can be extremely useful for studying other outputs of schools (graduates, cost, etc.) and does present an excellent framework for studying the relationship among inputs, outputs, and processes of schooling. This technique is one of the major tools of benefit cost analysis in education since it examines implicit resource or input tradeoffs and their effects on outputs. In this context production function theory contains as a subset the analytical optimization methodology of linear programming. This technique, discussed in Chapter 7, allows the analyst to maximize or minimize a linear objective function (production function) subject to a set of constraints. The production function concept is best described with isocost, isoquant curves or maps.

5-3 ISOQUANT MAPS*

For the purpose of illustration, consider the following problem. A school district is constructing a new building of q square footage. Available resources allow the district two options: Either build a single story structure, that is, minimize the quantity of steel used with a large amount of land allocated, or build a multistory structure using a small quantity of land and a larger quantity of steel.

This problem can be represented graphically as a surface that represents the most production that can be obtained from a given set of resources—land (X_1) and steel (X_2). This surface is called the production surface. It is the locus of technically efficient combinations of inputs for each level of outputs. If we let X_1 be the amount of land resource, X_2 be the amount of steel resource, and q be the square footage produced, a production function can be defined by

$$Q = f(X_1, X_2)$$

where Q is the maximum output possible with a given set of inputs. This production function itself can be represented in a three-dimensional diagram (Figure 5-3). In Figure 5-3a, points B, B', and B'' represent arbitrary combinations of inputs X_1 and X_2. (Note X_1B, X_2B notation for axes means the combination of X_1 and X_2 associated with B, etc.) Suppose we know from the above equation that with these combinations of inputs we can produce some maximum quantity of our output, square footage (i.e., $B*q$, $B'*q'$, $B''*q''$). The points $*q$, $*q'$, and $*q''$ are points on the production surface.

We can define a production function for q, f_q, on the production surface, where $f_q(X_1, X_2)$ is the maximum amount of q that can be produced with inputs X_1 and X_2. If we select a particular value of q, say $*q'$, then we can define a locus of points by

$$f_q(X_1, X_2) = *q'$$

This locus of points is called an isoquant or equal product line. For

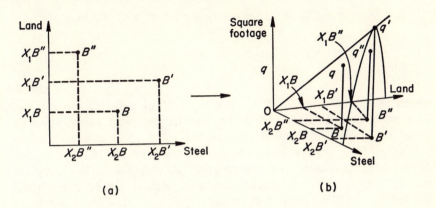

Figure 5-3. Production function analysis.

every value of q, we can plot an isoquant, thereby forming a family of isoquants. An isocost line is a line representing equal costs. The point of tangency between an isocost line and the isoquant is the optimal point. See Figure 5-4.

The isoquant is the intersection of the production function, and the plane at height $*q'$ over the $X_1 X_2$ plane of resources. Furthermore, all combinations of resources represented by an isoquant are technically efficient, for example, no combination of inputs is intrinsically better than any other from the point of view of physical design.

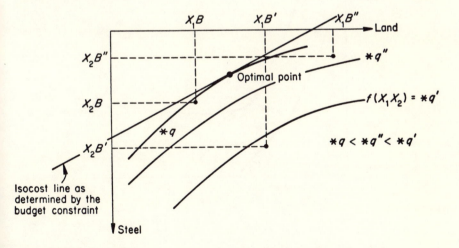

Figure 5-4. Optimization.

It is interesting to consider the rate of change of the isoquant

$$\frac{\partial X_i}{\partial X_j}$$

which is also known as the marginal rate of substitution (MRS). This ratio is sometimes called the rate of technical substitution in order to emphasize that it defines the relatively physical productivities of the inputs independent of their value. Note that the slope of the isoquant, or more properly its negative, is the marginal rate of substitution and shows how one product can be substituted for another holding output constant.

At optimal there is, by definition, no cost reduction possible by moving in either direction along an isoquant. This implies that the change in total cost ΔC relative to the change in output Δq for any incremental change in a resource ΔX_1 and ΔX_2 is equal for all resources that could change cost and output (see also Figure 5-5).

$$\frac{\Delta C/\Delta X_1}{\Delta q/\Delta X_1} = \frac{\Delta C/\Delta X_2}{\Delta q/\Delta X_2}$$

Thus, $\Delta C/\Delta q$ is equal for all resource inputs at optimum.

For the case where resources X_1 and X_2 each sell for a constant unit, price C_1 and C_2, respectively, then we have the conditions for

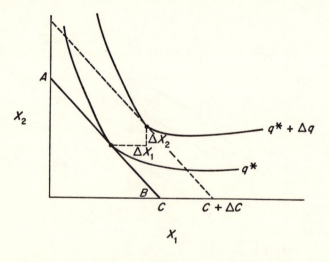

Figure 5-5. Change of cost for change in output for each input.

optimality as

$$\frac{\Delta q/\Delta X_2}{C_2} = \frac{\Delta q/\Delta X_1}{C_1} = \frac{MP_1}{C_1} = \frac{MP_2}{C_2}$$

The marginal product (*MP*) is defined as the incremental gain in output associated with an increment in resource input

$$\frac{\text{Change in output}}{\text{Change in resource input}} = MP_i = \begin{cases} \dfrac{\Delta Q}{\Delta X} \text{ (nonanalytical)} \\ \dfrac{\partial q}{\partial X} \text{ (if continuous)} \end{cases}$$

This means, in effect, that the effectiveness of a dollar spent on one resource is equal to the effectiveness of a dollar spent on any other input.

The criterion for optimality can now be restated in terms of the slope of the isoquant

$$\frac{MP_2}{MP_1} = \frac{C_2}{C_1}$$

or

$$\text{MRS} = \frac{-C_2}{C_1}$$

By definition the change of output (∂q) equals zero along the isoquant. Since marginal rates of substitution can only be defined in terms of any two resources while all others are fixed, we will restrict our attention to X_i and X_j, and the change of output can be expressed as

$$\partial q = MP_i\, \partial X_i + MP_j\, \partial X_j$$

Since ∂q or change of output equals zero along the isoquant, the equation can be reduced to

$$\frac{\partial X_i}{\partial X_j} = \frac{-MP_j}{MP_i}$$

The marginal rate of substitution of one resource for another is, therefore, defined and equal to the negative reciprocals of their marginal products. Resources ideally should be allocated among various inputs in a school until the marginal product divided by unit price is the same for each input; that is, MP/P_u for books, equipment, teachers, laboratories, etc., where MP is the marginal product and P_u is the price.

The problem in educational situations is that it is impossible to know how much is added to outputs by the addition of a given unit of input. However, we can achieve realistic real world approximation by using subjective probabilities.

Table 5-1 considers a resource allocation problem (Thomas 1962). Using expected value and subjective probabilities, we see the marginal product for each resource:

$$A = (0.1)\,(0.6) + (0.2)\,(0.8) + (0.4)\,(1.0) + (0.2)\,(1.2)$$
$$\quad + (1.4)\,(0.1) = 1.0$$
$$B = (0.3)\,(0.6) + (0.4)\,(0.8) + (0.2)\,(1.0) + (0.1)\,(1.2)$$
$$\quad + (0)\,(1.4) = .82$$
$$C = (0.1)\,(0.6) + (0.1)\,(0.8) + (0.2)\,(1.0)$$
$$\quad + (0.4)\,(1.2) + (0.2)\,(1.4) = 1.1$$

We then divide the marginal products for A, B, and C by their respective costs

$$A = 1.0/5\ = 0.2$$
$$B = 0.82/2 = 0.4$$
$$C = 1.1/6\ = 0.18$$

Thus, B is the preferred input (has the highest marginal product). For

Table 5-1. Resource Allocation Problem—Increments in Output[a]

Resource input	Cost per unit	Expected performance increment				
		< 0.7	0.7–0.89	0.9–1.09	1.1–1.29	⩾ 1.3
A	5	0.1	0.2	0.4	0.2	0.1
B	2	0.3	0.4	0.2	0.1	0
C	6	0.1	0.1	0.2	0.4	0.2
Midpoint of interval		0.6	0.8	1.0	1.2	1.4

[a]Source: J. Alan Thomas, The Productive School. New York: John Wiley & Sons, 1971. Reproduced with permission of the author and publisher.

our system, therefore, it will pay to shift to resource B until the MP's are equal.

The optimal combination of any two inputs U and V requires that the ratio of their marginal products be equal to the ratio of their prices:

$$\frac{MP_u}{MP_v} = \frac{P_u}{P_v}$$

or

$$\frac{MP_u}{P_u} = \frac{MP_v}{P_v}$$

Suppose one additional unit of u (teacher time) produces a performance increment of 15 points and costs $0.50, while an additional unit of input v (teaching machine) produces a performance increment of 12 points and costs $5.00. For each dollar of u we get 2 points while v yields 2.4 points. Therefore, a shift in resource inputs from u to v is most productive.

Since price plays such a dominant role in the determination of marginal product, it is important to focus on this variable in order to examine how changes in price of resource inputs affect the decision process.

Suppose the price of the inputs of labor (L) and machines (M) change. If cost of labor is C_L and the cost of machines C_M, then the units of labor and machines are defined to be:

$$\frac{C_L}{P_L} \qquad \frac{C_M}{P_M}$$

If both inputs change at the same rate (say P_L and P_M doubles), the ratio or slope of the isocost unit remains unchanged (AB in Figure 5-6).

Assume the price of labor P_L doubles, but the price of machines remains constant. The price change ratio P_M/P_L is reduced by half. The isocosts that are consistent with the new set of prices will then have a slope half as steep as the initial isocosts line. Since the price of machines is unchanged, the point C_M/P_M remains the same, as shown in Figure 5-6, with segment $A'B$. Thus, adjustments in the price of labor P_L (say teacher salaries) can be thought of as pivoting all

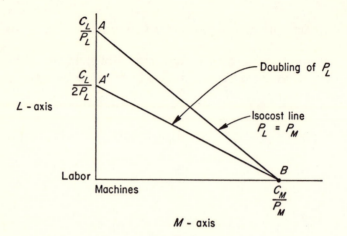

Figure 5-6. Pricing and its effect upon isocost line.

isocosts on their machine intercepts (point B) until each isocost line intercepts the L-axis as a point halfway between the origin and its initial L-intercept.

Obviously, q is no longer the least cost input combination for a given output x (as shown in Figure 5-7). The new least cost combination is now q' as shown in Figure 5-8. In order to retain the same level of production X, a higher amount of costs will have to be used. In Figure 5-8, $C'_M > C_M$ and $C'_L > C_L$.

Or alternatively, a lower level of output or production x' could

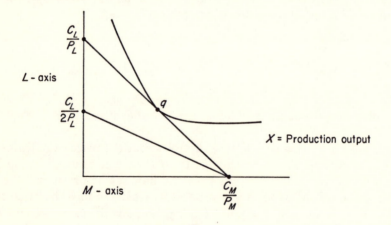

Figure 5-7. Effect of changes in prices on optimum point.

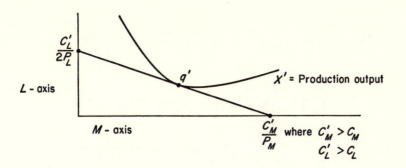

Figure 5-8. Effect of changes in prices on total costs to retain production output.

be specified and the new optimal combination q' would result (see Figure 5-9). Thus, as price changes in a system, there is a corresponding rise in the least cost or the cost of the optimal combination of resources. Note that price changes also lead to changes in the composition or mixture of inputs in a system.

Examining the sample problem relating the production process of instructional square footage for a school plant to tons of steel and acres of land used, we can define the isocost line for a given piece of steel C_S and acre of land C_A with a fixed budget C_O as in Figure 5-10. We define C_O/C_S as the number of tons of steel one could purchase at a price of C_S and C_O/C_A as the number of acres one could purchase at a price of C_A.

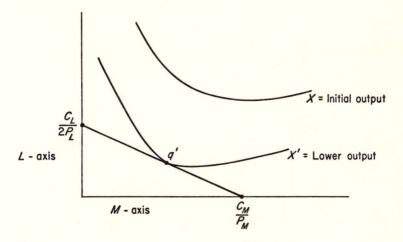

Figure 5-9. Adjusting production output to reflect changes in price.

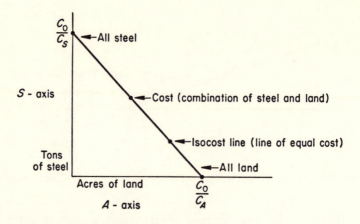

Figure 5-10. Isocost line for sample problem.

Since prices change (inflation, depression) due to market forces, it would be valuable to consider possible price changes in our analysis. If the price of steel, currently at C_S, rose to a higher level C_S' while the cost of land remained constant, the slope of the isocost line would decrease as shown in Figure 5-11. Subsequent isoquant or isocost analysis would yield a new solution reflecting a higher cost to produce the same output or lower output for the same cost as shown in Figure 5-12. If both C_S and C_A rose by the same rates to C_S' and C_A', then the slope of the isocost line would

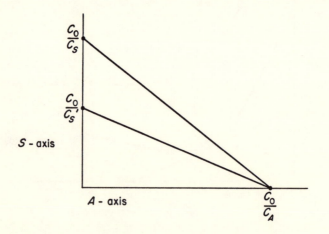

Figure 5-11. Isocost under price changes for sample problem.

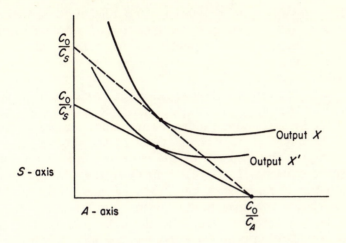

Figure 5-12. Change of prices and outputs for sample problem.

remain constant, but the level of production for a set amount of dollars would decrease, as shown in Figure 5-13. Thus, pricing is an extremely important aspect of microeconomic theory and dramatically influences the form of isoquant diagrams. The measurement of prices and costs will be discussed in Section 5-5.

5-4 INTRODUCTION TO MARGINAL ANALYSIS*

Marginal analysis in economics deals with rates of changes of outputs to changes in inputs and forms the foundation of what is

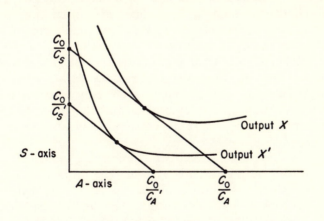

Figure 5-13. Effect of pricing on cost-output tradeoff.

commonly described as systems analysis related to optimization. Assume $q = f(x)$, where q is the quantity of output or product. The transformation from input value to output value can be represented by two different models, the input value model and the physical system model.

Up to now we were concerned with modeling the phsycial system. The purpose of marginal analysis is to combine the physical model with value models or functions for use in decision making. Assume that $v(q)$ is the value of the product, $X = (X_1, X_2, \ldots, X_N)$ is the quantity of the resources, $h(X)$ is the value of the resources used, $\Pi = v(q) - h(X)$ is the net value of the transformation of resources X into product P, and f is the production function relating resources used to output produced: $P = f(X)$. The systems analysis problem can, therefore, be presented as a constrained optimization problem where we maximize $\Pi = v(q) - h(X)$ subject to $P = f(X)$.

Marginal analysis is based on this type of optimization problem and is applicable only when these functions define a convex feasible space (see p. 203).

In essence, all of systems analysis can be reduced to two problems: (1) minimize the total cost or value of resources used while producing a required output and (2) maximize output subject to a fixed budget or limited resources. Small scale projects are usually of the second type: The system must meet or exceed a specified design. On the other hand, large scale investments tend to resemble the former.

The concepts of marginal analysis can now be applied to various types of production functions in order to examine different economic concepts, such as the law of diminishing marginal returns, returns to scale, and so on. First, we shall examine the law of diminishing marginal returns. In education, it might relate increasing teacher salaries to improving student output measures.

The laws of diminishing marginal returns simply says that the marginal product of any resource eventually decreases as the amount of the resource used increases and the quantity of other resources remains constant. This concept is illustrated in Figure 5-14.

To demonstrate the effect of diminishing marginal returns, consider the following economic system. The problem is how large should a substitute teacher pool be to meet the demand for substitute teachers in a school district. The output q is defined as the service level or the number of days out of 100 the substitute

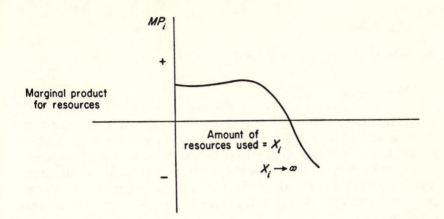

Figure 5-14. Law of diminishing returns.

teacher pool can meet demand and the input x_i is the number of teachers in the pool.

Note the ratio

$$\frac{\Delta q_1}{\Delta x_2} > \frac{\Delta q_2}{\Delta x_1}$$

from Figure 5-15. Because of the shape of the production curve,

$$\Delta q_1 \Delta x_1 > \Delta q_2 \Delta x_2$$

then since the change in inputs are equal,

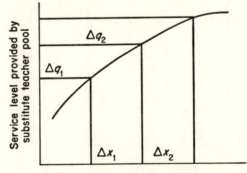

Number of substitute teachers in pool

Figure 5-15. Diminishing returns for a substitute teacher pool.

$$\Delta x_1 = \Delta x_2$$

the change of outputs must be different or

$$\Delta q_1 > \Delta q_2$$

Thus, the service level provided by the substitute teacher pool (percentage requests able to be met by the pool) has a diminishing return as the number of teachers in the substitute pool increases.

A large part of systems and economic analysis is concerned with resource mixes and the law of diminishing marginal returns, and this concept provides the foundation of cost effectiveness analysis.

To show how the concept of diminishing marginal returns can be applied to an educational planning situation, consider a problem involving the organization of special reading programs for the inner city (see Figure 5-16). Currently the district is spending at point X_0 and receiving performance P_0. An increase in cost ΔX would result in program performance of P'. An additional cost increase ΔX would result in performance level P''. Due to the nature of this cost performance relationship $\Delta P = f(\Delta X)$ or the curve itself; there is a diminishing rate of return (performance) with increase in X beyond $X_0 + \Delta X$.

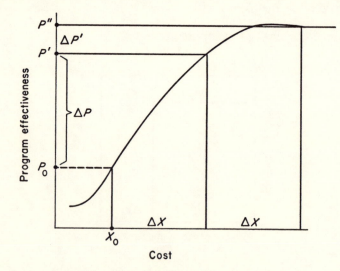

Figure 5-16. Cost–program effectiveness tradeoff.

Diminishing marginal returns characterized the rate of change of output when individual resource inputs were changed one at a time while other resources were held constant

$$MP_L = \frac{\partial y}{\partial X_L}$$

Suppose all resource inputs were changed proportionately, that is,

$$\lambda Y = f\,(\lambda X_1 + \lambda X_2 + \cdots + \lambda X_m)$$

Investigations of systems where all resources are changed proportionally are known as the returns-to-scale analysis. The returns-to-scale in any system can be increasing, decreasing, or constant, depending upon whether the rate of change in output is greater than, less than, or equal to the rate of change in inputs. Mathematically, this can be investigated as

$$\lambda^k Y = f(\lambda X_1, \lambda X_2, \cdots, \lambda X_m)$$

For the condition of increasing returns to scale the exponent k is greater than unity:

$$\lambda^k Y > Y$$

For constant returns to scale $k = 1$:

$$\lambda^k Y = Y$$

For diminishing returns to scale $k < 1$:

$$\lambda^k Y < Y$$

Returns-to-scale in an education planning sense might be illustrated as

$$Y = f(C, L)$$

where C is the cost per student, L is the library size, and Y is the reading achievement. If we doubled C and L, the resource inputs in the production function, we double the output Y, that is the average reading achievement. If Y exactly doubled as a result of this policy change, then we have achieved what is called constant returns-to-scale. If Y more than doubled, then we have increasing returns-to-scale. Finally, if Y less than doubled, we have diminishing returns-to-scale.

Geometrically, a production function on an isoquant with constant returns-to-scale can be visualized by a ray through the origin intersecting the isoquants; thus the slopes of the isoquants at these points are the same. The isoquants themselves are equally spaced as output expands, thus exhibiting a constant proportional relationship between increases in all inputs and increases in output. If the production function demonstrated increasing returns-to-scale, the isoquants would move closer together as the quantity of inputs expanded, since proportional increases in quantity require less than proportional increases in inputs. Finally, decreasing returns-to-scale in a production function would exhibit isoquants farther apart since proportional increases in quantity require more than proportional increases in inputs. It is possible, especially in studying the phenomenon of education, that a production function would exhibit all three effects in different output ranges.

If the law of diminishing returns is valid in a particular situation, then there are no increasing returns to scale, and all feasible combinations of inputs and outputs define a convex set. The concept of convexity is extremely important and many analytical techniques such as linear programming (to be discussed in Chapter 7) depend upon this assumption.

A convex set can be viewed as a line or a curve, such that a line joining any two points on the curve will be within the curve (see Figure 5-17). Convexity insures one optimum point, and when this point is determined, it is considered a global optimum instead of a local optimum. Proof of the characteristics of a convex region can be given as follows using Figure 5-18.

We define a convex curve ABC such that dy/dx is a monotonically decreasing function of x; that is, as x increases, dy/dx (the slope) decreases. As y increases, dy/dx gradually approaches zero. When either the end of the curve (for example, point B if we were considering only the section AB) or the condition $dy/dx = 0$ (point C) is reached, a maximum is obtained.

But when we reach the maximum at $dy/dx = 0$, is this actually the largest value of y that can be obtained? As we move toward increasing x, higher values of y could be obtained only if the slope (dy/dx) increased instead of decreased. But this cannot happen, since dy/dx is defined as monotonically decreasing. Thus, the

(a)   Convex

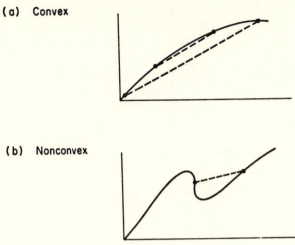

(b)   Nonconvex

(c)   Convex

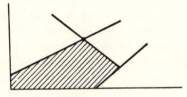

(d)   Nonconvex

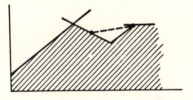

Figure 5-17.   Examples of convex and nonconvex sets.

maximum is a global maximum (that is, there is no higher point on the curve).

This property is not true for a nonconvex curve ($A'B'C'$ in Figure 5-18). Moving toward increasing x; dy/dx gradually increases and we can always find a higher point (larger y value) on the curve.

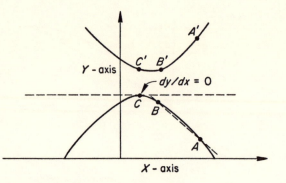

Figure 5-18. Convexity characteristics.

5-5 COSTS AND THEIR MEASUREMENT

Cost-effectiveness analysis is another important concept in micro-economics. Its main focus is to establish, as diagrammed in Figure 5-19, the relationship between the effectiveness or the system output and the costs necessary to achieve this output. It, therefore, is extremely important to be able to measure cost accurately.

For the sake of discussion, cost can be defined as the decrease in wealth or purchasing power resulting from a decision to use a

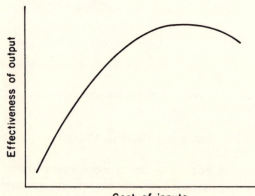

Figure 5-19. Cost-effectiveness analysis.

specified combination of inputs. In educational planning, costs can be money, teacher time, social cost, political costs, and so on. Most of this discussion will focus on monetary costs. We can state that

Cost = f (resources used)

or

Cost = $f(x_1, x_2, \cdots, x_n)$

or assuming a linear function

$C = c_1 x_1 + c_2 x_2 + \ldots + c_n x_n$

where C is the cost and c_i is the price of resource x_i. There is no single expression or meaning for the type of cost. Instead, there is a taxonomy of costs, which is useful for educational policy analysts and planners to understand. These cost comparisons are

1. fixed versus variable,
2. marginal versus average,
3. past versus future, and
4. opportunity versus outlay.

Fixed versus Variable

The distinction between fixed costs and variable costs is dependent upon the time period within which the potential decisions are to be implemented. For example, in the short run, the cost of a teacher may be considered a variable cost since the teacher can be hired or fired. In the long run, however, with present tenure laws, the cost of the teacher may be considered fixed. The best distinction between fixed and variable costs is probably made by describing variable costs as the costs assumed by the school district for the purpose of producing a specific item or teaching a specific group of students. These costs vary directly with the number of students involved. Other school district costs are fixed costs or costs that will be met regardless of whether or not they are used in production or teaching students. Thus, these costs are fixed costs per unit of time and do not vary with the decision to produce or not produce the item. Total cost is the sum of fixed and variable costs (see Figure 5-20).

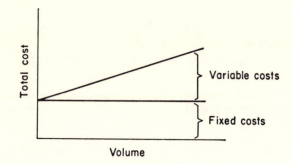

Figure 5-20. Fixed and variable costs.

Breakeven analysis involves the concepts of fixed and variable costs, but, in addition, considers a revenue source per unit volume (such as state tuition aid). The point of intersection between the marginal revenue and total cost curves is known as the breakeven point. See Figure 5-21.

Marginal versus Average

Marginal and average cost also depend upon the volume of production as depicted in Figure 5-22. Total cost can be represented as analogous to the breakeven function since it considers both fixed and variable costs: $TC = K + cn$, where TC is the total costs, K is the set up or fixed costs, c is the cost per unit, and n is

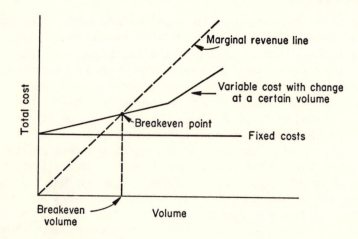

Figure 5-21. Breakeven analysis.

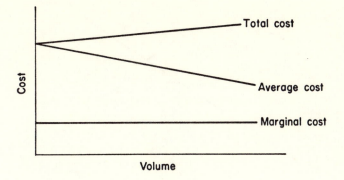

Figure 5-22. Marginal and average costs.

the number of units or output produced. Average cost is defined as

$$\frac{TC}{n} = \frac{K + cn}{n} = \frac{K}{n} + c$$

Note that

$$\lim_{n \to \infty} \frac{K}{n} + c = c$$

as n approaches infinity or the number of units gets very large. Therefore, the average cost curve is asymptotic to the marginal cost curve.

Marginal costs are the costs associated with each additional unit of production and are found by taking the first derivative of the total cost function with respect to n, where n is the number of units:

$$TC = K + cn$$
$$\frac{d(TC)}{dn} = c$$

As we can see, the marginal costs $d(TC)/dn$ equals c, where c is a constant. This is represented by means of a straight line in Figure 5-23. Again marginal costs and average costs become equal only when the volume is large.

With the use of average costs $\overline{c}$ in economic analysis, a problem results. Defining average cost as

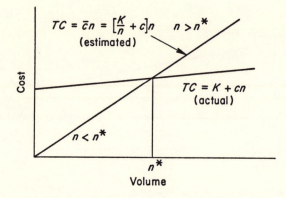

Figure 5-23. Estimates for average costs.

$$\bar{c} = \frac{K + cn}{n}$$

at output level n^*, total cost will be underestimated for low volumes and overestimated for high volumes. This is depicted in Figure 5-23.

The educational analyst, who is given an average cost per unit $\bar{c}$, can be led to believe that the cost of an additional unit is $\bar{c}$. Hence, the total cost is $TC = \bar{c}n$, and then he might incorrectly assess the cost implications of potential decisions. Marginal, total, and average costs do not have to be linear; in fact, most of these functions are nonlinear since they follow the law of diminishing returns. Typical cost curves are shown in Figure 5-24. Increasing

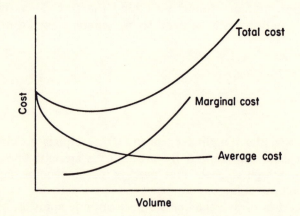

Figure 5-24. Plot of various types of costs.

marginal costs characterize the law of diminishing marginal returns in the production process. The effect of decreasing marginal productivity results in increasing marginal costs of a firm's output.

Past Cost versus Future Cost

The cost data in the account records of any school district are by definition a record of past costs. The educational policy analyst designing future educational programs actually needs a method for predicting future costs since costs greatly affect the selection of economically feasible long-range planning alternatives. Hence, the only truly relevant costs for the analyst are future costs. Past costs, of course, are simply a guide or source of information to be used in predicting future costs. The calculation of future costs to account for inflation will be described later.

Opportunity versus Outlay

Although costs are frequently thought of as dispersals of cash or money, they have in actuality a much broader meaning. The cost of using a resource on one project or system may be the cost of not having that resource available for more productive uses. In other words, the sacrifice may be in future earnings rather than a sacrifice of present cash. This indirect reduction in wealth is referred to as an opportunity cost and is contrasted to the direct reduction in wealth via a direct disbursement of cash, an outlay cost.

Summary of Types of Costs

The following definitions summarize the types of costs and their measurements that might be faced by educational planners and policy analysts:

1. average total cost (ATC) is the total money outlay per unit of output at a given level of output: ATC is defined as TC divided by the respective level of output x

$$ATC = \frac{TC}{x}$$

2. average fixed costs (AFC) is the money outlay on the fixed inputs per unit of output at a given level of output

$$AFC = \frac{TFC}{x}$$

3. average variable costs (AVC) is the cost of variable inputs per unit output

$$AVC = \frac{TVC}{x}$$

Note

$$ATC = AFC + AVC$$

4. marginal cost (MC) is the change in TC as the level of output is increased by one unit;

5. opportunity cost is the value of the product which could have been produced with resources currently employed in the production of another product;

6. total cost (TC) is the total money outlay for a given level of output;

7. total fixed cost (TFC) is the total money outlay on the fixed inputs used for a given level of output. Fixed inputs are factors of production whose quantities cannot be varied during the time period under analysis. Then, TFC may be defined as any type of outlay that is independent of the level of output; and

8. total variable costs (TVC) is the total money outlay on the variable inputs used for a given level of output. Variable inputs are all inputs not fixed. Note

$$TC = TFC + TVC$$

Present Value Analysis*

Costs and benefits in education accrue over time; therefore, we must find a means for comparing these values over time. The reduction of these streams of income to a base year is called present value analysis. Present value consists of using compound interest and compound discount procedures to reduce the stream of costs to a base year.

A dollar received today has a different value than a dollar received in 10 years. Hence, using the formula

$$\frac{a}{(1 + i)^t}$$

where t is the time period, i is the interest rate, and a is the amount of present dollars, the value of one dollar in 10 years at a

7% inflation rate can be determined

$$\frac{1}{(1 + 0.07)^{10}}$$

The income stream of y dollars per year for n years is given by

$$\frac{y_1}{(1 + i)} + \frac{y_2}{(1 + i)^2} + \cdots + \frac{y_n}{(1 + i)^n}$$

which is mathematically summarized by

$$\sum_{t=1}^{n} \frac{y_t}{(1 + i)^t}$$

where y_t is the income at time t and i is the inflation rate. Costs can be treated the same way

$$\sum_{t=1}^{n} \frac{x_t}{(1 + i)^t}$$

where x_t is the cost at time t and i is the inflation rate.

Note that an investment in an increment of education (an additional year of schooling) for an individual is worthwhile if the present value of additional benefits associated with the investment is greater than the present discounted value of additional costs. Mathematically, this relationship can be expressed as

$$V_0(y) = V_0(x) = \sum \frac{y_t}{(1 + i)^t} - \sum \frac{x_t}{(1 + i)^t} = 0$$

This formula defines the rate of return for an investment.* The internal rate of return for an investment is defined as that interest or return rate equating the present value of the investment to zero. In education, we can examine the rate of return for school by examining schooling costs versus future earnings discounted for inflation. Table 5-2 lists the internal rate of return for various

*For an excellent discussion of rate of return analysis see J. Hirshleifer (1970).

Table 5-2. Rate of Return Analysis Example[a]

Investment in schooling	Internal rate of return
Grade level	
9–10	9.5
11–12	13.7
13–14	5.4
15–16	15.6

[a]*Source*: Hansen, W. Lee. "Total and Private Rates of Return to Investment in Schooling," *Journal of Political Economy* 71(1963). Published by the University of Chicago Press. Reproduced with permission of the author and publisher.

levels of schooling for the United States and can be interpreted as follows: $100.00 invested in schooling for grades 9 and 10 yields $1,095.00 in earnings over a lifetime (discounted in current dollars) for a 9.5% return on investment.

The rate of return analysis concept can be illustrated by Figure 5-25, which shows the interest rate where costs intersect or equal benefits. Notice both costs and benefits are discounted to present discounted values (PDV) by means of PDV formulas. If we plot the net costs versus net benefits curve as in Figure 5-25b, the interest rate where the curve crosses the x-axis (i_a) is the rate of return for the investment.

The theoretical literature of economics defines net benefits as the consumers surplus for a particular price. The consumers surplus is in turn usually defined as the sum of the two differences between the price each consumer pays and what he is willing to pay. The shaded region in Figure 5-26 represents the extent to which the consumer feels that he is getting something more valuable than what he pays for, or the extent to which the product or service he receives is worth more to him than the price.

In summary, here are six measures of effectiveness related to benefit/cost analysis that are of use to educational policy analysts:

1. maximum benefits, that is, maximize benefits without regard to costs;
2. maximize net benefits, which are the total project benefits minus total costs when both benefits and costs are defined in terms of their net present values;
3. benefit/cost ratio, which is the division of the total benefits by the total costs;

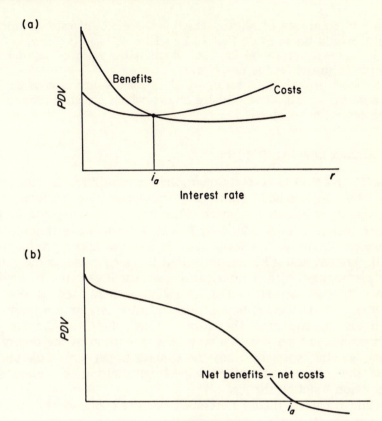

Figure 5-25. Solving for rate of return.

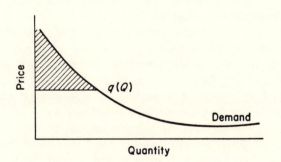

Figure 5-26. Benefits versus costs.

4. internal rate of return, which is the discount rate at which a project would break even; that is, benefit cost ratio is unity;
5. percent return on capital, which is the ratio of annual net benefits to initial capital costs; and
6. cost effectiveness ratio, which is the average cost of achieving a particular objective, usually one to which a realistic monetary value cannot be assigned.

5-6 HUMAN CAPITAL THEORY

Fritz Machlup (1970), mentioned that expenditures in education may be approached from the viewpoint of consumption, investment, waste, or hindrance. Education is consumption to the extent that it gives satisfaction; it is investment since it promotes future productivity; it is waste since it does not create productivity in the present and a hindrance in that it poorly matches individual job preferences with employment opportunities. Human capital theory focuses on education as an investment and is one of the major conceptual methodological contributions from economics.

It is appropriate, therefore, to conclude a chapter on microeconomic theory with a very brief discussion of the theory of human capital especially since the chapter began with a discussion of another conceptual-methodological contribution of economics—production function theory.

Human capital theory developed because neoclassical economic theories do not explain modern economic growth very well. In fact the "natural" or unexplained growth in economics led to formulation of the "human capital" concept as a dimension of production, along with physical capital. Human capital is defined as the increase in indiviudal human productive capacities (knowledge and skill), a qualitative dimension, which affects the fiscal capacities of an economy (see Becker 1964).

Education is assumed to contribute to the process of increasing human capacities; consequently, it is one of a set of factors in "human capital" formation affecting the stock capital, if only by acting as a limiting force. As education is viewed as increasing the stock capital (human) of a nation, it affects the rate (level and composition) of national economic development.

The basic assumption of human capital theory is that people can enhance their capability as producers and consumers by investing in themselves.* Research has found that the stock of

---

*Of course, the other purpose of education for an individual in addition to raising future income is that education presumably makes an individual a better person intellectually, culturally, and socially.

human capital rises relative to income and that there are differences in earning as a consequence of differential investment in
education. The theory also indicates that differences in investment
in human capital are the basic factors affecting inequality in the
distribution of personal income.

There are certain similarities between human capital investment
and physical capital investment. The common notion for both
investments is that an initial expenditure is undertaken with the
hope of higher net income in the future. If future earnings of
individuals due to educational investment are considered, the
United States has an estimated $1.2 trillion in educational forms of
human capital and $1.27 trillion in physical capital (Nicholson 1972).

The fine differences between human and physical capital are
important to understand. For example, it is more difficult to
estimate opportunity costs than direct costs in physical capital
investments. The risks involved in human capital investments are
much higher than in physical (payoff period is over a longer period
of time). Many human capital investments are irreversible; if one
has completed a Ph.D., say in education, it is almost too late to
earn an M.D. Finally, information available to the physical capital
investor is typically better both qualitatively and quantitatively
than the information available to the human capital investor.

Of course, there are additional dissimilarities between human
and physical capital investment due to our political–legal system.
Human capital cannot be sold or mortgaged. Discrimination and
other social maladies interact with human capital more than with
physical capital. Tax laws also discriminate against human capital
since the costs of education are usually not deductible, and when
human capital wears out or becomes obsolete, it cannot be
depreciated or deducted.

Human capital theory has been used to explain preferences of
students to pursue certain careers and to explain dropout rates in
education. Its most extensive application is in educational planning
at the national level. Specifically, how should underdeveloped
countries invest in alternative educational activities (vocational
education, secondary education, adult education, etc.) so that the
benefits to the economy versus the cost of the educational
program are maximized. In applying human capital theory to
education, we are concerned with educational expenditures as an
investment.

The rate-of-returns notion conceptualizes benefits as a measure
of economic (productive) worth and "costs" as the critical supply-
input variable. Relating benefits to costs, therefore, is a valuable
planning strategy providing cost per production units and

suggesting marginal rate of returns on investments. Investment in education, and returns on such investment, derive from human capital assumptions (1) that human productive capacities differ, (2) that they may be increased, (3) that education bears a direct (if not exclusive) relationship to human capital formation,* (4) that the benefits of education are linear, sequential and cumulative (measured by time in school), and so on. Krueger (1968), for example, demonstrated that half the difference in per capita income between the United States and less developed countries can be explained by differences in human capital endowments. An excellent illustration of how the notions of human capital can be applied to a developing economy can be found in Blaug (1970) and Bowles (1969). A discussion of Bowles' human capital model can be found in Chapter 7 on linear programming.

As previously discussed, there are certain growth formulas from methodologies of human capital theory that are important for educational policy analysts when attempting to determine future costs. Suppose it is necessary to determine what would be the annual teacher salary in 5 years if the present salary is $10,000.00 and a cost of living increase of 6% is negotiated by the teacher union each year of the contract. The growth of salary is similar to the growth of a bank account in that it uses the compound interest formula

$$A = P(1 + i)^m$$

where A is the amount of money at the end of time period N (salary after 5 years), P is the present amount of money (present salary), i is the interest rate or (cost of living increase), N is the number of compounding periods minus one, and m is the number of sequence terms ($m = N - 1$). Note $N - 1$ is needed because of the time sequence conditions as illustrated in Figure 5-27. Notice that four terms are in the sequence yet only three compounding periods have elapsed. Therefore, the number of compounding periods (N) always lags the number of sequence terms (m) by one.

The key term in the compounding formula is $(1 + i)^m$ or the geometric progression term. Table 5-3 records $(1 + i)^m$ for various

*It should be noted, however, that unlike other assets an individual can purchase, human capital cannot be sold, and is the most nonliquid of all assets. In addition, it depreciates totally upon the death of an individual and the acquisition of this asset takes longer than the acquisition of other types of assets.

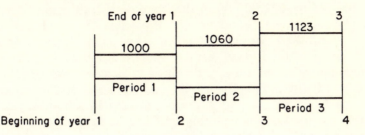

Figure 5-27. Time sequence conditions for 6% growth.

time periods m and inflation or cost of living rates i. Note the huge buildup in value toward the latter time periods at high inflation rates. This table can be viewed in two ways. A dollar today in salary will be worth what value in salary m years in the future, and a dollar today in purchasing power will require how many dollars in the future to be equivalent? Thus, from Table 5-3 we notice that a $10,000.00 salary becomes a $17,000.00 salary (assuming no step or merit increases) at an inflation rate of 5%. At a more realistic inflation rate of 7%, the original $10,000.00 salary more

Table 5-3. Projection of Future Costs Discounting for Inflation $(1 + i)^m$

| Year | Cost of living or inflation rate | | | | | |
	1%	2%	5%	7%	10%	12%
0	1.01	1.02	1.05	1.07	1.10	1.12
1	1.02	1.04	1.10	1.14	1.21	1.25
2	1.03	1.06	1.15	1.22	1.33	1.40
3	1.04	1.08	1.21	1.31	1.46	1.57
4	1.05	1.10	1.27	1.40	1.61	1.76
5	1.06	1.12	1.34	1.50	1.77	1.97
6	1.07	1.14	1.40	1.60	1.94	2.21
7	1.08	1.17	1.47	1.72	2.14	2.47
8	1.09	1.19	1.55	1.83	2.36	2.77
9	1.10	1.21	1.62	1.96	2.59	2.10
10	1.11	1.24	1.71	2.10	2.85	3.47
For 10,000 in year 0	11,110	12,400	17,100	21,000	28,500	34,700
The worth of a dollar in purchasing power in year 10	0.89	0.80	0.58	0.47	0.35	0.28

than doubles to $21,000.00 in this time period. In terms of school district indebtedness (bond issues), the value of one dollar today will be worth $0.47 or almost half in 10 years at 7% inflation rate.

Of course, the human capital economists base their theories and recommendations on exactly those notions of investments that consider inflation. The theory is used by economists to explain questions from will it pay a person to stay in school 4 years to graduate to questions concerning whether one should get married. The term "pay," of course, refers only to the material rewards not to the intrinsic rewards of schooling or marriage. Consider twin brothers both aged 20 and who both expect to retire at age 60. Brother A after military service desires to go back to school to become a teacher with a starting salary of $10,000.00 per year after 5 years of college. Brother B decides to become a maintenance man for the city at a starting pay of $6,000.00 per year. The question is will Brother A recoup the earnings that he has foregone (while in college) plus college costs—assume $1,000.00 per year. If Brother A can exceed in net future earnings what Brother B earns over his lifetime, the investment is worth it. A glance at Table 5-3 shows how dependent the return on investment for education is on the inflation rate—remember Brother A when he starts his work career has to make up approximately $35,000.00 in current dollars. If the inflation rate is low, Brother A can probably pass Brother B in earnings midway through his career. If the inflation rate is high, Brother A might never recoup those deferred earnings; hence, education, from a monetary sense, would be an unwise investment. (Remember the dollar would only be worth $0.28 in 10 years with a 12% inflation rate.)

An interesting type of problem for educational policy analysts dealing with school personnel entails the negotiations of cost of living benefits for teachers. Suppose the inflation rate is 7% and teachers receive a cost of living increase of 5%. Again, assuming no merit increase or promotion, the teacher in ten years would be earning $17,000.00 but the purchasing power of the dollar would decline to $0.47; therefore, the teacher only would be earning in terms of purchasing power $1,963.00 less than when he or she started—almost a 20% decline in purchasing power. Notice that at higher rates of inflation the decline is much worse. It is not surprising that inflation has played havoc with the traditional displacements or distance between economic classes. Inflation tends to close this social distance in addition to being a subtle way to raise taxes (more people move into higher tax brackets). Also governments can borrow money and pay back in dollars worth far less than the present value.

5-7 SUMMARY

Economists are deeply involved in educational policy and planning at all levels and rely heavily on principles of microeconomic theory, production theory, and human capital theory for their analysis. This chapter has attempted to provide those engaged in educational policy analysis with a capsule overview of these theories. Greater explication of these theories can be found in some of the references in the bibliography, especially Nicholson (1972). Note that a special section in the bibliography is devoted to educational production function studies.

Chapter 6

Program Evaluation and Review Techniques (PERT): Organization of Activities for Educational Management

6-1 INTRODUCTION

Educational policy analysts and evaluators are frequently placed in charge of coordinating a multitude of activities in an organization and are held responsible for meeting project schedules or deadlines. Some activities by their vary nature depend upon the successful completion of other activities, while some activities can be completed in parallel with others. For example, in evaluating a third grade reading program, the activity of analysis of data must follow the collection of data, while the activity of writing the preliminary chapters of the final report can be achieved in parallel with these activities.

A Gantt chart was an early means of planning and coordinating activities for a large project. In fact, many federal education grants, including Title III programs, require a Gantt chart of activities to be included in the proposal. Figure 6-1 shows a Gantt chart as being nothing more than a time line for task completion placed in

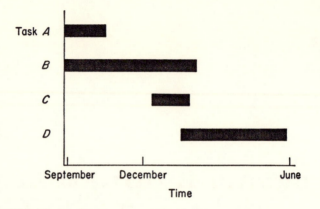

Figure 6-1. Typical Gantt bar chart including milestones.

bar graph format. This chart assists in defining and confirming estimated progress within tasks, but it does not indicate the interdependence of activities that are not within the same bar, nor does it identify critical activities required to complete the project.

Program Evaluation and Review Technique (PERT) analysis attempts to simulate systems of interrelated activities or projects for the purpose of coordination to meet project deadlines. PERT is a network model that extends the Critical Path Method (CPM) model to include a probabilistic evaluation for meeting project deadlines. Thus, while CPM endeavors to determine the expected time of completion for the total project, PERT goes further and endeavors to estimate variances associated with expected times of completion of all activities within the project (e.g., deals with uncertainty in the time estimates).

Unlike a Gantt chart, PERT depicts the interrelationship between activities as well as identifying critical activities within the project. PERT considers all elements in an overall project effort and succinctly communicates plans for the project by specifying the activities and the direction of work required to complete these activities. In addition, PERT provides a structural plan for determining total estimated time to complete all activities. Inherent in the PERT approach is an appraisal of the progress of the plan and a forecast of time problems to be encountered in meeting a schedule or project deadline.

A PERT analysis gives the policy analyst an indication of the earliest time of occurrence for a completed event. In addition, PERT provides answers to questions related to the latest time possible for completing an event (slack time) and the activities that constitute a critical path (no slack available). The activities along the defined critical paths must be completed on time if the project is to meet a schedule or a deadline. The probabilities of an event occurring on schedule are then calculated. Again, it is this latter feature that distinguishes PERT from CPM.

6-2 PERT NETWORKS AND PERT ANALYSIS

A PERT network can be viewed in Figure 6-2 as essentially a network consisting of arrows and circles. The circles represent significant completed events such as a prepared budget or a completed chapter of a dissertation. The lines represent the activity itself on the process of preparing a budget or the process of preparing a chapter. The tail of the arrow represents the beginning of the activity, and the head of the arrow indicates the end of activity and the direction of work.

PERT analysis begins with an estimate of the time required to complete an activity. The time estimates t_e refer to and are placed between circles. The circles represent the completed activities themselves. In Figure 6-3 it would take 10 days (or any time unit) to complete activity B. The time estimate itself is derived by eliciting the most likely pessimistic and optimistic times for completing an event. A formula is then used that considers this uncertainty in obtaining time estimates. Essentially, the time estimate t_e is a weighted average time to complete an event:

$$t_e = \frac{a + 4m + b}{6}$$

where a is the optimistic time to complete an event, b is the pessimistic time to complete an event, and m is the average or most likely time to complete an event.

Associated with each time estimate is a variance—that is, a

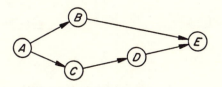

Figure 6-2. PERT network.

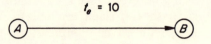

Figure 6-3. Time estimates in PERT. t_e is the time estimate to complete an activity.

measure of the uncertainty in the time estimate. Note that the greater the difference between optimistic and pessimistic times, the larger the uncertainty will be. Mathematically, the uncertainty is derived from the formula

$$\text{Variance} = \left(\frac{b-a}{6}\right)^2$$

Notice the time estimate for completion of an activity can be derived from a normal distribution as in Figure 6-4. As PERT analysis has been refined over the years, a beta distribution of time estimates is sometimes used for determining time estimates because it tends to provide a more conservative estimate for the time to complete an activity. In a beta distribution, the most likely time m to complete an event is closer to the pessimistic b time than the optimistic time a as in Figure 6-5. Figure 6-6 depicts a PERT network of events with the time estimates t_e to complete each activity in the network.

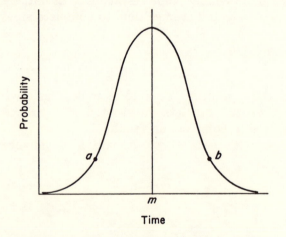

Figure 6-4. Normal distribution of expected times in PERT. a and b have equal chances of occurring, while m has the maximum chance of occurring.

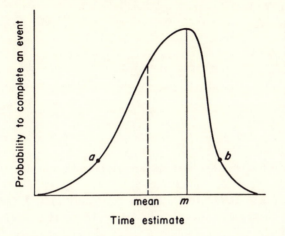

Figure 6-5. Beta distribution of expected times in PERT.

The earliest time to complete an event T_E is dependent upon estimated time to complete an activity t_e. Thus, in Figure 6-6 event E has paths ABE and AE with total t_e of 2 + 0 and 7, respectively. Thus, the earliest time to complete event E or T_E is the largest time estimate (sum of individual t_e) from all the paths leading to that event. (See Figure 6-7.)

This rule can be easily stated that when an event (such as E) has multiple arrowheads entering the event, then the largest time estimate along all paths leading to this event is used as the minimum time estimate to complete the activity. Thus, we see activities E and F with multiple arrowheads entering the activity. For event E the possible paths are AE and ABE with T_E's of 7 and 2, respectively; therefore, T_E of AE or 7 is chosen. For event

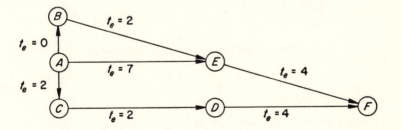

Figure 6-6. PERT network—estimated time to complete an event (t_e).

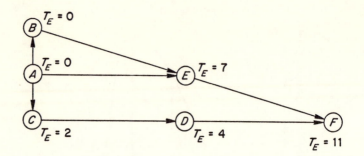

Figure 6-7. PERT network—earliest time to complete an event (T_E).

F we have path $ACDF$ for a T_E of 8 or path $ABEF$ (or AEF) for a T_E of 11; therefore, the T_E for path $ABEF$ is chosen or T_E is 11 for event F.

The latest time to complete an event T_L is the time above which a delay will be caused in all subsequent activities. In order to determine T_L, we work backwards from the last activity defined in the PERT network. As in Figure 6-8, we set T_L equal to T_E for the last event in the network and work backwards by subtracting the time estimates t_e.

We have a straightforward subtraction of t_e from T_E for each event along the paths until we come to event A, which has multiple tails of arrows emanating from the event. This situation is readily distinguishable from event E, which has multiple heads of arrows entering the event. For this type of situation, the T_L for all

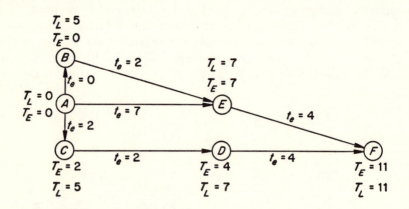

Figure 6-8. PERT network—latest time (T_L) to complete an event.

the various paths are calculated, and the smallest T_L value from the different paths is used as the latest time to complete the event.

Thus, event A has three tails of arrows emanating from itself. The three paths from the last event F are $FEBA$, FEA, and $FDCA$. The latest times T_L for each path are 5, 0, and 3, respectively. Therefore, the path FEA or the minimum T_L is used to determine the T_L for the event.

Slack time tells us how much free time or extra resources are associated with each activity. To determine slack time in a network, we subtract T_E from T_L for each event. Figure 6-9 shows the slack time for each event in the network. Notice events B, C, and D have slack time associated with completing their activities; hence, they do not have to be monitored as closely.

Finally, to determine the critical path in a network, we note all events that have $T_s = 0$ and "chain" the line representing the activities connecting these events. Thus, in Figure 6-10 the critical path is AEF. A delay in time in either A, E, or F activities will result in the project falling behind schedule and not meeting the project deadline. Also events B, C, and D have slack time where, if needed, resources can be taken and given to activities along the critical path.

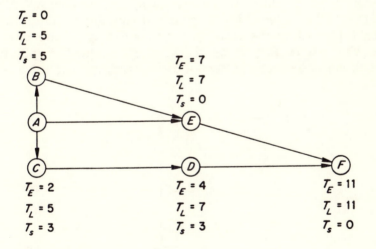

Figure 6-9. Determination of slack time (T_s).

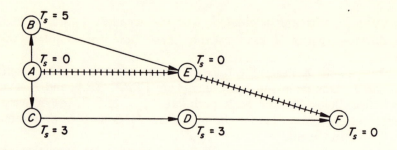

Figure 6-10. Critical path in PERT.

6-3 ILLUSTRATIVE PERT EXAMPLE

To illustrate PERT analysis from beginning (specification of the network with time estimate) to end (determination of probabilities of completing an event), consider the following network of activities for preparing a proposal for Title III. The network of activities to respond to the grant agency proposal requests (RFP) are defined in Figure 6-11.

Suppose event *A* is defined as reading the RFP, and event *F*, as submitting the grant proposal to the funding agency at the due date imposed by the RFP. Event *B* might be writing the preliminary proposal while event *C* might be seeking approval of all personnel to be included in the grant and checking facilities. Event *D* might be writing the final draft and receiving all inputs from those who will be funded by the grant if the grant is approved. Event *E* might be receiving school district approval and calculating

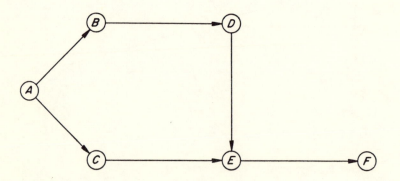

Figure 6-11. Simple PERT network for responding to the RFP.

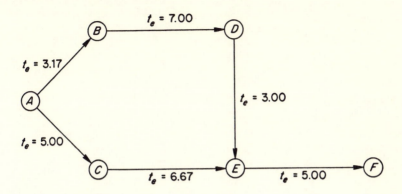

Figure 6-12. PERT network with time estimates.

the final budget. Finally, event F is the mailing of the grant proposal.

Suppose there were 20 days in which to mail the proposal and we were interested in the probability of meeting this deadline. Suppose we were also interested in the probability of completing event E in 15 days in addition to wanting to know those activities in the network of activities that constitute the critical path. The time estimates for each of the activities can be found in Figure 6-12. These estimates were derived by asking those "in a position to know" or those responsible for the activity the most likely, optimistic, and pessimistic times to complete each activity (see Table 6-1).

The t_e's and σ^2 are calculated using the formulas

$$t_e = \frac{a + 4m + b}{6}$$

$$= \frac{2 + 4(3) + 5}{6} = \frac{19}{6} = 3.17$$

Table 6-1. PERT Analysis Including Probability of Completion

Activity	Optimistic	Most likely	Pessimistic	t_e	σ^2
A–B	2	3	5	3.17	0.25
B–D	6	7	8	7.00	0.11
A–C	1	5	9	5.00	1.78
C–E	3	7	9	6.67	1.00
D–E	2	3	4	3.00	0.11
E–F	4	5	6	5.00	0.11

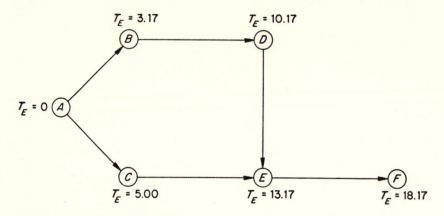

Figure 6-13. Earliest time estimate.

$$\sigma^2 = \left(\frac{b - a}{6}\right)^2 = \frac{3^2}{36} = 0.25$$

When the t_e's are placed in the PERT network with the flow of activities as defined, the network in Figure 6-12 results. From Figure 6-12, we can then calculate the earliest time T_E to complete an event by adding these time estimates for each activity. Note that event E has two arrows pointed into the event; therefore, the largest time estimate of the two paths $ABDE$ and ACE is used (see Figure 6-13).

The latest time (Figure 6-14) for the completion of each event is found by setting $T_L = T_E$ for the last event and working backwards—substracting t_e's for each activity. Note that event A has two tails; therefore, the smallest T_L is used from the paths FEC and $FEDB$.

Slack time T_s is found by subtracting, $T_L - T_E$. (See Figure 6-15.) All events where $T_s = 0$ are on the critical path. In this case, the critical path is $ABDEF$.

6-4 CALCULATION OF PROBABILITIES FOR COMPLETING EVENTS*

Suppose in the previous example we are interested in determining the probability of completing event E in 15 days. Note that the T_E for the completion of this event is 13–17 days.

First, only those activities along the critical path are analyzed

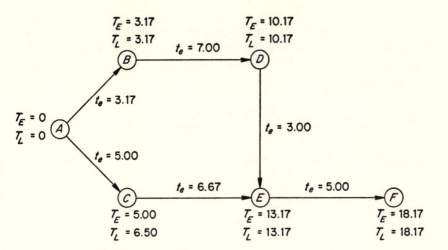

Figure 6-14. Latest time to complete activities.

for probability of completion since there is no slack time available for these activities. Second, it is reasonable to assume that an event such as E being completed on time (15 days) is dependent upon the uncertainty in time estimates of all activities up to event E or the σ^2 associated with events ABD.

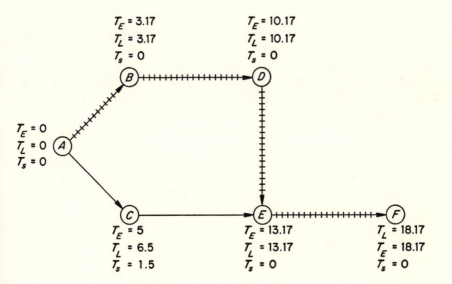

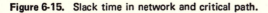

Figure 6-15. Slack time in network and critical path.

After converting these variances σ^2 to standard deviations by taking the square root, we can convert the time estimate and the scheduled completion date TS to a standard Z score. The formula for a Z score is

$$Z = \frac{TS - T_E}{\text{Standard deviation of sum of time estimates}}$$

For the PERT network we have

$$Z = \frac{15 - (13.17)}{\sqrt{0.25 + 0.11 + 0.11}}$$

or

$$Z = \frac{TS - T_E}{\sqrt{\sigma_1^2 + \sigma_2^2 + \cdots + \sigma_n^2}}$$

where $\sigma_1^2 \ldots \sigma_n^2$ are the variances of all events leading up to the event in question

$$Z = \frac{1.83}{\sqrt{0.47}} = 2.60$$

The scheduled date of completion is 2.6 standard deviations from the expected date; from a normal distribution, this standard score has a probability of 99.53 (see Chapter 2 for discussion of probabilities of the normal distribution). Thus, the chances are less than 1 out of 100 that event E cannot be completed in 15 days.

Notice if $TS = T_E$, then $Z = 0$, and the probability of completing the event at the earliest time T_E is 0.5. Also notice that as the uncertainty in time estimates of events previous to the event under analysis increases, the standard Z score decreases; hence, the probability is lowered on the chances for the event being completed on time. Thus, using the formulas

$$\sigma T_E = \left(\sum_{i=1}^{n} \sigma_{t_{e_i}2} \right)^{\frac{1}{2}}$$

$$Z = \frac{TS - T_E}{\sigma T_E}$$

we can determine the chances or probability of completing a project or an event in a project at a specified time period. The relationship of the calculated standard time estimate score and the normal distribution can be found in Figure 6-16. It follows that the actual event completion time can be considered as a normally distributed random variable as in Figure 6-16 with a mean of T_E and a standard deviation of σT_E. Therefore, counting the number of standard deviation units from the expected completion date and using the normal curve, we can calculate the probability of completing by the scheduled completion date TS.

Suppose we were interested in completing the entire project in 20 days, then we could calculate the chances of completing the project in this time period by the same process of summing the variancies for all events leading to the final event. In this example, we have

Event	σ^2
A	0.25
B	0.11
C	1.78
D	1.00
E	0.11
F	0.11

Summing the variances along the critical path until we reach the event in question and then using the formula, we derive the

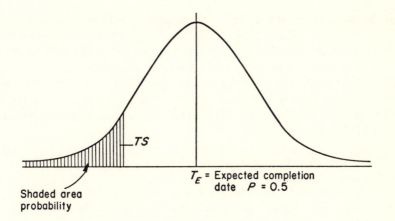

Figure 6-16. Probability of completing events.

number of standard deviations from the expected time for completion that the scheduled time for completion is located:

$$\sigma T_E = (\sigma T_A^2 + \sigma T_B^2 + \sigma T_E^2 + \sigma T_F^2)^{1/2}$$
$$\sigma T_E = (0.25 \ \ + 0.11 \ \ + 0.11 \ \ + 0.11)^{1/2}$$
$$\sigma T_E = (0.58)^{1/2}$$
$$Z = \frac{TS - T_E}{(0.58)^{1/2}} = \frac{20 - 18.17}{(0.58)^{1/2}} = 5.773966$$
$$P = 0.9987$$

Chances are less than 1 in 100 of not completing the project in 20 days. While PERT analysis has a quantitative component, the policy analyst must be aware of the sensitivity of this analytical procedure to errors in the data used in the analysis.

The weaknesses from an analytical perspective of the PERT methodology have been outlined in research by MacCrimmon and Ryavec (1962) and Van Slyke (1963) performed at The RAND Corporation. In the former research study, mathematical analysis was performed on the sensitivity of the standard assumptions used in PERT analysis, namely the time and variance estimates for the activities. The magnitude and direction of errors introduced by these assumptions were analyzed in relation to their effect upon determining the critical path.

6-5 PERT COST/PERT TIME

The literature of management frequently references the terms PERT cost and PERT time. PERT cost is a more recent development than the original PERT time concept and includes cost as well as a time variable in its analysis. When resources can be transferred from paths where there is slack to a critical path without necessitating added cost, the decision to shift resources is relatively simple. There are four methods of determining costs for use in PERT cost analysis:

1. an expected cost estimate derived by a formula similar to deriving expected time,
2. a single cost estimate for the expected actual cost,
3. use of optimum time cost curves such as found in Figure 6-17, and
4. three separate cost estimates.

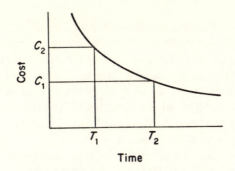

Figure 6-17. Time–cost relationship in PERT
cost.

The time–cost curve represents a relationship between time to complete an activity and costs incurred. The cost to complete an activity under "crash" conditions or minimum time might be represented by the point T_1 and C_2, where the cost under normal time conditions would be the point T_2 and C_1. The fourth approach provides three possible time–cost combinations. The three combinations "most efficient," "direct date," and "shortest time" plans are rated as low-, medium-, and high-risk alternatives for accomplishing the project.

6-6 APPLICATIONS OF PERT TO EDUCATIONAL POLICY AND PLANNING

One novel application of PERT to educational policy and planning involved the use of network analysis to obtain estimates of teaching-learning time (Pratzner 1972). Specifically, PERT was used to determine the optimal time a teacher would allow for teaching a particular task to achieve specified criterion performance. It was assumed that a general way of estimating the actual time, which should be allowed for learning, was essential if there were ever to be a technology of curriculum construction.

Using Gagné's method of task analysis, three time estimates were secured from each of the teachers or curriculum developers involved in the work (most likely, optimistic, and pessimistic). The base for time estimates was in terms of contact minutes for the particular task being considered. There were two paths described leading from start (S) to performance criterion (P). Expected times, variability (standard deviations), and ranges (in minutes) of allowable time for 68% (1 SD) and 95% (2 SD) probability of completion were given for each path section. Total expected time was equal to 256.7 minutes. Although the same material, information, or content in the learning structure will never take exactly the same amount of teaching-learning time, there was a 68% chance that in the long run the total sequence of activities will be completed within a total of 35 minutes either side of the expected time, and a 95% chance of completion within a total of 70 minutes either side of the expected time.

Finally, although not explicitly defining a critical path, scheduling problems that may result from delays in the system, specified task completion dates, and so on, were discussed. Possible solutions included: making new estimates for remaining activities and reducing one remaining activity time, proportionately reducing two or more of the remaining activity times.

Another application of PERT in education was the use of this technique for planning the sequence of activities and time allocation for the completion of a doctoral dissertation (Pullis and Rice 1972). In this article the authors began with a complete explanation of the PERT technique. PERT was then applied to the construction of a plan for completing a dissertation by developing a comprehensive network of 20 events and 25 activities that were considered typical of a doctoral dissertation. A table of times was then computed to describe the critical path for this event.

PERT was suggested as a technique for use in the planning of large-scale educational research and evaluation studies (Case 1969). In this study, PERT was used to coordinate the set of activities associated with a longitudinal study of disadvantaged school children. The project had seven component parts, or task forces, with a task force leader designated for each. Each task force was to provide a way to assess a different aspect of the preschool child or his environment. The main objective of the project was to identify the components of early education in preschool and primary grades that are associated with children's cognitive, perceptual, and personal-social development. In the initial seven task force networks there were 220 work items or events.

Case noted three problems in this large scale implementation of PERT. First, there was a problem of gaining enough time before the project started to prepare a plan that was consistent and acceptable to all concerned. The second problem was keeping the PERT system up-to-date. The third problem, which was not independent of the first two, was that PERT materials were not sufficiently used as a basis for reviewing and revising project plans.

Case concluded that a PERT system, implemented well ahead of project start and kept responsive to project developments, provides visibility of the structure of the project not available by other means. Everyone concerned with the project sees how the pieces of the project fit together in support of the general project objectives. With this readily available grand view of the project, ramifications of any changes are quickly assessed and massive changes are more easily handled. The visibility aids in maintaining communication up and down and across project organizational lines, with a PERT network acting as an impersonal entity to represent the wills of all project participants. The conclusion was that such visibility, using PERT in a well-conceived project, will make it more likely that the project objectives will be accomplished.

6-7 SUMMARY

PERT is a simple technique that is used for coordinating a project consisting of a large number of activities. For projects involving hundreds of activities, computer algorithms exist for performing the PERT analysis. The analyst, however, should be aware of three critical flaws in the PERT method. First, the network itself must be defined completely and unambiguously, and in addition must be consistent with the realistic flow of activities for the project. Second, the time estimates for the completion of activities must be valid. Even with the use of weighted time formulas and beta distributions, there can be substantial error in the time estimates and PERT analysis is totally dependent upon these time estimates. Third, the analyst must weigh the consequences of using PERT. If there is a penalty for not completing a project on time, such as commonly found in the business, industrial, and military sectors of the economy, the PERT approach becomes more important as a technique for coordinating activities in the project. In fact, we could use the expected value concept of probability theory (probability multiplied by penalty) and trade-off time, cost, or profit in order to indicate optimal strategies for shifting resources to conclude the project on the scheduled date versus having the project fall behind schedule and incurring a small penalty cost.

PERT offers a system for integrating planning, rapidly evaluating program status, identifying potential trouble spots, and reallocating resources. Educational research projects often involve many tasks, performed by many people, over long periods of time.

The administrative coordination involved is quite comprehensive. By applying PERT techniques, the educational administrator will be better able to assess problems and to attend to their correction. It is another valuable decision-making tool which can be realistically and effectively utilized by the educational policy analyst.

Chapter 7

Linear Programming: Allocation of Resources for Educational Management

7-1 INTRODUCTION

One of the most important and practical techniques from a field of mathematics called operations research, in terms of its usefulness to the problems in educational planning, is linear programming. Linear programming is important for solving problems where resources must be allocated among competing activities or consumers of these resources and where there is a specified criterion for measuring overall system effectiveness. The goal of linear programming then is to allocate resources to these activities in order to maximize this specified measure of effectiveness subject to resource constraints. The entire process is referred to as optimization.

Man has long been interested in, and intrigued by, optimization type problems. Euclid, for instance, in the third century B.C. set forth a number of optimization problems in his *Elements*, such as the problem of finding the longest and shortest straight line segments that can be drawn from a given point to the circumference of a given circle.

Problems of optimizing a linear function, subject to a set of linear constraints, have been considered in one form or another for centuries, but it was not until 1947 that the general problem of linear programming was formulated. At that time members of the United States Department of the Air Force (Marshall K. Wood and George Dantzig) had been requested to study the possibility and feasibility of applying scientific and mathematical methods and techniques to the solution of problems of allocating and programming the conduct of the war and the organization of national defense.

A research group known as Project SCOOP (Scientific Computation of Optimum Programs) was formed under the direction of Marshall Wood. In 1947, while a member of the Project SCOOP group, Dantzig made his initial statement of the linear programming type problem. The simplex technique was firsted presented in comprehensive form in 1953 by Charnes, Cooper, and Henderson in *An Introduction to Linear Programming*. The simplex technique has been revised in order to produce more efficient solutions of the general linear programming problem. Among the revised and new computational techniques are:

1. the dual simplex technique,
2. the revised simplex technique,
3. the composite simplex technique,
4. the primal dual algorithm, and
5. the Fusch multiplex method

Most linear programming algorithms, built into the program libraries of electronic digital computers, use one of the above-mentioned techniques to arrive at solutions to linear programming type problems.

Table 7-1 demonstrates the evolution of linear programming algorithms or computational procedures in the past 20 years. Larger problems are now being solved in much less time. (Note that in the third column rows represent resource constraints while columns represent variables.)

7-2 RELATIONSHIP BETWEEN MULTIVARIATE ANALYSIS AND LINEAR PROGRAMMING*

There is a strong relationship between multivariate analysis (MVA) and linear programming (LP). Both MVA and LP are concerned

Table 7-1. Evolution of Linear Programming Codes

Machine	Year	Constraints/variables (rows/columns)	Time
SEAC	1951	10/20	15 minutes
CPC	1952	27/80	7 hours
701	1953	18/34	20 minutes
701 (RAND)	1953	100/200	2.5 hours
704	1954	100/200	1 hour
7090	1958	300/600	1 hour
7044	1964	300/600	45 minutes
7094	1964	?00/600	2 minutes
360/75	1966	⌐00/600	1 minute
360/75	1972	1200/6000	

with an analysis of multivariate information and the subsequent optimization of some function of the variables. Multivariate analysis is concerned with estimating the linear model parameters from data and then fitting the model structures with the criterion of minimization of deviation without constraints, as a measure of effectiveness. On the other hand, mathematical programming, which includes linear programming as a subset, is concerned with finding optimal policies within known constraints and then optimizing an objective function of n variables subject to a set of constraints. Mathematically, optimize $f(x_1, x_2, \ldots, x_n)$ subject to $g_i(x_1, x_2, \ldots, x_n) = 0$, where $i = 1, \ldots, m$; $x_j \geqslant 0$; $j = 1, \ldots, n$; and $n < m$.

In linear programming we have a linear objective function subject to a set of linear constraints. Mathematically, optimize $Z = \Sigma c_i x_i$ subject to $\Sigma a_{ij} x_j = b_i$, where $i = 1, \ldots, m$; $j = 1, \ldots, n$; and $m < n$. In linear regression, we are concerned with the estimation of the coefficients $B = (b_1, b_2, \ldots, b_n)$ of a linear relationship between a dependent variable Y, and a set of independent variables $X = (x_1, x_2, \ldots, x_n)$; that is,

$$y = \sum_{j=1}^{n} b_j x_j + a$$

In regression, estimation is performed on a set of $m > n$ multivariate observations on y and x with the objective function being defined as the residual errors of model specification. Mathematically, we want to minimize

$$R = (R_1, R_2, \ldots, R_m)$$

where

$$R_i = y_i - \sum_{j=1}^{m} b_j x_{ij} - a$$

Any one of three "objective functions" of the residuals can be considered dependent upon the estimation criteria:

1. minimize ΣR_i^2,
2. minimize $\Sigma |R_i|$, and
3. minimize max $|R_i|$.

Thus, the typical least-squares model 1 normally leads via differentiation to a set of simultaneous equations in the b's, while models 2 and 3 are solved by *MP* (Mathematical Programming) since they cannot be solved by differentiation. Figure 7-1 describes how multivariate analysis and linear mathematical programming are related. In Section 7-6 the use of linear programming as an alternative to regression is discussed.

7-3 BASIC ASSUMPTIONS OF LINEAR PROGRAMMING

The basic assumptions of linear programming as distinguished from other forms of mathematical programming are:

1. all equations must be linear in form, for example,

$$y = ax$$

or

$$y = a_1 x_1 + a_2 x_2$$

not

$$y = ax^k$$

and not

$$y = a_1 x_1 x_2$$

2. the objective function (or production function) must bound

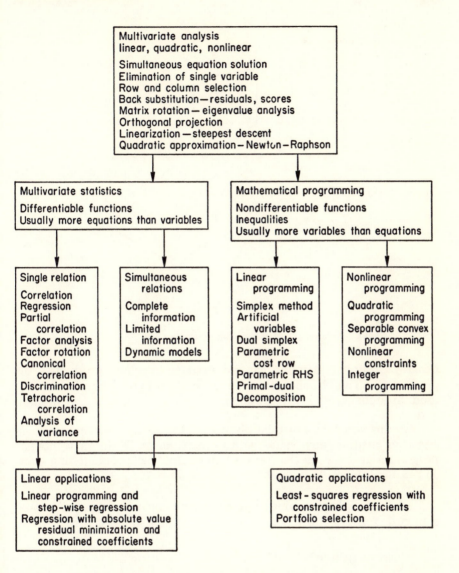

Figure 7-1. Relationship between multivariate analyses and mathematical programming. *Source*: P. Wegner "Relations Between Multivariate Statistics and Mathematical Programming," *Applied Statistics*, vol. 12, no. 3, 1965. Reproduced with permission of the author and publisher.

a convex set. A convex region has the property that all points on a line joining any two points of the region lie within the region. (See Figure 7-2.)

3. the variables in the linear programming model must be additive, that is, it must be possible to substitute inputs for each

(a)   Convex set

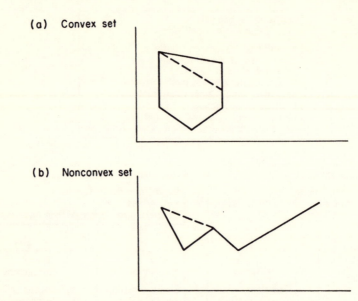

(b)   Nonconvex set

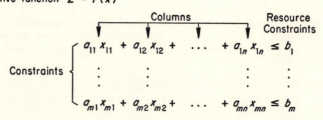

Figure 7-2.   Example of convex and nonconvex sets.

other. An hour of labor can be used to produce product 1 or product 2. This implies that, in general, resource inputs can be used interchangeably for producing various outputs of the model, and

4. the variables must be divisible. That is, they are continuous and can assume any value within their range. Note that integer programming is a special type of mathematical programming that allows for integer or noncontinuous solutions.

All linear programming type problems can be expressed in the standard format shown in Figure 7-3. Using matrix form, these

Objective function $Z = f(x)$

$$\text{Constraints} \begin{cases} a_{11}x_{11} + a_{12}x_{12} + \cdots + a_{1n}x_{1n} \le b_1 \\ \vdots \qquad \vdots \qquad \quad \vdots \qquad \vdots \\ a_{m1}x_{m1} + a_{m2}x_{m2} + \cdots + a_{mn}x_{mn} \le b_m \end{cases}$$

Columns

Resource Constraints

Figure 7-3.   Standard format for all linear programming problems.

equations in Figure 7-3 can be defined as

$$Z = CX$$
$$AX \leqslant B$$

where

C = 1 × n row vector
X = n × 1 column vector
A = m × n coefficient matrix (tradeoff matrix)
B = m × 1 column vector

The following two-variable linear programming problem illustrates the essential characteristics of linear programming and how the above narrative is transformed into a set of linear equations.

Suppose we were interested in maximizing a profit scheme whereby we produce two products (handbags and shoes) with a profit of $15.00 and $24.00 per item, respectively. To produce these products, raw materials (measured in yards of leather) and manufacturing equipment (measured in machine hours) are needed. Suppose we have 19 yards of leather material; and each handbag requires 4 yards and each pair of shoes requires 6 yards. In addition, to manufacture one pair of shoes requires 3 machine hours of time and to manufacture one handbag requires 6 hours of time. Suppose the total available machine time is 12 hours. The question is, How many handbags and shoes do we make to maximize the profit?

Figure 7-4 shows the problem translated into a set of linear relations in symbol form. In matrix form the model is expressed as

$$C = [c_1 \ c_2] = [15, 24] \quad 1 \times 2 \text{ row vector}$$

$$X = \begin{bmatrix} x_1 \\ x_2 \end{bmatrix} \qquad\qquad 2 \times 1 \text{ column vector of decision variables}$$

$$B = \begin{bmatrix} b_1 \\ b_2 \end{bmatrix} = \begin{bmatrix} 19 \\ 12 \end{bmatrix} \qquad 2 \times 1 \text{ column vector of resource constraints}$$

$$A = \begin{bmatrix} a_{11} a_{12} \\ a_{21} a_{22} \end{bmatrix} = \begin{bmatrix} 4 & 6 \\ 6 & 3 \end{bmatrix} \qquad 2 \times 2 \text{ tradeoff matrix}$$

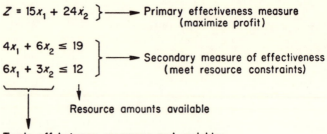

$Z = 15x_1 + 24x_2$ } ———▶ Primary effectiveness measure
(maximize profit)

$4x_1 + 6x_2 \leq 19$

$6x_1 + 3x_2 \leq 12$ } ———▶ Secondary measure of effectiveness
(meet resource constraints)

Resource amounts available

Trade-off between resources and variables

Figure 7-4. Illustrative linear programming problem. x_1 is the number of handbags produced and x_2 is the number of pairs of shoes produced.

7-4 ILLUSTRATIVE EXAMPLE
OF LINEAR PROGRAMMING

A simple two-variable educational application of linear pro-gramming illustrates the steps involved in solving a linear pro-gramming problem and is amenable to the graphical approach for its solution. Suppose an administrator in a school district desires to allocate funds to finance two experimental educational programs. Program 1 might be an experimental reading program, while program 2 might be an experimental mathematics program. The school district has set aside a block of time during the school day for both programs. In addition, a limited amount of school district resources, development time, funds, preparation time, and so on have to be allocated to both programs. The object is to allocate these fixed resources so that some school district priority or objective is maximized. Note that the problem was intentionally limited to a situation involving only two competing activities in order to clarify the essential features of the linear programming method and to utilize the graphical approach in solving the problem.

The first step it to mathematically formulate the problem into linear equations. These equations constitute what is called the constraint set of the linear programming model. The model is completed when the objective function, or the desired criterion of effectiveness, is specified.

Part I—Formulation of the Constraint Set

Let X be the minutes per day allocated to program 1 (reading) and Y be the minutes per day allocated to program 2 (mathematics).

Suppose that the minimum and maximum minutes per day devoted to either program 1 or 2 are 40 and 90 minutes, respectively, with the total time per day devoted to both programs being allowed to vary between 90 and 120 minutes. Mathematically, the maximum and minimum constraints for the individual programs are specified by means of the following equations

$$X \geqslant 40$$
$$Y \geqslant 40$$
$$X \leqslant 90$$
$$Y \leqslant 90$$

This type of constraint might reflect an opinion of curriculum specialists that below 40 minutes and above 90 the programs would be ineffective, for example, above 90 minutes boredom and restlessness might set in and below 40 minutes there would not be enough time to get started on the lesson. Figures 7-5 and 7-6 show the graphs of these constraint equations.

The shaded regions in Figures 7-6a and 7-6b outline the feasible regions for X and for Y. Any combination of X and Y that lies in the shaded region in Figure 7-6c is a feasible solution (a solution that satisfies *all* constraints). This shaded region is also known as the convex set of feasible solutions. The feasible region becomes further limited when the following equations are added

$$X + Y \leqslant 120$$
$$X + Y \geqslant 90$$

This might reflect a constraining condition inherent in the school scheduling practices, for example, at least 90 and no more than

(a) $X \leq 90$ (b) $Y \leq 90$

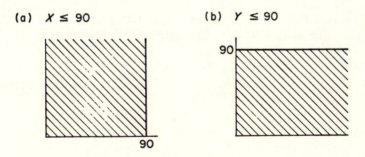

Figure 7-5. Upper bound time constraints.

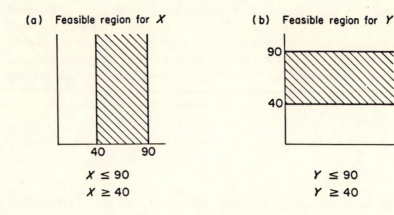

(a) Feasible region for X

$X \leq 90$
$X \geq 40$

(b) Feasible region for Y

$Y \leq 90$
$Y \geq 40$

(c) Convex set of feasible solutions

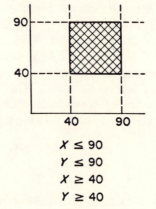

$X \leq 90$
$Y \leq 90$
$X \geq 40$
$Y \geq 40$

Figure 7-6. Upper and lower bound time constraints.

120 minutes per day are available for the experimental programs together. Figure 7-7 shows the graphical interpretation of these further constraints.

Combining all eight figures (Figures 7-5 to 7-7), Figure 7-8 shows the resulting feasible region. The equations that form the feasible region in Figure 7-8b are

$X \geqslant 40$
$Y \geqslant 40$ $X + Y \geqslant 90$
$X \leqslant 90$ $X + Y \leqslant 120$
$Y \leqslant 90$

(a) Upper bound

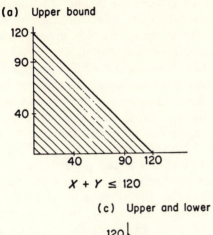

$X + Y \leq 120$

(b) Lower bound

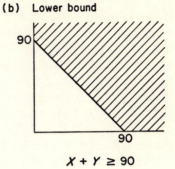

$X + Y \geq 90$

(c) Upper and lower

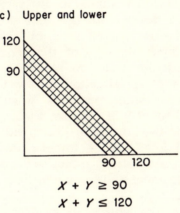

$X + Y \geq 90$

$X + Y \leq 120$

Figure 7-7. Upper and lower bound total time constraints.

(a) Each time constraint shown

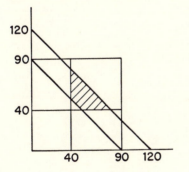

(b) Convex set of feasible solutions

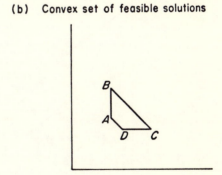

Figure 7-8. Total time constraint set.

Notice that while any solution (values for X and Y) that falls in the shaded region ($ABCD$) is a feasible solution, there is only one unique optimal solution. The optimal solution always lies at one of the vertices ($ABCD$) of the feasible region or convex set. For example, depending upon the slope of the objective function, the maximization of the objective function might lie at point B or C, while the minimization of the objective function might be at point A or D. Note that the objective function is a straight line of the form $Y = AX + B$. By changing the intercept value b, we can obtain a family of parallel lines. This is illustrated in Figure 7-9.

Let X equal the variables or activities in the problem; A, slope of the objective function; B_i, the y-intercept ($i = 1, 2, \ldots$); and, Y, the value of the objective function. By varying B, a family of parallel lines can be drawn with the same slope, but different x- and y-intercepts. The one highest value of B, which generates that unique line that intersects one of the vertices of the feasible region, is the maximum value for the objective function. Depending upon the problem situation, this value could be a maximum, such as l_2 intersecting vertex D. When using the graphical approach, the usual procedure is to set the intercept value to zero and draw the objective function, then with a ruler trace the parallel lines until the line is found that yields the largest y-intercept for a maximization or smallest y-intercept for a minimization. These maximum and minimum lines must touch one of the vertices of the convex set.

Continuing with the illustrative problem, certain additional

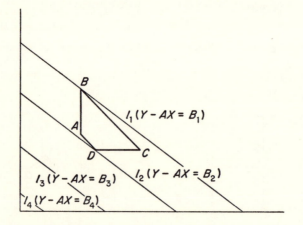

Figure 7-9. Determining optimal solution.

school district constraints should perhaps be considered. Assume the preparation time allocated for the teaching staff by the school district is 6 hours per week. Further, assume program 1 consumes this resource at the rate of 2 minutes of preparation time per week for each minute of instruction per day and program 2 consumes 5 minutes of preparation time per week for each minute of instruction per day. Mathematically, this can be expressed as:

$$2X + 5Y \leqslant (6)(60)$$

Suppose the amount of school district time that has been allocated for the development of both programs is specified at 15 hours. Furthermore, suppose program 1 consumes this resource at the rate of 9 minutes per year for each minute of instruction per day for program 1, and 4 minutes per year for each minute of instructional time per day for program 2. Mathematically, this can be expressed as:

$$9X + 4Y \leqslant (15)(60)$$

One of the most important conditions that might have to be considered in educational decision making is the limitation placed by school district financial resources. In this problem, suppose the school administrator must allocate a fixed amount of funds between programs 1 and 2. Assume that the school district has budgeted $4,500.00 to financially support both programs. Suppose program 1 consumes $12.00 per hour of class time, while program 2 consumes $10.00 per hour class time. Mathematically, this relationship can be defined assuming a 225 day school year in the constraint set as:

$$225 \left(\frac{12}{60}X + \frac{10}{60}Y \right) \leqslant 4500$$

or

$$45X + 37.5Y \leqslant 4500$$

Part II—Determination of the Objective Function

In order to complete the linear programming model, the school administrator is faced with the problem of determining what criterion of effectiveness for the school district is to be maximized or minimized. Does the district desire to minimize the total costs of the programs, maximize the time per day devoted to program 1, minimize teacher preparation time, and so on? Assume the criterion of effectiveness or objective function decided by the district for this illustrative example is to maximize the total amount of time per day devoted to both programs. Mathematically, this objective function for the district is expressed as

Maximize $X + Y$

Thus, with the inclusion of the objective function or criterion of effectiveness, the model is completed. The constraint set and the objective function will, of course, determine the optimal solution. The following is a summary of the model used in this simple application. Maximize $X + Y$ (the criterion of effectiveness maximization of time devoted to programs X and Y) subject to the following constraints*

upper and lower bound constraints on time permitted for both programs taken one at a time
1. $X \geqslant 40$
2. $Y \geqslant 40$
3. $X \leqslant 90$
4. $Y \leqslant 90$
upper and lower bound constraint for the sum of time devoted to both programs
5. $X + Y \geqslant 90$
6. $X + Y \leqslant 120$
7. preparation time constraint $2X + 5Y \leqslant 360$
8. development time constraint $9X + 4Y \leqslant 900$
9. school district budget constraint $45X + 37.5Y \leqslant 4500$

where X is the amount of time devoted to the reading program and Y is the amount of time devoted to the mathematics program. The solution to the above model is

$$X = 60.00 \quad \text{Program 1}$$
$$Y = 48.00 \quad \text{Program 2}$$
$$X + Y = 108.00 \quad \text{Total time}$$

*Note this is an expanded constraint set from the constraints described in Figure 7-9.

Table 7-2. Alternate Optimal Solutions Obtained by Parameterizing School
District Resources (Change = +$200.00)

	Original funding	+200	+400	+600
Program 1 (minutes)	60	66.7	73.3	80
Program 2 (minutes)	48	45.3	42.7	40
Total (minutes)	108	112	116	120
School resources required	4500	4700	4900	5100

These results indicate that, in order to maximize the total amount
of time devoted to both programs while still working within the
given constraints, 60 minutes per day should be alloted for program
1 and 48 minutes per day for program 2 for a total of 108 minutes.
Due to the increased complexity of the constraint set, the problem
was solved using a computer linear programming algorithm.

By parameterizing (allowing changes in) selected variables in
the model, alternate optimal solutions can be obtained. Examples
are shown in Tables 7-2 and 7-3.

7-5 LINEAR PROGRAMMING APPLICATIONS
TO THE DESIGN OF A SCHOOL DISTRICT
SALARY SCHEDULE*

Linear programming models do not necessarily have to concern
resource allocation per se. The following is an illustration of the
linear programming methodology applied to the design of a salary
schedule for a school district (Bruno 1971). Because of the
complexity of the problem and the number of variables, a computer
solution is required. The salary model considers in hierarchical order

Table 7-3. Alternate Optimal Solutions Obtained by Parameterizing School
District Resources (Change = −$100.00)

	Original funding	−100	−200	−300	−400
Program 1 (minutes)	60	56.7	53.3	50.0	46.7
Program 2 (minutes)	48	49.3	50.7	52.0	53.3
Total (minutes)	108	106	104	102	100
School resources required	4500	4400	4300	4200	4100

five job classifications based upon the premise of area of responsibility—school district-wide, school-wide, department-wide, class-
wide, and individual student-wide. For this district the hierarchical
ordering (in terms of salary from high to low) is defined as: (1)
Superintendent, (2) Administrator, (3) Department heads, (4)
Teachers, and (5) Teacher Aides.

The model is based upon two groups of parameters: (1) the
factors to be considered in salary evaluation and (2) the characteristics which describe each factor. For example, the factors
could be:

1. X_1—difficulty of assignment
2. X_2—supply–demand for skill of person
3. X_3—supervisory responsibility
4. X_4—level of education
5. X_5—work experience
6. X_6—special distinctions or awards
7. X_7—college units
8. X_8—in-service hours
9. X_9—relative additional workload
10. X_{10}—special bonus

The linear programming approach is particularly applicable since
there is no limit to the number of factors that can be considered
by the model. This application also illustrates how this most
widely used of all optimization techniques can be used for dealing
with educational problems of design and conflict resolution as well
as problems in resource allocation.

The characteristics that constitute each factor are then ordinally ranked. For the education factor we could have the
following values:

Relative weight	Characteristic
5	Ph.D.
4	M.A.
3	M.E.
2	B.A.
1	A.A.

For the difficulty of the assignment factor we could define the
following characteristics where X_1 is the difficulty of assignment:

Relative weight	Characteristic
$3X_1$	Difficult
$2X_1$	Normal
X_1	Privileged

A concept to remember is that a factor with two few related characteristics will not sufficiently distinguish among differences in ability. Too many characteristics for a factor result in ambiguity.

Thus, there are two basic equations for the salary model: one to represent the theoretically highest paid individual for the job classification and one to represent the theoretically lowest paid individual.

Mathematically, the theoretically highest λ_j and lowest σ_j salaries for each function or job classification are defined as

$$\alpha_1 X_1 + \alpha_2 X_2 + \cdots + \alpha_n X_n = \lambda_j$$
$$\beta_1 X_1 + \beta_2 X_2 + \cdots + \beta_{n-1} X_{n-1} = \sigma_j$$

where α_i are the highest rated characteristics i associated with factors appropriate to function j; β_i are the lowest rated characteristics i associated with factors appropriate to function j; X_i are the factors i associated with function j; λ_j is the theoretically highest or maximum salary for function j; σ_j is the theoretically lowest or minimum salary to be paid within function j; and n is the number of factors considered in the evaluation.

Additional constraints on the model could include: the percentage spreads between functions j and $j + 1$

$$\sigma_j \geqslant w_1 \lambda_{j+1}$$
$$\sigma_j \leqslant w_2 \lambda_{j+1}$$

or the percentage spreads within each function j

$$\sigma_j \geqslant v_1 \lambda_j$$
$$\sigma_j \leqslant v_2 \lambda_j$$

where $w_1 w_2$ and $v_1 v_2$ are the desired percentage spreads, σ_j is the lowest salary for function j, and λ_j is the highest salary for function j. For example, the highest paid teacher can be defined as getting 1.10% of lowest paid administrator salary.

Budgetary constraints on the amount of resources available to the school district can be expressed as

$$\Sigma\Sigma N_{ik} n_{ik} X_i \leqslant \psi$$

where N_{ik} is the number of school district employees having characteristic k of factor i, X_i is the salary weight for factor i used in the salary evaluation, n_{ik} is the relative rating given to characteristic k of factor i, and ψ is the total amount of school district resources available for salaries.

Additional constraints may be added to the model to bound the solution so that σ_5 is the beginning salary in the district, λ_1 is the top salary in the district, $\lambda_k - \lambda_{k+1}$ is the minimum dollar spreads between salaries between level k and $k + 1$, and $X_i \leqslant B_i$ is the upper bound constraints on salary weight given any one factor. Once the model is solved for X_i the salary for an individual member in the school organization can be found by application of the following formula

$$\Sigma Y_{ij} X_i = S$$

where S is the individual salary, Y_{ij} is the relative weight of characteristic j found in factor i possessed by the individual, and X_i is the weight for factor i derived from the model.

In summary, beginning with the following preliminary considerations:

1. objectives or priorities of the school district,
2. job classifications in the school district,
3. factors required to perform job, and
4. characteristics that constitute each factor.

the following constraints can be developed:

1. theoretically highest and lowest salaries for each function (expressed as a variable),
2. maximum and minimum percentage spreads in salary within each job classification,
3. maximum and minimum percentage spreads between job functions to permit salary overlap,
4. absolute dollar spreads between highest salaries in each job classification,
5. consideration of school district resources,

6. maximum and minimum salaries (optional), and
7. upper and lower bounds on each factor weight in the model.

Possible objective functions for the salary model can include:

1. maximizing beginning teacher salary,
2. maximizing top teacher salary,
3. maximizing the salary weight given any factor,
4. maximizing the salary weights for those factors related to pupil performance, and
5. minimizing school district costs.

Consider an illustrative application of the salary model for a school district with the following personnel:

> 6 Superintendents
> 30 Administrators
> 90 Department heads
> 1200 Teachers
> 60 Teacher aides

The district has only $13,500,000.00 to spend on salaries, and it has set an objective to maximize the salary weight of the difficulty of the learning environment factor. Thus, we desire to maximize X_1 (maximize the salaries given school district personnel assigned to difficult learning environments) subject to the following 46 equation constraint set (see Table 7-4). Notice the coefficients in equation (33) were derived by means of an inventory of personnel with associated characteristics. This procedure is summarized in Table 7-5.

The optimum solution (using the MPS 360 linear programming algorithm) is given in Table 7-6. The salary weights associated with each factor X_i that produced the salary schedule are given in Table 7-7. To determine an individual salary, we use the salary equation from the model

$$\Sigma \alpha_i X_i$$

where α_i is the relative weight for the characteristic possessed by the individual for factor i and X_i is the weight for factor i determined by the model. Table 7-8 shows the salary calculation for a teacher

Table 7-4. Constraint Set for Salary Schedule Problem

Organizational hierarchy constraints

Superintendent[a]	$3X_1 + 3X_2 + 7X_3 + 5X_4 + 5X_5 + 2X_6 + 5X_7 + 5X_9 + 5X_{10} = \lambda_1$ (1)
(Function 1)	$X_1 + X_2 + 6X_3 + 3X_4 + 2X_5 + X_6 + X_7 + 5X_9 = \sigma_1$ (2)
Administrator[a]	$3X_1 + 3X_2 + 5X_3 + 5X_4 + 5X_5 + 2X_6 + 5X_7 + 4X_9 + 4X_{10} = \lambda_2$ (3)
(Function 2)	$X_1 + X_2 + 4X_3 + 3X_4 + X_5 + X_6 + X_7 + 4X_9 = \sigma_2$ (4)
Department head[b]	$3X_1 + 3X_2 + 3X_3 + 5X_4 + 7X_5 + 2X_6 + 8X_7 + 7X_8 + 3X_9 + 3X_{10} = \lambda_3$ (5)
(Function 3)	$X_1 + X_2 + 3X_3 + 2X_4 + X_5 + X_6 + X_7 + X_8 + 3X_9 = \sigma_3$ (6)
Teacher[b]	$3X_1 + 3X_2 + 2X_3 + 5X_4 + 7X_5 + 2X_6 + 8X_7 + 8X_8 + 2X_9 + 2X_{10} = \lambda_4$ (7)
(Function 4)	$X_1 + X_2 + 2X_3 + 2X_4 + X_5 + X_6 + X_7 + X_8 + 2X_9 = \sigma_4$ (8)
Teacher aide[b]	$3X_1 + 3X_2 + X_3 + 2X_4 + 5X_5 + 2X_6 + 5X_7 + 6X_8 + X_9 + X_{10} = \lambda_5$ (9)
(Function 5)	$X_1 + X_2 + X_3 + X_4 + X_5 + X_6 + X_7 + X_8 + X_9 = \sigma_5$ (10)

Percentage salary spreads within each job classification

$$\sigma_1 \geqslant 0.50\,\lambda_1 \quad (11)$$
$$\sigma_1 \leqslant 0.80\,\lambda_1 \quad (12)$$
$$\sigma_2 \geqslant 0.50\,\lambda_2 \quad (13)$$
$$\sigma_2 \leqslant 0.75\,\lambda_2 \quad (14)$$
$$\sigma_3 \geqslant 0.50\,\lambda_3 \quad (15)$$
$$\sigma_3 \leqslant 0.75\,\lambda_3 \quad (16)$$
$$\sigma_4 \geqslant 0.50\,\lambda_4 \quad (17)$$
$$\sigma_4 \leqslant 0.75\,\lambda_4 \quad (18)$$
$$\sigma_5 \geqslant 0.50\,\lambda_5 \quad (19)$$
$$\sigma_5 \leqslant 0.75\,\lambda_5 \quad (20)$$

Percentage salary overlaps between job classifications

$$\lambda_2 \geqslant 1.05\,\sigma_1 \quad (21)$$
$$\lambda_2 \leqslant 1.20\,\sigma_1 \quad (22)$$
$$\lambda_3 \geqslant 1.05\,\sigma_2 \quad (23)$$
$$\lambda_3 \leqslant 1.20\,\sigma_2 \quad (24)$$
$$\lambda_4 \geqslant 1.10\,\sigma_3 \quad (25)$$
$$\lambda_4 \leqslant 1.30\,\sigma_3 \quad (26)$$
$$\lambda_5 \geqslant 1.10\,\sigma_4 \quad (27)$$
$$\lambda_5 \leqslant 1.30\,\sigma_4 \quad (28)$$

Minimum dollar spreads between the highest salaries for each job classification

$$\lambda_1 - \lambda_2 \geqslant 3500 \quad (29)$$
$$\lambda_2 - \lambda_3 \geqslant 3000 \quad (30)$$
$$\lambda_3 - \lambda_4 \geqslant 2500 \quad (31)$$
$$\lambda_4 - \lambda_5 \geqslant 2000 \quad (32)$$

School district resources available to support the salary structure

$$2992X_1 + 2873X_2 + 2892X_3 + 3126X_4 + 5432X_5$$
$$+ 1422X_6 + 5736X_7 + 3950X_8 + 2880X_9 + 284X_{10} = \psi \quad (33)$$

Table 7-4. Constraint Set for Salary Schedule Problem (*Cont.*)

School district resources available to support the salary structure

$$\psi = \$13,500,000 \quad (34)$$
$$\sigma_s \geqslant 4500 \qquad\quad (35)$$
$$\lambda_1 \leqslant 23,500 \qquad (36)$$

Upper and lower bounds placed upon the value of each factor in the model[c]

$$100 \leqslant X_1 \leqslant 1000 \quad (37)$$
$$100 \leqslant X_2 \leqslant 1000 \quad (38)$$
$$100 \leqslant X_3 \leqslant 1500 \quad (39)$$
$$100 \leqslant X_4 \leqslant 1000 \quad (40)$$
$$100 \leqslant X_5 \leqslant 500 \quad (41)$$
$$100 \leqslant X_6 \leqslant 1500 \quad (42)$$
$$100 \leqslant X_7 \leqslant 500 \quad (43)$$
$$100 \leqslant X_8 \leqslant 500 \quad (44)$$
$$100 \leqslant X_9 \leqslant 2000 \quad (45)$$
$$100 \leqslant X_{10} \leqslant 1000 \quad (46)$$

[a]Note that factor X_8, inservice credits, is not included in the salary evaluations for these personnel.

[b]Note that the factor X_5, work experience, has its highest relative weight among these personnel; that is, in these two classifications you would expect to find individuals with the greatest relevant experience.

[c]The upper and lower bounds for the factors used in this model were arbitrarily set. In any direct application of the model, these lower bounds would result from negotiations with teachers unions, PTAs, and other concerned groups. These lower bounds could also be parameterized and alternate optimal salary determined.

Table 7-5. Factors Included in the Model with Relative Weight, Characteristics, and Number of School District Personnel Possessing Each Characteristic[a]

Factor	Variables	Relative weight and characteristics	Number of employees possessing this characteristic	Weighted total for each characteristic
Learning environment	X_1	3 Difficult	220	660
		2 Medium	1166	2332
		1 Easy	0	0
				2992
Subject matter or special skills	X_2	3 High Priority	236	708
		2 Medium	1015	2030
		1 Low Priority	135	135
				2873

Table 7-5.   Factors Included in the Model with Relative Weight, Characteristics, and Number of School District Personnel Possessing Each Characteristic[a] *(Cont.)*

Factor	Variables	Relative weight and characteristics	Number of employees possessing this characteristic	Weighted total for each characteristic
Supervisory responsibility	X_3	7 Single district-wide	1	7
		6 District-wide	5	30
		5 Single school-wide	5	25
		4 School-wide	25	100
		3 Department-wide	90	270
		2 Class-wide	1200	2400
		1 Student	60	60
				2892
Highest academic degree attained	X_4	5 Ph.D. or Ed.D.	20	100
		4 M.A.	120	480
		3 M.Ed.	100	300
		2 B.A.	1100	2200
		1 A.A.	46	46
				3126
Work experience	X_5	7 12– years	16	112
		6 10–12 years	100	600
		5 8–10 years	300	1500
		4 6– 8 years	400	1600
		3 4– 6 years	500	1500
		2 2– 4 years	50	100
		1 0– 2 years	20	20
				5432
Special awards and distinctions	X_6	2 With	36	72
		1 Without	1350	1350
				1422
College credits completed in addition to degree	X_7	8 36–	10	80
		7 31–35	15	105
		6 26–30	80	480
		5 21–25	370	1850
		4 16–20	470	1880
		3 11–25	325	975
		2 6–10	140	280
		1 0– 5	86	86
				5736
Service units completed	X_8	7 30–	3	21
		6 26–30	3	18
		5 21–25	90	450
		4 16–20	202	808
		3 11–15	700	2100
		2 6–10	201	402
		1 0– 5	151	151
				3950
Additional workload in the hierarchy	X_9	5 District-wide	6	30
		4 School-wide	30	120
		3 Department-wide	90	270

Table 7-5. Factors Included in the Model with Relative Weight, Characteristics, and Number of School District Personnel Possessing Each Characteristic[a] *(Cont.)*

Factor	Variables	Relative weight and characteristics	Number of employees possessing this characteristic	Weighted total for each characteristic
		2 Class-wide	1200	2400
		1 Student	60	60
				2880
Extra salary for those personnel at the top of each salary classification	X_{10}	5 Superintendents	0	0
		4 Administrators	1	4
		3 Department heads	5	150
		2 Teachers	50	100
		1 Teacher aides	30	30
				284

[a]Depending upon school district needs and philosophy, each characteristic within each factor can be weighted. For example, a year of experience for an administrator must be weighted twice that for a teacher. This study, however, will assume equal weights for each characteristic in each factor for all job functions in a school district.

with a given set of characteristics and Table 7-9 shows the salary calculation for an administrator with a given set of characteristics.

Solving the model with different objective functions will, of course, yield different salary schedules. Table 7-10 lists salary schedules with the objective functions to (1) maximize factor X_i (school district personnel in difficult learning environments), (2) maximize beginning teacher salary, and (3) maximize top teacher salary.

Table 7-6. Optimum Solution—Objective Function: Factor X_1 (Difficulty of Learning Environment)

Function	Description	Salary ($)
1 Highest	Superintendents	22,757
Lowest		17,254
2 Highest	Administrators	18,618
Lowest		13,015
3 Highest	Department heads	15,618
Lowest		10,377
4 Highest	Teachers	12,918
Lowest		7,738
5 Highest	Teacher aides	9,118
Lowest		5,000

Table 7-7. Optimal Salary Weights for the Various Factors

Factor	Description	Value	Activity level at[a]
X_1	Difficulty of the instructional environment	$ 495.83	BS
X_2	Subject matter priority	$ 100.00	LL
X_3	Supervisory responsibility	$1500.00	UL
X_4	Highest academic degree	$ 100.00	LL
X_5	Work experience	$ 100.00	LL
X_6	Special awards or distinctions	$1365.63	BS
X_7	Academic additional credits	$ 100.00	LL
X_8	Additional inservice units	$ 100.00	LL
X_9	Relative additional workload	$1138.54	BS
X_{10}	Extra bonus for school district service	$ 161.45	BS

[a]BS = in the basis; LL = at the imposed lower limit; UL = at the imposed upper limit.

Table 7-8. Salary Calculation for a Particular Teacher

Characteristics	Rating	Weight	Total
Difficult assignment	$3X_1$	496	$1,488
Medium subject matter priority	$2X_2$	100	200
Teacher	$2X_3$	1,500	3,000
Masters degree	$4X_4$	100	400
Five years experience	$3X_5$	100	300
No special distinction	$1X_6$	1,365	1,365
Ten additional college units	$2X_7$	100	200
Fifteen in-service units	$2X_8$	100	200
Normal workload for teachers	$2X_9$	1,139	2,278
Total salary			$9,431

Table 7-9. Salary Calculation for a Particular Administrator

Characteristic	Rating	Weight	Total
Difficult assignment	$3X_1$	496	$1,488
Medium subject matter priority	$2X_2$	100	200
Principal of a school	$5X_3$	1,500	7,500
Doctor's degree	$5X_4$	100	500
Five years experience	$3X_5$	100	300
No distinctions	X_6	1,365	1,365
Two additional college units	X_7	100	100
Normal workload for administrators	$4X_9$	1,139	4,556
Total salary			$16,009

Table 7-10. Comparison of Salary Schedules with Various
Objective Functions

			1	2	3
Superintendent	Top	1	22,757	23,500	23,500
	Bottom		17,254	17,908	17,820
Administrator	Top	2	18,618	19,635	19,674
	Bottom		13,015	13,943	13,895
Department head	Top	3	15,618	16,635	16,674
	Bottom		10,377	11,016	10,972
Teacher	Top	4	12,918	13,321	13,358[a]
	Bottom		7,738	8,084[a]	8,060
Aides	Top	5	9,118	8,892	8,881
	Bottom		5,000	5,051	5,032

[a]Indicates objective function.

7-6 APPLICATIONS OF LINEAR PROGRAMMING IN EDUCATION

Linear programming has been suggested as a means for distributing state funds in school finance programs (Bruno 1971). In this study the major "criterion for evaluating effectiveness" was to minimize financial commitment at the state level with minimal effect upon total funds allocated for education at the school district level. In essence, state costs were to be reduced without sacrificing basic state educational objectives as reflected in the minimal financial educational support.

In this study a linear programming model was derived using variables such as the foundation level, state-mandated tax rate, and basic minimum aid provision. The objective function was to minimize state funds required to support educational expenditures at the local level subject to constraints such as:

1. maintenance of current foundation level and
2. insurance that each district in the system receives its minimum amount.

Constraint equations and linear functions for each constraint were presented. The model was able to meet its criterion for effectiveness through reduction in state costs while maintaining the present foundation level.

In another illustration (McNamara 1971) linear programming was used by state educational planners as an aid to evaluate decisions concerning the allocation of vocational education funds to local school districts. A linear programming model was developed to supply decision makers with information on alternative programs and courses of action.

The solution to the model provided a knowledge of the consequences of particular resource allocation strategy. These consequences were expressed in terms of the number of future graduates that would be produced to fill critical occupational strategies that exist in the labor market.

The following constraints were used to develop the model:

1. unmet demands of the labor market area,
2. budget constraints, and
3. constraints on the existing additional capacity of the public schools.

Linear programming has also been applied to problems in the allocation of resources in instruction (Besel 1972). In this study, linear programming was used for the statistical development of an allocation model "for instructional systems which have instructional programs that can be structured in terms of behavioral objectives, instructional activities and required achievement levels."

Using Carroll's model it was hypothesized "that a learner will achieve an objective to the extent that he spends the time he needs." The assumption from Carroll's model was that "most learning objectives can be achieved by all but the mentally retarded and emotionally disabled."

The problem issue addressed was to design instructional resource allocations so that the students will have the time to achieve. The following variables in the linear model were identified:

1. the estimated time required for a student to achieve a certain objective if a certain instructional alternative is employed;
2. the time allocated for a student to achieve the objective using a certain instructional alternative;
3. the aptitude of a student for learning that objective;
4. the efficiency of alternative instruction for achieving a certain activity which is evaluated in terms of the student; and
5. the perseverance of a student for an instructional alternative to reach a certain objective.

Constraints were then established for these variables:

   1. do not assign a student whose perseverance is less than the time required to learn;
   2. the number of feasible instructional alternatives for achieving an objective;
   3. the maximum amount of student time that can be allocated to instruction during the planning period;
   4. the amount of time for a specific instructional activity;
   5. the number of students in a group activity; and
   6. the amount of instructional time available for a teacher.

This model developed at the Southwest Regional Laboratory for Educational Research presents a means to statistically allocate resources to an instructional system based upon the constraints of those resources available and the ability of the student.

Linear programming has also been used as an alternative to multiple linear regression (Campbell and Ignizio 1972). In this study two different methods using College Entrance Examination Board (CEEB) tests to predict a college student's future performance were employed. The students' performance in college was predicted both by the least-squares method and by a linear programming method. For each sample, the residuals (the actual grades minus the predicted grades) in both methods were compared.

The least-squares method had two key disadvantages: It was biased by extreme cases and its analysis was relatively difficult and time consuming. The linear programming method was not as biased by extreme cases and was more easily employed. The linear programming model proved to be more accurate in analyzing the data and in predicting for the two samples.

The general equation the authors used for prediction was

$$Q_P = a_1 x_1 + a_2 x_2 + b$$

The least-squares method calculated the variables as

$$Q_P = -0.0335 a_1 + 0.0421 a_2 + 2.31$$

The linear programming method produced the prediction equation as

$$Q_P = -0.0179 a_1 + 0.0520 a_2 + 0.905$$

The a_1 in the formula was the average Scholastic Aptitude Test (SAT) score, while the a_2 was the average on the CEEB tests. For both samples used, the linear programming model was found to be the better predicting vehicle (on the basis of a smaller absolute sum of residuals in each sample).

Another application of linear programming to education combines the "human capital" concept from microeconomic theory with the benefit cost feature implicit in linear programming type optimization models. The Bowles model (1967), based upon educational data from Nigeria, illustrates how linear programming can be used at a macro or state planning level.

In the Bowles model, the educational system was represented as a set of production activities. Variables included enrollments, importing teachers, and training students abroad. Two types of constraints were considered: exogenous (e.g., money, population of age group) and endogenous (e.g., teachers, buildings, student advancements).

The objective function for the model was to maximize contribution of education to national income subject to constraints based on educational production technology and given resource availability. This was measured by the increment in discounted lifetime earnings attributable to additional years of education. So the net benefit coefficient was the student's lifetime earnings (opportunity cost and educational cost).

The constraints to the model included teachers, enrollments, construction, expatriate teachers, and political restrictions. There were, for example, 32 constraints of teacher type corresponding to one per year for the following inputs: Grade III teachers, Grade II teachers, Nigerian Certificates of Education teachers, and university graduates. There were also 32 constraints of the student enrollment type also corresponding to one per year for the following inputs: primary school leavers, craft school leavers, secondary school leavers, and university leavers. Additional political constraints required that each activity was between 0.7 and 1.3 of its previous value.

7-7 SUMMARY

Linear programming is an iterative optimization technique developed specifically for the computer environment, and is a subset of production function theory in economics. It guarantees that an optimal solution will be found after a finite number of steps, provided the production function bounds a convex region and is piecewise linear and regular. The basic form of the linear programming problem consists of two parts: an objective function and constraint equations. The above function defines in linear equation form the criterion used to evaluate the effectiveness of the resource allocation. The constraint set defines the limits in resources at the disposal of the decision maker. Sensitivity analysis can also be performed on the coefficients of the objective function (pricing). Thus the assumptions in the model can be subjected to a sensitivity analysis, and the decision maker can be provided with information concerning the range over which the obtained solution will remain optimal.

Applications of linear programming to education in problem areas of resource allocation and design of a salary schedule were provided to illustrate the versatility of this technique. The reader is directed to the extensive literature on the application of linear programming to education. The relatively large number of applications to educational policy and planning demonstrate its value to educational policy analysts.

Chapter 8

Lorenz Curve Analysis: Measurement of Inequality in Educational Systems

8-1 INTRODUCTION

Because of recent court interest in education, there are many situations in which educational policy analysts are called upon to determine whether some system or educational practice in a school district is inequitable. For example, various desegregation plans for a school district can be compared on the basis of whether they are more equitable than the present attendance pattern in terms of racial balance. It is essential, when dealing with problems of this type, for the policy analyst to develop quantitative measures of inequality. This chapter discusses a relatively straightforward method for measuring the inequality that might be an inherent feature of some educational policy. The technique is an economics-based procedure called Lorenz curve analysis. The interpretation of various characteristics of Lorenz curves provides the educational policy maker with an impressive means for mathematically measuring inequality.

From a mathematical perspective there are various ways to examine inequality. First, one can compare individual inequalities. Suppose P is a measure of power; we can compare the power of Tom versus the power of Robert

$$P_T - P_R \quad \text{or} \quad \frac{P_T}{P_R}$$

and conclude that Tom is some amount more powerful or some number of times more powerful than Robert. Second, one might compare power in terms of its difference from some average power, or in terms of a ratio of power to some average power

$$\frac{P_T}{\bar{P}} \quad \text{or} \quad \frac{P_R}{\bar{P}}$$

and conclude that Tom or Robert is so many times more powerful than the average power.

This latter type of measurement (the ratio of power) is called a ratio of advantage, and it forms one of the most important indices for Lorenz curve analysis. Individual power or influence v_i is compared by means of a ratio with the average power of the system $\bar{v}$. Where the ratio is greater than unity, the individual holds more power than the average; when the ratio is less than unity, the individual assumes less than average power. Ratios of advantage ($v_i/\bar{v}$) can also be thought of as contextually defined indices of individual privilege or discrimination.

Cumulating values held by certain proportions of the population is the central idea in the assessment of the overall inequality of a particular value distribution. If the individual ratio of advantage measures are made cumulative, the observer can measure the fraction of total power held by various proportions of the population. When presented geometrically, the cumulative measures suggest a great variety of individual and collective measures of inequality.

If the cumulative distribution of the amount of power is plotted as an ordinate against the cumulative frequency distribution of the individuals possessing the power, the resulting curve is a Lorenz curve. The cumulation is usually expressed as a percentage of the total quantity, total number of individuals, and so on; and from the curve, it is possible to make statements such as: "$x\%$ of the people hold $y\%$ of the power." It is also possible to study the variations of these figures through time, or at different sites, by plotting successive curves on the same graph.

The cumulative value distributions begin ordinally ranking all individuals according to their ratios of advantage. Ratios for groups of individuals are calculated by an equivalent procedure—namely, dividing the percentage of values these groups hold by the percentage of population they represent.

8-2 LORENZ CURVE METHODOLOGY

The method of Lorenz curve analysis begins by ranking all individuals according to their ratios of advantage which, in turn, are found by dividing the percentages of power these individuals hold by the percentage of populations they represent. For example, consider five individuals with the following wealth:

Individual	Wealth
1	10,800
2	4,800
3	4,800
4	4,800
5	4,800
Total wealth	30,000
Average	6,000

Table 8-1 calculates the ratios of advantage, cumulative percentage of population, and wealth of the individuals. Table 8-1 is then rank ordered by ratios of advantage yielding Table 8-2; and the cumulative percent wealth or power is plotted against the cumulative percent population as the y- and x-axis, respectively.

Table 8-1. Ratio of Advantage, Percent of Population, and Percent of Wealth

Individual	Ratio of advantage[a]	Percent of population	Percent of wealth
1	9/5	20	36
2	4/5	20	16
3	4/5	20	16
4	4/5	20	16
5	4/5	20	16

[a]Ratio of advantage can be calculated in two ways: from $v_i/\bar{v}$ when working with individuals, e.g., for individual 1, 10,800/6,000 = 9/5 and from % power when working with groups or individuals, e.g., 36/20 = 9/5.

Table 8-2. Percentages To Be Plotted for Lorenz Analysis

Individual	Percent wealth	Cumulative percent wealth	Percent population	Cumulative percent population
2	16	16	20	20
3	16	32	20	40
4	16	48	20	60
5	16	64	20	80
1	36	100	20	100

When values from Table 8-2 are plotted (cumulative percent wealth y-axis and cumulative percent population x-axis), the Lorenz curve results (Figure 8-1). From Figure 8-2, we can determine the minimal majority or the percentage of people who hold 50% or more of the wealth or power. The minimal majority is determined by noting the point of intersection of the Lorenz curve with the horizontal line (dotted in Figure 8-1) where power equals 50%. The x value of this line subtracted from 100% is the minimal majority. In the above illustration the minimal majority is approximately 40%. The 45° line is the line of mathematical equality and the shaded area between the 45° line and the curve is called

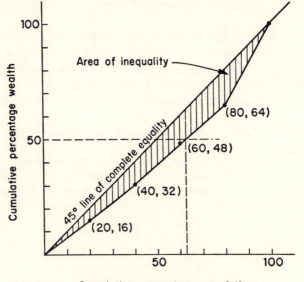

Figure 8-1. Illustrative Lorenz curve.

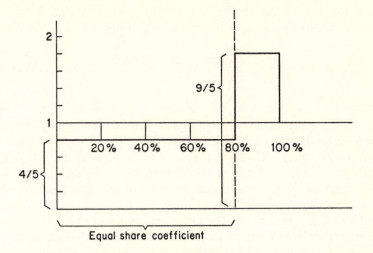

Figure 8-2. Determining equal share coefficient.

the area of inequality. By plotting the ratios of advantage on an ordinal scale, we can determine the equal share coefficient, that is, the percentage of people receiving less than their fair share or having ratio of advantage less than one. This is illustrated in Figure 8-2, which shows that 80% of the population in the example being considered are getting less than their fair share of wealth or power.

Finally, we might be interested in knowing the exact amount of inequality. The Gini index (also called Gini coefficient) is a mathematical representation of the inequality represented by this Lorenz curve. Notice that the area shaded in the Lorenz curve or the area beneath the 45° line and above the Lorenz curve in Figure 8-1 is the total area of inequality. The mathematical procedure for finding this area entails finding the total area under the 45° line or $A = \frac{1}{2} XV$ where X is the cumulative percent of population divided by 100 and V is the cumulative percent of wealth or power divided by 100.

In order to standardize the Gini coefficient so it varies between zero and one (perfect equality-perfect inequality) we divide the shaded area by the total area (below the 45°line) and define this as the Gini index

$$\frac{\text{Area shaded}}{\text{Total area}} = \text{Gini index}$$

Since the total area (under the 45° line) is $\frac{1}{2}XV$ and XV is unity, the Gini index is equal to precisely two times the area shaded

$$\text{Gini index} = \frac{\text{Area shaded}}{\frac{1}{2}\,XV} = \frac{\text{Area shaded}}{\frac{1}{2}\,(1.00)} = 2\,(\text{Area shaded})$$

Notice that as the area of inequality approaches zero, then the Gini index approaches zero; and the area of inequality approaches the area under the 45° line or half the total area, the Gini index approaches unity. Thus, if there is perfect equality (shaded area would equal zero), the Gini coefficient would equal zero. With total inequality (shaded area equal to total area) the Gini coefficient would be $\frac{1}{2}XV$, divided by $\frac{1}{2}XV$ or 1.

The Gini index sums, for each individual in the population, the difference between where he is on the Lorenz curve and where he would be expected to be in the case of democratic equality. The simplest method for determining the area of inequality is to use a geometric approach and sum the areas of the various triangles and squares defined by the Lorenz curve (see Figure 8-3). This total area is then subtracted from the total area between the 45° line

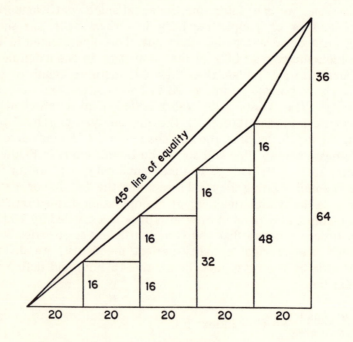

Figure 8-3. Deriving the area of inequality.

and the x-axis and multiplied by 2 to determine the Gini index. Note that in the calculations, proportions of wealth and population (values less than 1.00; that is, percentage/100) are used instead of percentage figures. Thus, the area of the whole square is $1.00 \times 1.00 = 1.00$, and the area under the $45°$ degree line is $\frac{1}{2}(1.00)(1.00) = 0.5$. Area would then be equal to

$\frac{1}{2}$ (1.00) (1.00) − [½ (0.16) (0.20) + (0.20) (0.16)
+ (0.32) (0.20) + ½ (0.16) (0.20) + ½ (0.20) (0.16)
+ (0.48) (0.20) + ½ (0.20) (0.16) + (0.64) (0.20)
+ ½ (0.36) (0.20)]

which would be equal to

0.5000 − (0.0160 + 0.0320 + 0.0640 + 0.0160 + 0.0160 + 0.0960
+ 0.0160 + 0.1280 + 0.0360)

Area = 0.5000 − 0.4200 = .0800

The area is then multiplied by two to derive the Gini index

(2) (0.0800) = 0.160

This method of summing areas can be written as a formula as follows

$$\text{Gini index} = 2 \left[0.5 - \left(\frac{1}{2} \sum_{i=1}^{n} PP_i PW_i + \sum_{i=2}^{n} PP_i CPW_{i-1} \right) \right]$$

where $\frac{1}{2}\sum_{i=1}^{n} PP_i PW_i$ is the areas of triangles, $\sum_{i=2}^{n} PP_i CPW_{i-1}$ is the areas of rectangles, PP is the percent population/100, PW is the percent wealth/100, and CPW is the cumulative percent wealth/100. Substituting the data from the example into the formula gives

Gini index = 2[0.5 − ½ ((0.16) (0.20) + (0.16) (0.20)
            + (0.16) (0.20) + (0.16) (0.20) + (0.36) (0.20))
            + (0.20) (0.16) + (0.20) (0.32) + (0.20) (0.48)
            + (0.20) (0.64)]
            = 0.160

Another method to find the area under the curve is to use the calculus. The Lorenz curve can be approximated with an exponential of the form $y = ce^x$. We know the beginning point (0,0)

and end point (1,1). We would only need some intermediate point to roughly approximate the shape of the curve. Using integration and $y = x$ as the 45° line, we have the y of the line y_L minus the y of the curve y_c integrated from 0 to 1 or

$$\int_0^1 (y_L - y_c)\, dx = \int_0^1 (x - ce^x)\, dx$$

or

$$\frac{x^2}{2} - ce^x = 0.5 - ce^x + c$$

where c controls the shape of the curve. Note that this procedure is only valid if the Lorenz curve is fairly smooth and can be approximated by an exponential curve.*

The most important outputs of Lorenz curve analysis are ratios of advantage (equal to the slopes of the curve) which are defined as

$$\Delta V/\Delta P = \frac{\text{Change in value}}{\text{Change in population}}$$
$$= \frac{\text{Percentage of total value held}}{\text{Percentage of total population represented}}$$

The equal share coefficient is another interpretable result of Lorenz curve analysis. Notice that when the slope of the Lorenz curve equals or begins to exceed unity, people to the right of the curve get more than an equal share, people to the left of this point therefore get less than their fair share. The equal share coefficient

---

*Another common method for approximating the area of inequality is to sum the areas of rectangles representing cumulatively the inequality of each individual or group. This can be written as a formula (Alker 1965)

$$\text{Gini index} = 2 \sum_{i=1}^{N} (X_i - Y_i)\, \Delta X_i$$

which is twice the sum of rectangles with heights $X_i - Y_i$ and widths ΔX_i, where $X_i = i/N$, $Y_i = \sum_{k \leqslant i} V_k/V$, and $\Delta X_i = X_i - X_{i-1}$. Applying this formula to the previous example gives

$$\begin{aligned}
\text{Gini index} &= 2\,\Sigma(\text{cum. \% of people} - \text{cum. \% wealth})\,(\text{\% of people}) \\
&= 2\,[(0.20 - 0.16)\,(0.20) + (0.40 - 0.32)\,(0.20) + (0.60 - 0.48) \\
&\quad (0.20) + (0.80 - 0.64)\,(0.20)] \\
&= 0.160
\end{aligned}$$

is, consequently, defined as the percentage of the population getting less than equal share of the power.

The minimal majority is defiend as the smallest percentage of people getting 50% of the value, that is in essence, the elite (or percent of population) who get the most power. The minimal majority in Figure 8-2 is 20%.

As previously mentioned, the Gini index represents the total amount of inequality in the population. Inequality is measured for each individual as the difference between the Lorenz curve and where the indiviual would be in a situation of complete equality. The Gini index is two times the sum of this inequality for all individuals in the population. In general, school policy makers are interested in reducing the Gini index to values approximating zero.

8-3 SCHOOL DISTRICT APPLICATION
OF LORENZ CURVE METHODOLOGY

To illustrate the Lorenz curve methodology for measuring inequality, consider the following problem facing an educational policy maker in a school district. Suppose there were five high schools in the district with the following total expenditures and total number of students as shown in Table 8-3. The ratios of advantage, percent of total, and cumulative percent of total for both budget and number of students are then calculated as in Table 8-4. A ranking of school sites in increasing ratios of advantage is shown in Table 8-5. A plot of Table 8-5 forms the Lorenz curve shown in Figure 8-4.

The Gini index is then found by measuring the area between the 45° line of perfect equality and the Lorenz curve. The area of the total triangle (0.5000) under the 45° line minus the area under the Lorenz curve yields the area of inequality. Using the geometric approach to find this area, the Gini index is 0.187.

Table 8-3. Expenditures and Number
of Students by School Site

School	Budget	Students
A	1,950,000	5200
B	333,004	3000
C	909,179	4000
D	2,300,000	5800
E	381,603	2000

Table 8-4. Cumulative Percent Distributions

School site	Budget	Percents	Students	Percents	Slope[a]	Cumulative percent
A	1,950,000	32	5,200	26	1.23	71
B	333,004	6	3,000	15	0.4	25
C	909,179	16	4,000	20	0.8	45
D	2,300,000	39	5,800	29	1.33	100
E	381,603	7	2,000	10	0.7	10
Total ($)	5,873,786	100%	20,000	100%		
Average	1,174,757					

[a]Slope = ratio of advantage = % budget/% students.

Table 8-5. Ranking of School Sites

	Budget			Pupils	
	Percents	Cumulative percent	Ratio of adv.	Percents	Cumulative percent
School B	06	06	0.4	15	15
School E	07	13	0.7	10	25
School C	16	29	0.8	20	45
School A	32	61	1.23	26	71
School D	39	100	1.33	29	100

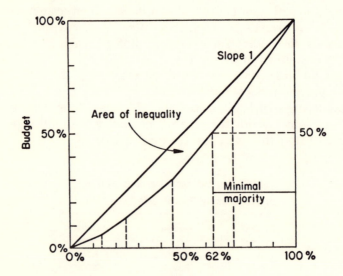

Figure 8-4. Lorenz curve.

In summary the four important outputs of Lorenz curve analysis are:

1. minimal majority—What percentage of populaton gets more than 50% of value?
2. equal share coefficient—What percentage of the population gets less than its fair share?
3. line of complete equality—Slope = 1, and
4. Gini coefficient—Gini index = 2 × area shaded in Figure 8-1

$$\frac{\text{Area shaded}}{\text{½ total area}} = \text{Gini coefficient}$$

For example, a Gini coefficient of 0.15 indicates that the distribution of wealth is 15% away from theoretical total equality. In the example presented here (Figure 8-4) the principal Lorenz curve outputs are

minimal majority	38%
equal share coefficient	45%
Gini coefficient	0.187

8-4 OTHER APPLICATIONS OF LORENZ CURVE ANALYSIS

Lorenz curve analysis is especially useful for measuring inequalities in wealth distribution and inequalities in representation in government. In Reynolds vs. Lims (Silva 1961), a legal suit was presented to uphold the fundamental principle of representative government in this country (one of equal representation for equal numbers of people without regard to race, sex, or economic status). The following Lorenz analysis is presented in Figure 8-5. Note that in Figure 8-5 the minimal majority was 35%. This means 35% of the state population have potential majority control. Also, the top 8% of the population has 20% of the representative strength in the legislature.

An analysis of the equal share coefficient showed as in Figure 8-6 that 77% of the people were under represented or had ratios of advantage less than one. The legal interpretation of the above figure is that 77% of the population is underrepresented and that 90% of the representation is held by 72% of the people. A Gini index was calculated for the Lorenz curve in Figure 8-5 and found to be 0.22. This indicated that the current legislative apportionment program was 0.22 away from complete equality.

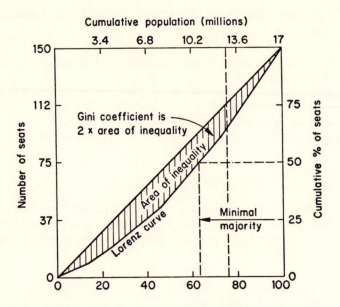

Figure 8-5. Lorenz analysis of apportionment. *Source*: Alker (1965). Reproduced with permission of the author.

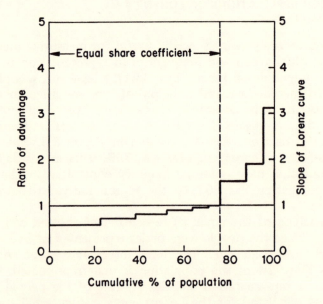

Figure 8-6. Equal share coefficient in legislative apportionment. *Source*: Alker (1965). Reproduced with permission of the author.

In another study involving school desegregation plans for a school district, the following data were collected and Lorenz curves were drawn for situations reflecting complete balance, the proposed plan, current busing plan, and maximum feasible imbalance. These results are summarized in Table 8-6. The Lorenz curves for the various busing plans nicely showed the progress of the district toward providing equitable educational opportunities via improving racial balance in the district. Figure 8-7 summarizes the Lorenz curves for the different situations or patterns of racial imbalance.

The Gini index for the present plan was 0.25, and the maximum feasible imbalance (total segregation) of the Gini index was 0.40. Calculation of the Gini index for the proposed plan yielded a value of 0.07, which is a marked improvement (0.07/0.25

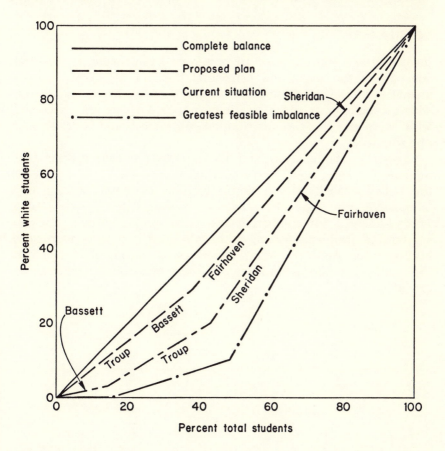

Figure 8-7. Alternate patterns of racial balance. *Source*: Alker (1965). Reproduced with permission of the author.

Table 8-6. Data on School Desegregation Plans[a]

Number of students	White	Percent of total white	Nonwhite	Total	Percent of all students
Bassett	55	3	555	610	17
Troup	419	19	514	933	27
Sheridan	741	34	148	889	25
Fairhaven	968	44	140	1,108	31
Total	2,183		1,357	3,540	

[a]*Source*: Alker (1965). Reproduced with permission of the author.

over 28%) over the present plan toward achieving maximum equality.

8-5 SUMMARY

Inequality and concentration of power are basic themes and central concepts in the social and behavioral sciences. Economists study inequities in the distribution of wealth, income, taxes, and so on, whereas sociologists and educational policy analysts are concerned with inequities in the distribution of educational services and opportunity.

Lorenz curve analysis and its important output measures of minimal majority, equal share coefficient, and Gini index presents the policy analyst with a simple method for demonstrating any inequitable distribution of power or resources in a system. Using Lorenz analysis for comparing alternative proposed plans for the solution of problems dealing with imbalance in a system provides insights into selecting alternative courses of action, which result in the most equitable distribution of wealth or resources that can be provided.

Delphi Techniques: Elicitation of Expert Opinion for Setting Organizational Goals

9-1 INTRODUCTION

The old adage "two heads are better than one," or, the extrapolated, "n heads are better than one," characterizes a type of technology for dealing with group opinion that has been utilized for centuries. This traditional method for arriving at decisions depended upon committees, the members of which were involved in face-to-face interaction. Several problems with this procedure are easily identified:

1. in every group there are "talkative" and "quiet" members. Group consensus is highly influenced by the dominant members of the group, whether or not the dominant members are, in fact, the most knowledgeable;

2. a considerable amount of the discussion in a group is typically not related to the topic, that is, irrelevant to the basic problem issue and perhaps even biased. This problem has been labeled as "semantic noise"; and

3. in any group, there is a tendency to yield to group pressure or to the opinions of a supposed expert. This pressure tends to negate the opinions of the less articulate indiviudals, even though their opinions may be well founded.

In 1953, Norman C. Dalkey and Olaf Helmer began research with a set of procedures, subsequently labeled Delphi because, like the ancient oracle, it has been employed to obtain opinions about the future (Dalkey et al. 1972). Interest in Delphi was slow in developing on a general basis for about 10 years, but the mid-60s saw extensive use of the technique primarily by industry in forecasting technological developments. It was also used by a wide variety of organizations for the formulation of policy in such areas as education, convict incarceration, transportation, and public health. It has also been used to predict the quality of life in the 21st century, the future of science, and future developments in computer technology.

Delphi still uses the "*n* heads are better than one" adage, but replaces the direct face-to-face interaction with a well-planned program of sequential questionnaires administered individually and with guaranteed anonymity. Each questionnaire (usually three or four questionnaires are administered sequentially) is followed by dissemination of information derived from the individual respondents (experts). In many cases these experts are asked to give reasons for their particular opinions. Each successive questionnaire is, therefore, a refinement of the previous one, and generally the predictions tend to compress or reach closure. This technique permits participants to confront the ideas of the others without doing personal battle and permits all opinions to have equal exposure.

In essence Delphi is a technique in which responses are systematically elicited from a group of experts until they arrive at a consensus concerning some organizational problem in forecasting. For a detailed discussion of the methodological foundations of the technique see Brown (1968) and Dalkey and Helmer (1963) and Dalkey (1967).

The format for a Delphi investigation is always the same. First, a group of experts are selected and each member completes a specially designed and structured questionnaire. Second, the responses of each individual on the questionnaire are reported (usually interquartile ranges are given), and the panel are asked to reevaluate their responses based upon information provided by the analysis of responses. Third, the entire cycle is repeated; if some experts are not in the middle quartile range, they can be asked to justify their estimates or to provide other members of the committee with information they possess that justified their extreme (out of range of the middle two quartiles) response.

Respondents might also be asked to present reasons for revisions of their original estimates. In addition, they might be asked to critique reasons presented by other members of the group and to specify which arguments were convincing and why. These arguments and counterarguments would then be summarized in writing and included in the decision framework for each individual in the next round.

9-2 CHARACTERISTICS OF DELPHI

Delphi has three principal characteristics which make it useful as a technique for educational policy:

1. Anonymous response—Opinions of members of the group are obtained by formal questionnaires, thus avoiding confrontation;
2. Iteration and controlled feedback—Interaction is effected by a systematic exercise conducted in several iterations, with carefully controlled feedback; and
3. Statistical group response—The group opinion is defined as an appropriate aggregate of individual opinions on the final round. The technique has features designed to minimize the biasing effects of dominant individuals, of irrelevant communication, and of group pressure toward conformity.

It is the anonymous response and controlled feedback features that make Delphi extremely efficient in organizations where "experts' " time is at a premium thereby making committee meetings costly and inefficient. Delphi is also effective in organizations where there are dominant individuals who tend to become ego-involved with certain policy issues and in order to save face defend their positions to their utmost just for the sake of winning a point. Thus, Delphi is a rapid, efficient method for "picking the brains" of a group of knowledgeable people called experts, which involve much less effort for a participant than a committee. The feedback and analysis of responses provide a high level of interest, thus stimulating motivation toward organizational over personal interests. Because of the anonymity of the experts, there are fewer ego-involved responses, less defense of these responses (because names are not attached to the response), and less inhibition from those members of the organization who can contribute a great deal of information and insight but who are intimidated at face-to-face committee meetings. In summary Delphi tries to minimize:

1. influence of dominant indiviudals—Opinions may be inordinately influenced by effective speakers, higher-ranking personnel, and so on;
2. noise—Semantic noise dealing with individual or group interests, rather than the specific problem-solving task, may be irrelevant and biasing;
3. group pressure for conformity—Individual judgments can be dramatically distorted as a result of group pressure; and
4. concern for self-image in group—An individual may be unwilling to change an opinion that has been publicly expressed.

Since one key element in successful studies employing Delphi techniques is panel of experts' selection, it is appropriate to present some guidelines as to the panel composition. Suppose we desired a forecasting panel for a school district planning situation. As forecast needs vary from concrete to abstract, the importance of empirical data diminishes rapidly. In addition, forecasters with specialized skills must be replaced by informed generalists capable of understanding without empirical data but with disciplined imaginations to evaluate diversified sources of qualitative information. As the forecast becomes more abstract, the use of interdisciplinary teams of experts becomes more important. Campbell and Hitchin present an interesting set of heuristics for panel selection in Delphi studies (see Table 9-1).

Consider the following example of Delphi methodology. Suppose an administrator is interested in determining years in the future a $30,000.00 teacher salary would be reality.

First, select a panel of experts. An expert could be defined to include anyone who contributes relevant inputs (generally a highly educated or experienced person). Administer a questionnaire to each expert, asking for a prediction of how soon teachers could be earning $30,000.00 a year. Suppose there were ten experts and the number of years given by these experts as the time required for teacher salaries to reach $30,000.00 per year were recorded to be:

Expert	No. of years in the future	Expert	No. of years in the future
1	5	6	2
2	6	7	4
3	5	8	5
4	8	9	6
5	1	10	6

Table 9-1. Important Factors in Selection of Panel of Experts[a]

Specific corporate orientation to the future	Judgment				Diversity of participants		Imagination	
	Empirical data	Specialized expertise	Less specialized expertise	Informal generalists	Close to specialized fields and interests	Widely diversified and inter-disciplinary	Extrap-olative	Creative conjecture
a. Broadened applications of existing technologies	High	High	High	Low	High	Low	High	Medium
b. New alternatives evolving from existing knowledge	Medium	Medium to high	High	Medium	Medium	Medium	Medium	Medium
c. New alternatives evolving from new knowledge derived from trends of research, analysis, and social developments	Low	Medium	High	High	Medium to low	High	Medium to low	High
d. New alternatives evolving from new knowledge derived strictly from responsible, educated conjecture	Low	Medium to low	High	High	Low	High	Low	High
e. New alternatives from creative conjecture, not discernible from any existing knowledge	Low	Low	High	High	Low	High	Low	High

aSource: R. Campbell and D. Hitchin (1968). "The Delphi Technique: Implementation in the Corporate Environment." *Management Services*, vol. 5, no. 6. Reproduced with permission of the author and publisher. Copyright 1968 by the American Institute of Certified Public Accountants, Inc.

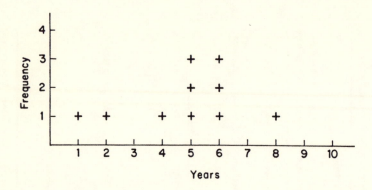

Figure 9-1. Results from Round 1.

A plot of the frequency responses is given in Figure 9-1.

Next, the above information would be provided these experts, who would then be asked to reassess their responses. On the basis of this new information Expert 5 might be asked to justify his extreme response if the position is maintained.

The second iteration is shown in Figure 9-2. In this second round, an expert with an extreme response gave as justification the reason that the inflation rate will be more than 10%. In the next round, this information is given to the experts with justifications for extreme responses and they are again asked to reassess their responses. The results are shown in Figure 9-3. The iterative process is repeated until a consensus is reached. In summary, the steps to be followed for a Delphi investigation are:

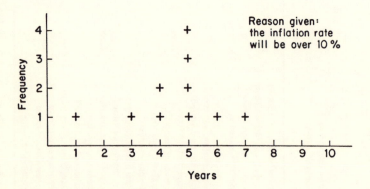

Figure 9-2. Results from Round 2.

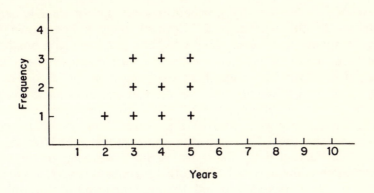

Figure 9-3. Results from Round 3.

1. group of experts is selected,
2. each member completes a structured questionnaire,
3. results are combined (usually interquartile range),
4. panel is provided with responses and asked to recalculate response. Arguments and counterarguments for extreme veiws are summarized, and
5. cycle is repeated. If some experts are not in the middle quartile ranges, they can be asked to justify their "guesstimates" until a consensus is reached.

9-3 EXPERIMENTS ON DELPHI

To establish the validity of the Delphi approach, research has been conducted at The RAND Corporation on the technique. See Dalkey et al. (1972) for a complete summary of this research.

The experiences at the RAND Corporation have shown the following results (Dalkey 1968a and 1968b):

1. face-to-face discussion is not efficient compared with more formalized communication;
2. there is pronounced convergence of opinion with iteration;
3. improvement in accuracy of estimate may be expected with iteration (especially where a range is estimated rather than a simple point); and
4. the larger the group, the more accurate and reliable the answer.

Many questions remain to be answered before assessing the validity of the technique. For example, how much of the convergence is due to the procedures used, rather than a better estimation of the true answer? Refined analysis has shown the median response to be more powerful than the mean as a predictor of the true answer (where that was known). Another area of research in Delphi concerns how the effects of group pressure (even though anonymous) can be dampened further, and the movement toward the true answer amplified.

The most recent studies (Dalkey and Rourke 1971) have focused on the use of Delphi with value judgments. With values (rather than factual data) there can be little assurance of accuracy because there is no standard of "truth" for measurement. However, analysis of these studies has led to the conclusion that Delphi is useful with value judgments as well as factual material. The state of the art has been advanced by the identification of three conditions that are important for assuming a given Delphi exercise is involving judgment rather than a capricious expression of personal attitudes:

1. there will be a normal distribution of responses;
2. there will be group reliability (i.e., a similar grouping of experts would get similar results); and
3. there will be change and convergence on iteration with feedback.

Another important area of analysis on the Delphi technique is the attempt to identify the most competent experts in the exercise based on their own self-ratings of competence on each item of the questionnaire. The results of these experiments, however, are mixed. Earlier studies by Dalkey (1968b) indicated that an indiviudal's self-rating of his competence on items was not highly correlated with his accuracy. More recent studies (Dalkey et al. 1970a and 1970b), however, have indicated that a self-rating index can be developed from an average of the individual self-ratings. This index is a valid indication of the mean accuracy of the group responses. This is demonstrated in Figures 9-4 and 9-5. Thus, some measure of the accuracy of an exercise is possible.

While serious questions remain to be answered and refinements of the technique have yet to be developed, the value of Delphi for educational policy and planning is promising. In fact, for future problems such as setting goals and priorities for school districts, Delphi is possibly the best way of studying the problems.

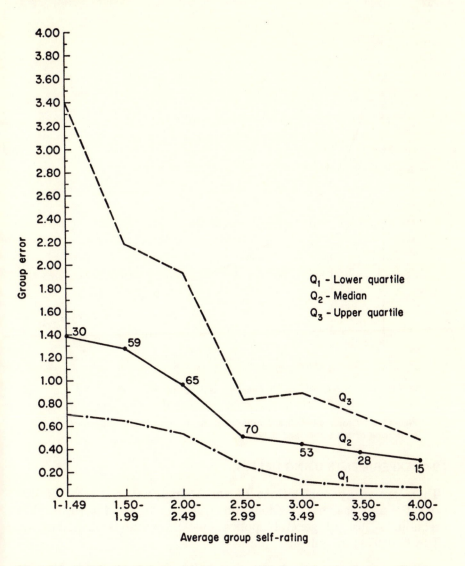

Figure 9-4. Relationship between average group self-rating and group accuracy. *Source:* Dalkey et al. (1970a). Reproduced with permission of the author and publisher.

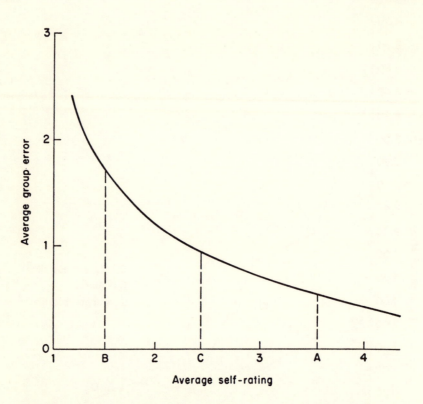

Figure 9-5. Group self-rating. *Source*: Dalkey et al. (1970a). Reproduced with permission of the author and publisher.

9-4 EXPERIMENTS USING DELPHI

There are many applications of the Delphi method; some of the specific applications in education will be discussed later in this section. A list of general applications of Delphi is suggested by Turoff (1971) as follows:

1. forecasting,
2. examining the significance of historical events,
3. gathering current and historical data,
4. putting together the structure of a model,
5. delineating the pros and cons associated with potential decision and policy options, and
6. developing causal relationships in economic or social phenomena.

Helmer (1966) suggests the following problem situations for using Delphi in the field of education:

1. a district superintendent intends to institute a curriculum reform project and may wish to solicit opinions among selected administrators and teachers within his district;
2. a state educational planning office might decide on a building program after first consulting and determining needs of local superintendents;
3. the priorities in a university's long-range expansion program are established by reconciling the views of its various academic departments; and
4. administrators, departmental representatives, or other panels at many levels in a school district help establish a comprehensive program of educational innovations.

Concerning the use of Delphi in studying educational innovations, Helmer specifically proposes the following steps:

1. establishment of appropriate goals through the Delphi method,
2. suggestions for potential educational innovations related to the goals,
3. estimate of dollar cost of each item in the resulting list of contemplated innovations, and
4. cost-benefit analysis.

Concerning this last step of cost benefit analysis, Helmer remarks that when costs and benefits are clearly measureable in objective terms, there is no need to resort to the use of mere opinions. However, benefits resulting from the choice of given policy alternatives especially in education can almost never be measured unambiguously; even in the case of costs, it is usually only the dollars that can sometimes be predicted; whereas, social costs may be as elusive as the benefits. For this purpose, the type of consensus of individual judgments obtained by the Delphi method can be helpful in obtaining an appraisal for benefits and cost.

Many studies have been employed using Delphi techniques. The following studies demonstrate some of the varied applications of this technique:

1. A pilot Delphi experiment was conducted in an Educational Innovations Seminar held at the Institute of Government and Public Affairs, UCLA (Adelson et al. 1967, Helmer 1966). Three

groups were used for the experiment. Among their collective opinions for priorities in education were the following:

    a. teacher salaries ought to be raised substantially in order to improve the quality of education; and

    b. significant amounts should be allotted toward increasing student participation either through educational leaves for adults or by sending children to public school prior to age 5.

2. In 1967 a study using Delphi for long-range social forecasting was conducted at RAND (Haydon 1967). The study involved more than 80 experts—engineers, mathematicians, economists, physical scientists, social scientists, writers, and so on. Delphi was utilized for the examination of the future in six areas: scientific breakthroughs, population growth, automation, space progress, the probability and prevention of war, and future weapon systems.

3. Olaf Helmer (1967), one of the primary developers of Delphi, describes the use of Delphi in predicting the future of science, utilizing about 20 prominent scientists. Consensus predictions were made about many events, including, economical desalination of sea water, automated language translators, reliable weather forecasts, biochemicals to stimulate growth of new organs and limbs, chemical control of the aging process, and two-way communication with extraterrestrials.

4. In the context of penal corrections forecasting was necessary to determine the demand for correctional facilities and manpower. Delphi was used as a means of anticipating policy changes affecting the corrections population (McLean 1971).

5. Students from the University of California at Los Angeles were subjects in an experiment assessing the appropriateness of Delphi for formulating group value judgments (Dalkey et al. 1972). The responders generated and rated value categories relating to higher education and the quality of life. This experiment furnished support for the conclusion that Delphi procedures were appropriate for processing value material as well as factual material.

6. A Delphi study in the future of higher education was conducted at the National Center for Higher Education Management Systems (NCHEMS) by the Ford Foundation. There were 385 respondents and these represented a wide cross-section of the population, which is concerned with education: congressmen, governors, state legislators, lay board members, students, faculty, deans, finance officers, college and university presidents, members of the press, and consultants in postsecondary education. The study involved the use of five questionnaires and dealt with the possible changes which might take place in higher education. Huckfeldt (1972) summarized the results:

    a. postsecondary education will become more readily accessible to all; and

    b. more students will drop in and out of the system throughout their lifetimes and will participate in programs that lead to vocations.

9-5 SUMMARY

Judgment of experts may be used in any planning situation where it is necessary to choose among several alternative courses of action and no theory has been developed that would evaluate the consequences of the proposed courses of action. Experts are used because they possess a large store of background knowledge and a cultivated sensitivity to the problem. The expert's intuitive insight is what is required. Consensus of experts is required because individual experts usually diagree, and policy makers are unwilling to rely on the judgment of a single specialist.

In addition, there are variables used as inputs to models in social systems for which no adequate measure exists. An example might be a policy decision model requiring measures of social and cultural conditions at some school site when there are no historical records available. The obvious recourse is the efficient use of the intuition and judgment of a group of persons who are keen observers and have lived in the area for a long period of time.

The use of expertise is not a retreat from objectivity. Judgment and informed opinion have always played a crucial role in human enterprises. Expert judgment can be incorporated into the structure of an investigation and can be made subject to some of the safeguards that are commonly used to assure objectivity in any scientific inquiry.

Education, as one of the "inexact sciences," has suffered from the lack of a well-defined theoretical framework. Yet decisions are demanded and futuristic policies are desirable. Society is placing pressure on educators to be more effective decision makers. If we believe that intuition is one of the untapped resources available to solve problems, then the Delphi method can be one method for systematically developing intuition as a useful resource. It should be noted that beyond the leaders of education, government, and business, it is possible that the intuitive judgment of students and parents may be a vast resource of ideas for what is best for the "client"—the student.

The value of Delphi in accurately predicting the future has yet to be adequately assessed, although few would disagree that the process has solved some of the problems encountered in the committee approach. In education, Delphi has great potential as a method of studying the process of thinking about the future. By using Delphi, learning to adapt to change, which is perhaps equally as important as specific training, can be accomplished. Delphi forces educators to think about the future in a more complex way than they would ordinarily. Finally, Delphi is a tool that may assist in establishing priorities in education by identifying those priorities of individual members of a segment of society who ultimately influence the course and direction of education.

Appendices–Standard
Statistical Tables

Table 1. Random Numbers[a]

```
10 09 73 25 33    76 52 01 35 86    34 67 35 48 76    80 95 90 91 17    39 29 27 49 45
37 54 20 48 05    64 89 47 42 96    24 80 52 40 37    20 63 61 04 02    00 82 29 16 65
08 42 26 89 53    19 64 50 93 03    23 20 90 25 60    15 95 33 47 64    35 08 03 36 06
99 01 90 25 29    09 37 67 07 15    38 31 13 11 65    88 67 67 43 97    04 43 62 76 59
12 80 79 99 70    80 15 73 61 47    64 03 23 66 53    98 95 11 68 77    12 17 17 68 33

66 06 57 47 17    34 07 27 68 50    36 69 73 61 70    65 81 33 98 85    11 19 92 91 70
31 06 01 08 05    45 57 18 24 06    35 30 34 26 14    86 79 90 74 39    23 40 30 97 32
85 26 97 76 02    02 05 16 56 92    68 66 57 48 18    73 05 38 52 47    18 62 38 85 79
63 57 33 21 35    05 32 54 70 48    90 55 35 75 48    28 46 82 87 09    83 49 12 56 24
73 79 64 57 53    03 52 96 47 78    35 80 83 42 82    60 93 52 03 44    35 27 38 84 35

98 52 01 77 67    14 90 56 86 07    22 10 94 05 58    60 97 09 34 33    50 50 07 39 98
11 80 50 54 31    39 80 82 77 32    50 72 56 82 48    29 40 52 42 01    52 77 56 78 51
83 45 29 96 34    06 28 89 80 83    13 74 67 00 78    18 47 54 06 10    68 71 17 78 17
88 68 54 02 00    86 50 75 84 01    36 76 66 79 51    90 36 47 64 93    29 60 91 10 62
99 59 46 73 48    87 51 76 49 69    91 82 60 89 28    93 78 56 13 68    23 47 83 41 13

65 48 11 76 74    17 46 85 09 50    58 04 77 69 74    73 03 95 71 86    40 21 81 65 44
80 12 43 56 35    17 72 70 80 15    45 31 82 23 74    21 11 57 82 53    14 38 55 37 63
74 35 09 98 17    77 40 27 72 14    43 23 60 02 10    45 52 16 42 37    96 28 60 26 55
69 91 62 68 03    66 25 22 91 48    36 93 68 72 03    76 62 11 39 90    94 40 05 64 18
09 89 32 05 05    14 22 56 85 14    46 42 75 67 88    96 29 77 88 22    54 38 21 45 98
```

[a]*Source*: From The RAND Corporation, *A Million Random Digits with 100,000 Normal Deviates* (Glencoe, Ill., Free Press, 1955). This table is reproduced with permission from The RAND Corporation.

Table 1. Random Numbers (Continued)

```
91 49 91 45 23    68 47 92 76 86    46 16 28 35 54    94 75 08 99 23    37 08 92 00 48
80 33 69 45 98    26 94 03 68 58    70 29 73 41 35    53 14 03 33 40    42 05 08 23 41
44 10 48 19 49    85 15 74 79 54    32 97 92 65 75    57 60 04 08 81    22 22 20 64 13
12 55 07 37 42    11 10 00 20 40    12 86 07 46 97    96 64 48 94 39    28 70 72 58 15
63 60 64 93 29    16 50 53 44 84    40 21 95 25 63    43 65 17 70 82    07 20 73 17 90

61 19 69 04 46    26 45 74 77 74    51 92 43 37 29    65 39 45 95 93    42 58 26 05 27
15 47 44 52 66    95 27 07 99 53    59 36 78 38 48    82 39 61 01 18    33 21 15 94 66
94 55 72 85 73    67 89 75 43 87    54 62 24 44 31    91 19 04 25 92    92 92 74 59 73
42 48 11 62 13    97 34 40 87 21    16 86 84 87 67    03 07 11 20 59    25 70 14 66 70
23 52 37 83 17    73 20 88 98 37    68 93 59 14 16    26 25 22 96 63    05 52 28 25 62

04 49 35 24 94    75 24 63 38 24    45 86 25 10 25    61 96 27 93 35    65 33 71 24 72
00 54 99 76 54    64 05 18 81 59    96 11 96 38 96    54 69 28 23 91    23 28 72 95 29
35 96 31 53 07    26 89 80 93 54    33 35 13 54 62    77 97 45 00 24    90 10 33 93 33
59 80 80 83 91    45 42 72 68 42    83 60 94 97 00    13 02 12 48 92    78 56 52 01 06
46 05 88 52 36    01 39 09 22 86    77 28 14 40 77    93 91 08 36 47    70 61 74 29 41

32 17 90 05 97    87 37 92 52 41    05 56 70 70 07    86 74 31 71 57    85 39 41 18 38
69 23 46 14 06    20 11 74 52 04    15 95 66 00 00    18 74 39 24 23    97 11 89 63 38
19 56 54 14 30    01 75 87 53 79    40 41 92 15 85    66 67 43 68 06    84 96 28 52 07
45 15 51 49 38    19 47 60 72 46    43 66 79 45 43    59 04 79 00 33    20 82 66 95 41
94 86 43 19 94    36 16 81 08 51    34 88 88 15 53    01 54 03 54 56    05 01 45 11 76

98 08 62 48 26    45 24 02 84 04    44 99 90 88 96    39 09 47 34 07    35 44 13 18 80
33 18 51 62 32    41 94 15 09 49    89 43 54 85 81    88 69 54 19 94    37 54 87 30 43
80 95 10 04 06    96 38 27 07 74    20 15 12 33 87    25 01 62 52 98    94 62 46 11 71
79 75 24 91 40    71 96 12 82 96    69 86 10 25 91    74 85 22 05 39    00 38 75 95 79
18 63 33 25 37    98 14 50 65 71    31 01 02 46 74    05 45 56 14 27    77 93 89 19 36

74 02 94 39 02    77 55 73 22 70    97 79 01 71 19    52 52 75 80 21    80 81 45 17 48
54 17 84 56 11    80 99 33 71 43    05 33 51 29 69    56 12 71 92 55    36 04 09 03 24
11 66 44 98 83    52 07 98 48 27    59 38 17 15 39    09 97 33 34 40    88 46 12 33 56
48 32 47 79 28    31 24 96 47 10    02 29 53 68 70    32 30 75 75 46    15 02 00 99 94
69 07 49 41 38    87 63 79 19 76    35 58 40 44 01    10 51 82 16 15    01 84 87 69 38

09 18 82 00 97    32 82 53 95 27    04 22 08 63 04    83 38 98 73 74    64 27 85 80 44
90 04 58 54 97    51 98 15 06 54    94 93 88 19 97    91 87 07 61 50    68 47 66 46 59
73 18 95 02 07    47 67 72 62 69    62 29 06 44 64    27 12 46 70 18    41 36 18 27 60
75 76 87 64 90    20 97 18 17 49    90 42 91 22 72    95 37 50 58 71    93 82 34 31 78
54 01 64 40 56    66 28 13 10 03    00 68 22 73 98    20 71 45 32 95    07 70 61 78 13

08 35 86 99 10    78 54 24 27 85    13 66 15 88 73    04 61 89 75 53    31 22 30 84 20
28 30 60 32 64    81 33 31 05 91    40 51 00 78 93    32 60 46 04 75    94 11 90 18 40
53 84 08 62 33    81 59 41 36 28    51 21 59 02 90    28 46 66 87 95    77 76 22 07 91
91 75 75 37 41    61 61 36 22 69    50 26 39 02 12    55 78 17 65 14    83 48 34 70 55
89 41 59 26 94    00 39 75 83 91    12 60 71 76 46    48 94 97 23 06    94 54 13 74 08

77 51 30 38 20    86 83 42 99 01    68 41 48 27 74    51 90 81 39 80    72 89 35 55 07
19 50 23 71 74    69 97 92 02 88    55 21 02 97 73    74 28 77 52 51    65 34 46 74 15
21 81 85 93 13    93 27 88 17 57    05 68 67 31 56    07 08 28 50 46    31 85 33 84 52
51 47 46 64 99    68 10 72 36 21    94 04 99 13 45    42 83 60 91 91    08 00 74 54 49
99 55 96 83 31    62 53 52 41 70    69 77 71 28 30    74 81 97 81 42    43 86 07 28 34

33 71 34 80 07    93 58 47 28 69    51 92 66 47 21    58 30 32 98 22    93 17 49 39 72
85 27 48 68 93    11 30 32 92 70    28 83 43 41 37    73 51 59 04 00    71 14 84 36 43
84 13 38 96 40    44 03 55 21 66    73 85 27 00 91    61 22 26 05 61    62 32 71 84 23
56 73 21 62 34    17 39 59 61 31    10 12 39 16 22    85 49 65 75 60    81 60 41 88 80
65 13 85 68 06    87 64 88 52 61    34 31 36 58 61    45 87 52 10 69    85 64 44 72 77
```

Table 1. Random Numbers (Continued)

```
38 00 10 21 76   81 71 91 17 11   71 60 29 29 37   74 21 96 40 49   65 58 44 96 98
37 40 29 63 97   01 30 47 75 86   56 27 11 00 86   47 32 46 26 05   40 03 03 74 38
97 12 54 03 48   87 08 33 14 17   21 81 53 92 50   75 23 76 20 47   15 50 12 95 78
21 82 64 11 34   47 14 33 40 72   64 63 88 59 02   49 13 90 64 41   03 85 65 45 52
73 13 54 27 42   95 71 90 90 35   85 79 47 42 96   08 78 98 81 56   64 69 11 92 02

07 63 87 79 29   03 06 11 80 72   96 20 74 41 56   23 82 19 95 38   04 71 36 69 94
60 52 88 34 41   07 95 41 98 14   59 17 52 06 95   05 53 35 21 39   61 21 20 64 55
83 59 63 56 55   06 95 89 29 83   05 12 80 97 19   77 43 35 37 83   92 30 15 04 98
10 85 06 27 46   99 59 91 05 07   13 49 90 63 19   53 07 57 18 39   06 41 01 93 62
39 82 09 89 52   43 62 26 31 47   64 42 18 08 14   43 80 00 93 51   31 02 47 31 67

59 58 00 64 78   75 56 97 88 00   88 83 55 44 86   23 76 80 61 56   04 11 10 84 08
38 50 80 73 41   23 79 34 87 63   90 82 29 70 22   17 71 90 42 07   95 95 44 99 53
30 69 27 06 68   94 68 81 61 27   56 19 68 00 91   82 06 76 34 00   05 46 26 92 00
65 44 39 56 59   18 28 82 74 37   49 63 22 40 41   08 33 76 56 76   96 29 99 08 36
27 26 75 02 64   13 19 27 22 94   07 47 74 46 06   17 98 54 89 11   97 34 13 03 58

91 30 70 69 91   19 07 22 42 10   36 69 95 37 28   28 82 53 57 93   28 97 66 62 52
68 43 49 46 88   84 47 31 36 22   62 12 69 84 08   12 84 38 25 90   09 81 59 31 46
48 90 81 58 77   54 74 52 45 91   35 70 00 47 54   83 82 45 26 92   54 13 05 51 60
06 91 34 51 97   42 67 27 86 01   11 88 30 95 28   63 01 19 89 01   14 97 44 03 44
10 45 51 60 19   14 21 03 37 12   91 34 23 78 21   88 32 58 08 51   43 66 77 08 83

12 88 39 73 43   65 02 76 11 84   04 28 50 13 92   17 97 41 50 77   90 71 22 67 69
21 77 83 09 76   38 80 73 69 61   31 64 94 20 96   63 28 10 20 23   08 81 64 74 49
19 52 35 95 15   65 12 25 96 59   86 28 36 82 58   69 57 21 37 98   16 43 59 15 29
67 24 55 26 70   35 58 31 65 63   79 24 68 66 86   76 46 33 42 22   26 65 59 08 02
60 58 44 73 77   07 50 03 79 92   45 13 42 65 29   26 76 08 36 37   41 32 64 43 44

53 85 34 13 77   36 06 69 48 50   58 83 87 38 59   49 36 47 33 31   96 24 04 36 42
24 63 73 87 36   74 38 48 93 42   52 62 30 79 92   12 36 91 86 01   03 74 28 38 73
83 08 01 24 51   38 99 22 28 15   07 75 95 17 77   97 37 72 75 85   51 97 23 78 67
16 44 42 43 34   36 15 19 90 73   27 49 37 09 39   85 13 03 25 52   54 84 65 47 59
60 79 01 81 57   57 17 86 57 62   11 16 17 85 76   45 81 95 29 79   65 13 00 48 60

03 99 11 04 61   93 71 61 68 94   66 08 32 46 53   84 60 95 82 32   88 61 81 91 61
38 55 59 55 54   32 88 65 97 80   08 35 56 08 60   29 73 54 77 62   71 29 92 38 53
17 54 67 37 04   92 05 24 62 15   55 12 12 92 81   59 07 60 79 36   27 95 45 89 09
32 64 35 28 61   95 81 90 68 31   00 91 19 89 36   76 35 59 37 79   80 86 30 05 14
69 57 26 87 77   39 51 03 59 05   14 06 04 06 19   29 54 96 96 16   33 56 46 07 80

24 12 26 65 91   27 69 90 64 94   14 84 54 66 72   61 95 87 71 00   90 89 97 57 54
61 19 63 02 31   92 96 26 17 73   41 83 95 53 82   17 26 77 09 43   78 03 87 02 67
30 53 22 17 04   10 27 41 22 02   39 68 52 33 09   10 06 16 88 29   55 98 66 64 85
03 78 89 75 99   75 86 72 07 17   74 41 65 31 66   35 20 83 33 74   87 53 90 88 23
48 22 86 33 79   85 78 34 76 19   53 15 26 74 33   35 66 35 29 72   16 81 86 03 11

60 36 59 46 53   35 07 53 39 49   42 61 42 92 97   01 91 82 83 16   98 95 37 32 31
83 79 94 24 02   56 62 33 44 42   34 99 44 13 74   70 07 11 47 36   09 95 81 80 65
32 96 00 74 05   36 40 98 32 32   99 38 54 16 00   11 13 30 75 86   15 91 70 62 53
19 32 25 38 45   57 62 05 26 06   66 49 76 86 46   78 13 86 65 59   19 64 09 94 13
11 22 09 47 47   07 39 93 74 08   48 50 92 39 29   27 48 24 54 76   85 24 43 51 59

31 75 15 72 60   68 98 00 53 39   15 47 04 83 55   88 65 12 25 96   03 15 21 91 21
88 49 29 93 82   14 45 40 45 04   20 09 49 89 77   74 84 39 34 13   22 10 97 85 08
30 93 44 77 44   07 48 18 38 28   73 78 80 65 33   28 59 72 04 05   94 20 52 03 80
22 88 84 88 93   27 49 99 87 48   60 53 04 51 28   74 02 28 46 17   82 03 71 02 68
78 21 21 69 93   35 90 29 13 86   44 37 21 54 86   65 74 11 40 14   87 48 13 72 20
```

Table 1. Random Numbers (Continued)

41	84	98	45	47	46	85	05	23	26	34	67	75	83	00	74	91	06	43	45	19	32	58	15	49
46	35	23	30	49	69	24	89	34	60	45	30	50	75	21	61	31	83	18	55	14	41	37	09	51
11	08	79	62	94	14	01	33	17	92	59	74	76	72	77	76	50	33	45	13	39	66	37	75	44
52	70	10	83	37	56	30	38	73	15	16	52	06	96	76	11	65	49	98	93	02	18	16	81	61
57	27	53	68	98	81	30	44	85	85	68	65	22	73	76	92	85	25	58	66	88	44	80	35	84
20	85	77	31	56	70	28	42	43	26	79	37	59	52	20	01	15	96	32	67	10	62	24	83	91
15	63	38	49	24	90	41	59	36	14	33	52	12	66	65	55	82	34	76	41	86	22	53	17	04
92	69	44	82	97	39	90	40	21	15	59	58	94	90	67	66	82	14	15	75	49	76	70	40	37
77	61	31	90	19	88	15	20	00	80	20	55	49	14	09	96	27	74	82	57	50	81	69	76	16
38	68	83	24	86	45	13	46	35	45	59	40	47	20	59	43	94	75	16	80	43	85	25	96	93
25	16	30	18	89	70	01	41	50	21	41	29	06	73	12	71	85	71	59	57	68	97	11	14	03
65	25	10	76	29	37	23	93	32	95	05	87	00	11	19	92	78	42	63	40	18	47	76	56	22
36	81	54	36	25	18	63	73	75	09	82	44	49	90	05	04	92	17	37	01	14	70	79	39	97
64	39	71	16	92	05	32	78	21	62	20	24	78	17	59	45	19	72	53	32	83	74	52	25	67
04	51	52	56	24	95	09	66	79	46	48	46	08	55	58	15	19	11	87	82	16	93	03	33	61
83	76	16	08	73	43	25	38	41	45	60	83	32	59	83	01	29	14	13	49	20	36	80	71	26
14	38	70	63	45	80	85	40	92	79	43	52	90	63	18	38	38	47	47	61	41	19	63	74	80
51	32	19	22	46	80	08	87	70	74	88	72	25	67	36	66	16	44	94	31	66	91	93	16	78
72	47	20	00	08	80	89	01	80	02	94	81	33	19	00	54	15	58	34	36	35	35	25	41	31
05	46	65	53	06	93	12	81	84	64	74	45	79	05	61	72	84	81	18	34	79	98	26	84	16
39	52	87	24	84	82	47	42	55	93	48	54	53	52	47	18	61	91	36	74	18	61	11	92	41
81	61	61	87	11	53	34	24	42	76	75	12	21	17	24	74	62	77	37	07	58	31	91	59	97
07	58	61	61	20	82	64	12	28	20	92	90	41	31	41	32	39	21	97	63	61	19	96	79	40
90	76	70	42	35	13	57	41	72	00	69	90	26	37	42	78	46	42	25	01	18	62	79	08	72
40	18	82	81	93	29	59	38	86	27	94	97	21	15	98	62	09	53	67	87	00	44	15	89	97
34	41	48	21	57	86	88	75	50	87	19	15	20	00	23	12	30	28	07	83	32	62	46	86	91
63	43	97	53	63	44	98	91	68	22	36	02	40	08	67	76	37	84	16	05	65	96	17	34	88
67	04	90	90	70	93	39	94	55	47	94	45	87	42	84	05	04	14	98	07	20	28	83	40	60
79	49	50	41	46	52	16	29	02	86	54	15	83	42	43	46	97	83	54	82	59	36	29	59	38
91	70	43	05	52	04	73	72	10	31	75	05	19	30	29	47	66	56	43	82	99	78	29	34	78
94	01	54	68	74	32	44	44	82	77	59	82	09	61	63	64	65	42	58	43	41	14	54	28	20
74	10	88	82	22	88	57	07	40	15	25	70	49	10	35	01	75	51	47	50	48	96	83	86	03
62	88	08	78	73	95	16	05	92	21	22	30	49	03	14	72	87	71	73	34	39	28	30	41	49
11	74	81	21	02	80	58	04	18	67	17	71	05	96	21	06	55	40	78	50	73	95	07	95	52
17	94	40	56	00	60	47	80	33	43	25	85	25	89	05	57	21	63	96	18	49	85	69	93	26
66	06	74	27	92	95	04	35	26	80	46	78	05	64	87	09	97	15	94	81	37	00	62	21	86
54	24	49	10	30	45	54	77	08	18	59	84	99	61	69	61	45	92	16	47	87	41	71	71	98
30	94	55	75	89	31	73	25	72	60	47	67	00	76	54	46	37	62	53	66	94	74	64	95	80
69	17	03	74	03	86	99	59	03	07	94	30	47	18	03	26	82	50	55	11	12	45	99	13	14
08	34	58	89	75	35	84	18	57	71	08	10	55	99	87	87	11	22	14	76	14	71	37	11	81
27	76	74	35	84	85	30	18	89	77	29	49	06	97	14	73	03	54	12	07	74	69	90	93	10
13	02	51	43	38	54	06	61	52	43	47	72	46	67	33	47	43	14	39	05	31	04	85	66	99
80	21	73	62	92	98	52	52	43	35	24	43	22	48	96	43	27	75	88	74	11	46	61	60	82
10	87	56	20	04	90	39	16	11	05	57	41	10	63	68	53	85	63	07	43	08	67	08	47	41
54	12	75	73	26	26	62	91	90	87	24	47	28	87	79	30	54	02	78	86	61	73	27	54	54
60	31	14	28	24	37	30	14	26	78	45	99	04	32	42	17	37	45	20	03	70	70	77	02	14
49	73	97	14	84	92	00	39	80	86	76	66	87	32	09	59	20	21	19	73	02	90	23	32	50
78	62	65	15	94	16	45	39	46	14	39	01	49	70	66	83	01	20	98	32	25	57	17	76	28
66	69	21	39	86	99	83	70	05	82	81	23	24	49	87	09	50	49	64	12	90	19	37	95	68
44	07	12	80	91	07	36	29	77	03	76	44	74	25	37	98	52	49	78	31	65	70	40	95	14

Table 1. Random Numbers (Continued)

41	46	88	51	49	49	55	41	79	94	14	92	43	96	50	95	29	40	05	56	70	48	10	69	05
94	55	93	75	59	49	67	85	31	19	70	31	20	56	82	66	98	63	40	99	74	47	42	07	40
41	61	57	03	60	64	11	45	86	60	90	85	06	46	18	80	62	05	17	90	11	43	63	80	72
50	27	39	31	13	41	79	48	68	61	24	78	18	96	83	55	41	18	56	67	77	53	59	98	92
41	39	68	05	04	90	67	00	82	89	40	90	20	50	69	95	08	30	67	83	28	10	25	78	16

25	80	72	42	60	71	52	97	89	20	72	68	20	73	85	90	72	65	71	66	98	88	40	85	83
06	17	09	79	65	88	30	29	80	41	21	44	34	18	08	68	98	48	36	20	89	74	79	88	82
60	80	85	44	44	74	41	28	11	05	01	17	62	88	38	36	42	11	64	89	18	05	95	10	61
80	94	04	48	93	10	40	83	62	22	80	58	27	19	44	92	63	84	03	33	67	05	41	60	67
19	51	69	01	20	46	75	97	16	43	13	17	75	52	92	21	03	68	28	08	77	50	19	74	27

49	38	65	44	80	26	60	42	35	54	21	78	54	11	01	91	17	81	01	74	29	42	09	04	38
06	31	28	89	40	15	99	56	93	21	47	45	86	48	09	98	18	98	18	51	29	65	18	42	15
60	94	20	03	07	11	89	79	26	74	40	40	56	80	32	96	71	75	42	44	10	70	14	13	93
92	32	99	89	32	78	28	44	63	47	71	20	99	20	61	39	44	89	31	36	25	72	20	85	64
77	93	66	35	74	31	38	45	19	24	85	56	12	96	71	58	13	71	78	20	22	75	13	65	18

38	10	17	77	56	11	65	71	38	97	95	88	95	70	67	47	64	81	38	85	70	66	99	34	06
39	64	16	94	57	91	33	92	25	02	92	61	38	97	19	11	94	75	62	03	19	32	42	05	04
84	05	44	04	55	99	39	66	36	80	67	66	76	06	31	69	18	19	68	45	38	52	51	16	00
47	46	80	35	77	57	64	96	32	66	24	70	07	15	94	14	00	42	31	53	69	24	90	57	47
43	32	13	13	70	28	97	72	38	96	76	47	96	85	62	62	34	20	75	89	08	89	90	59	85

64	28	16	18	26	18	55	56	49	37	13	17	33	33	65	78	85	11	64	99	87	06	41	30	75
66	84	77	04	95	32	35	00	29	85	86	71	63	87	46	26	31	37	74	63	55	38	77	26	81
72	46	13	32	30	21	52	95	34	24	92	58	10	22	62	78	43	86	62	76	18	39	67	35	38
21	03	29	10	50	13	05	81	62	18	12	47	05	65	00	15	29	27	61	39	59	52	65	21	13
95	36	26	70	11	06	65	11	61	36	01	01	60	08	57	55	01	85	63	74	35	82	47	17	08

49	71	29	73	80	10	40	45	54	52	34	03	06	07	26	75	21	11	02	71	36	63	36	84	24
58	27	56	17	64	97	58	65	47	16	50	25	94	63	45	87	19	54	60	92	26	78	76	09	39
89	51	41	17	88	68	22	42	34	17	73	95	97	61	45	30	34	24	02	77	11	04	97	20	49
15	47	25	06	69	48	13	93	67	32	46	87	43	70	88	73	46	50	98	19	58	86	93	52	20
12	12	08	61	24	51	24	74	43	02	60	88	35	21	09	21	43	73	67	86	49	22	67	78	37

19	61	27	84	30	11	66	19	47	70	77	60	36	56	69	86	86	81	26	65	30	01	27	59	89
39	14	17	74	00	28	00	06	42	38	73	25	87	17	94	31	34	02	62	56	66	45	33	70	16
64	75	68	04	57	08	74	71	28	36	03	46	95	06	78	03	27	44	34	23	66	67	78	25	56
92	90	15	18	78	56	44	12	29	98	29	71	83	84	47	06	45	32	53	11	07	56	55	37	71
03	55	19	00	70	09	48	39	40	50	45	93	81	81	35	36	90	84	33	21	11	07	35	18	03

98	88	46	62	09	06	83	05	36	56	14	66	35	63	46	71	43	00	49	09	19	81	80	57	07
27	36	98	68	82	53	47	30	75	41	53	63	37	08	63	03	74	81	28	22	19	36	04	90	88
59	06	67	59	74	63	33	52	04	83	43	51	43	74	81	58	27	82	69	67	49	32	54	39	51
91	64	79	37	83	64	16	94	90	22	98	58	80	94	95	49	82	95	90	68	38	83	10	48	38
83	60	59	24	19	39	54	20	77	72	71	56	87	56	73	35	18	58	97	59	44	90	17	42	91

24	89	58	85	30	70	77	43	54	39	46	75	87	04	72	70	20	79	26	75	91	62	36	12	75
35	72	02	65	56	95	59	62	00	94	73	75	08	57	88	34	26	40	17	03	46	83	36	52	48
14	14	15	34	10	38	64	90	63	43	57	25	66	13	42	72	70	97	53	18	90	37	93	75	62
27	41	67	56	70	92	17	67	25	35	93	11	95	60	77	06	88	61	82	44	92	34	43	13	74
82	07	10	74	29	81	00	74	77	49	40	74	45	69	74	23	33	68	88	21	53	84	11	05	36

21	44	58	27	93	24	83	19	32	41	14	19	97	62	68	70	88	36	80	02	03	82	91	74	43
72	51	37	64	00	52	22	59	23	48	62	30	89	84	81	29	74	43	31	65	33	14	16	10	20
71	47	94	50	27	76	16	05	74	11	13	78	01	36	32	52	30	87	77	62	88	87	43	36	97
83	21	05	14	66	09	08	85	03	95	26	74	30	53	06	21	70	67	00	01	99	43	98	07	67
68	74	99	51	48	94	89	77	86	36	96	75	00	90	24	94	53	89	11	43	96	69	36	18	86

Table 1. Random Numbers (Continued)

05	18	47	57	63	47	07	58	81	58	05	31	35	34	39	14	90	80	88	30	60	09	62	15	51
13	65	16	25	46	96	89	22	52	40	47	51	15	84	83	87	34	27	88	18	07	85	53	92	69
00	56	62	12	20	00	29	22	40	69	25	07	22	95	19	52	54	85	40	91	21	28	22	12	96
50	95	81	76	95	58	07	26	89	90	60	32	99	59	55	71	58	66	34	17	35	94	76	78	07
57	62	16	45	47	46	85	03	79	81	38	52	70	90	37	64	75	60	33	24	04	98	68	36	66
09	28	22	58	44	79	13	97	84	35	35	42	84	35	61	69	79	96	33	14	12	99	19	35	16
23	39	49	42	06	93	43	23	78	36	94	91	92	68	46	02	55	57	44	10	94	91	54	81	99
05	28	03	74	70	93	62	20	43	45	15	09	21	95	10	18	09	41	66	13	78	23	45	00	01
95	49	19	79	76	38	30	63	21	92	82	63	95	46	24	72	43	49	26	06	23	19	17	46	93
78	52	10	01	04	18	24	87	55	83	90	32	65	07	85	54	03	46	62	51	35	77	41	46	92
96	34	54	45	79	85	93	24	40	53	75	70	42	08	40	86	58	38	39	44	52	45	67	37	66
77	96	33	11	51	32	36	49	16	91	47	35	74	03	38	23	43	52	40	65	08	45	89	53	66
07	52	01	12	94	23	23	80	17	48	41	69	06	73	28	54	81	43	77	77	10	05	74	23	32
38	42	30	23	09	70	70	38	57	36	46	14	81	42	58	29	23	61	21	52	05	08	86	58	25
02	46	36	55	33	21	19	96	05	55	33	92	80	18	17	07	39	68	92	15	30	72	22	21	02
15	88	09	22	61	17	29	28	81	90	61	78	14	88	98	92	52	52	12	83	88	58	16	00	98
71	92	60	08	19	59	14	40	02	24	30	57	09	01	94	18	32	90	69	99	26	85	71	92	38
64	42	52	81	08	16	55	41	60	16	00	04	28	32	29	10	33	33	61	68	65	61	79	48	34
79	78	22	39	24	49	44	03	04	32	81	07	73	15	43	95	21	66	48	65	13	65	85	10	81
35	33	77	45	38	44	55	36	46	72	90	96	04	18	49	93	86	54	46	08	93	17	63	48	51
05	24	92	93	29	19	71	59	40	82	14	73	88	66	67	43	70	86	63	54	93	69	22	55	27
56	46	39	93	80	38	79	38	57	74	19	05	61	39	39	46	06	22	76	47	66	14	66	32	10
96	29	63	31	21	54	19	63	41	08	75	81	48	59	86	71	17	11	51	02	28	99	26	31	65
98	38	03	62	69	60	01	40	72	01	62	44	84	63	85	42	17	58	83	50	46	18	24	91	26
52	56	76	43	50	16	31	55	39	69	80	39	58	11	14	54	35	86	45	78	47	26	91	57	47
78	49	89	08	30	25	95	59	92	36	43	28	69	10	64	99	96	99	51	44	64	42	47	73	77
49	55	32	42	41	08	15	08	95	35	08	70	39	10	41	77	32	38	10	79	45	12	79	36	86
32	15	10	70	75	83	15	51	02	52	73	10	08	86	18	23	89	18	74	18	45	41	72	02	68
11	31	45	03	63	26	86	02	77	99	49	41	68	35	34	19	18	70	80	59	76	67	70	21	10
12	36	47	12	10	87	05	25	02	41	90	78	59	78	89	81	39	95	81	30	64	43	90	56	14

Table 2. Normal Distribution, Ordinates, and Central Areas[a]

Ordinates Y at $\pm z$, and areas A between $-z$ and $+z$, of the normal distribution

z	X	Y	A	$1-A$	z	X	Y	A	$1-A$
0	μ	.399	.0000	1.0000	±1.50	$\mu\pm1.50\sigma$	.1295	.8664	.1336
$\pm\ .05$	$\mu\pm\ .05\sigma$	.398	.0399	.9601	±1.55	$\mu\pm1.55\sigma$	.1200	.8789	.1211
$\pm\ .10$	$\mu\pm\ .10\sigma$	.397	.0797	.9203	±1.60	$\mu\pm1.60\sigma$	.1109	.8904	.1096
$\pm\ .15$	$\mu\pm\ .15\sigma$	.394	.1192	.8808	±1.65	$\mu\pm1.65\sigma$	.1023	.9011	.0989
$\pm\ .20$	$\mu\pm\ .20\sigma$	.391	.1585	.8415	±1.70	$\mu\pm1.70\sigma$	.0940	.9109	.0891
$\pm\ .25$	$\mu\pm\ .25\sigma$	.387	.1974	.8026	±1.75	$\mu\pm1.75\sigma$	.0863	.9199	.0801
$\pm\ .30$	$\mu\pm\ .30\sigma$	.381	.2358	.7642	±1.80	$\mu\pm1.80\sigma$	.0790	.9281	.0719
$\pm\ .35$	$\mu\pm\ .35\sigma$	.375	.2737	.7263	±1.85	$\mu\pm1.85\sigma$	.0721	.9357	.0643
$\pm\ .40$	$\mu\pm\ .40\sigma$	.368	.3108	.6892	±1.90	$\mu\pm1.90\sigma$	.0656	.9426	.0574
$\pm\ .45$	$\mu\pm\ .45\sigma$	.361	.3473	.6527	±1.95	$\mu\pm1.95\sigma$	.0596	.9488	.0512
$\pm\ .50$	$\mu\pm\ .50\sigma$	.352	.3829	.6171	±2.00	$\mu\pm2.00\sigma$	.0540	.9545	.0455
$\pm\ .55$	$\mu\pm\ .55\sigma$	.343	.4177	.5823	±2.05	$\mu\pm2.05\sigma$	.0488	.9596	.0404
$\pm\ .60$	$\mu\pm\ .60\sigma$	.333	.4515	.5485	±2.10	$\mu\pm2.10\sigma$	.0440	.9643	.0357
$\pm\ .65$	$\mu\pm\ .65\sigma$	.323	.4843	.5157	±2.15	$\mu\pm2.15\sigma$	.0396	.9684	.0316
$\pm\ .70$	$\mu\pm\ .70\sigma$	.312	.5161	.4839	±2.20	$\mu\pm2.20\sigma$	.0355	.9722	.0278
$\pm\ .75$	$\mu\pm\ .75\sigma$	.301	.5467	.4533	±2.25	$\mu\pm2.25\sigma$	.0317	.9756	.0244
$\pm\ .80$	$\mu\pm\ .80\sigma$	.290	.5763	.4237	±2.30	$\mu\pm2.30\sigma$	.0283	.9786	.0214
$\pm\ .85$	$\mu\pm\ .85\sigma$	.278	.6047	.3953	±2.35	$\mu+2.35\sigma$	.0252	.9812	.0188
$\pm\ .90$	$\mu\pm\ .90\sigma$	.266	.6319	.3681	±2.40	$\mu\pm2.40\sigma$	.0224	.9836	.0164
$\pm\ .95$	$\mu\pm\ .95\sigma$	.254	.6579	.3421	±2.45	$\mu\pm2.45\sigma$	.0198	.9857	.0143
±1.00	$\mu\pm1.00\sigma$	.242	.6827	.3173	±2.50	$\mu\pm2.50\sigma$	.0175	.9876	.0124
±1.05	$\mu\pm1.05\sigma$	.230	.7063	.2937	±2.55	$\mu\pm2.55\sigma$	.0154	.9892	.0108
±1.10	$\mu\pm1.10\sigma$	.218	.7287	.2713	±2.60	$\mu\pm2.60\sigma$	.0136	.9907	.0093
±1.15	$\mu\pm1.15\sigma$	.206	.7499	.2501	±2.65	$\mu\pm2.65\sigma$	.0119	.9920	.0080
±1.20	$\mu\pm1.20\sigma$	.194	.7699	.2301	±2.70	$\mu\pm2.70\sigma$	.0104	.9931	.0069
±1.25	$\mu\pm1.25\sigma$	.183	.7887	.2113	±2.75	$\mu\pm2.75\sigma$	.0091	.9940	.0060
±1.30	$\mu\pm1.30\sigma$	.171	.8064	.1936	±2.80	$\mu\pm2.80\sigma$	.0079	.9949	.0051
±1.35	$\mu\pm1.35\sigma$	.160	.8230	.1770	±2.85	$\mu\pm2.85\sigma$	.0069	.9956	.0044
±1.40	$\mu\pm1.40\sigma$	.150	.8385	.1615	±2.90	$\mu\pm2.90\sigma$	.0060	.9963	.0037
±1.45	$\mu\pm1.45\sigma$	.139	.8529	.1471	±2.95	$\mu\pm2.95\sigma$	.0051	.9968	.0032
±1.50	$\mu\pm1.50\sigma$	.130	.8664	.1336	±3.00	$\mu\pm3.00\sigma$	.0044	.9973	.0027
					±4.00	$\mu\pm4.00\sigma$	.0001	.99994	.00006
					±5.00	$\mu\pm5.00\sigma$	.000001	.9999994	.0000006

z	X		Y	A	$1-A$	z	X	Y	A	$1-A$
$\pm\ .000$	μ		.3989	.0000	1.0000	±1.036	$\mu\pm1.036\sigma$	.2331	.7000	.3000
$\pm\ .126$	$\mu\pm$	$.126\sigma$	.3958	.1000	.9000	±1.282	$\mu\pm1.282\sigma$	.1755	.8000	.2000
$\pm\ .253$	$\mu\pm$	$.253\sigma$	.3863	.2000	.8000	±1.645	$\mu\pm1.645\sigma$	.1031	.9000	.1000
$\pm\ .385$	$\mu\pm$	$.385\sigma$	.3704	.3000	.7000	±1.960	$\mu\pm1.960\sigma$	.0584	.9500	.0500
$\pm\ .524$	$\mu\pm$	$.524\sigma$	.3477	.4000	.6000	±2.576	$\mu\pm2.576\sigma$	.0145	.9900	.0100
$\pm\ .674$	$\mu\pm$	$.674\sigma$	.3178	.5000	.5000	±3.291	$\mu\pm3.291\sigma$	.0018	.9990	.0010
$\pm\ .842$	$\mu\pm$	$.842\sigma$	.2800	.6000	.4000	±3.891	$\mu\pm3.891\sigma$	.0002	.9999	.0001

[a]*Source*: From *Introduction to Statistical Analysis* by W. Dixon and F. Massey. Copyright 1969 by McGraw-Hill, Inc. Used with permission of McGraw-Hill Book Company.

Table 3. Cumulative Normal Distribution[a]

z	X	Area	z	X	Area
−3.25	$\mu - 3.25\sigma$	.0006	−1.00	$\mu - 1.00\sigma$	.1587
−3.20	$\mu - 3.20\sigma$	.0007	− .95	$\mu - .95\sigma$	.1711
−3.15	$\mu - 3.15\sigma$	.0008	− .90	$\mu - .90\sigma$	.1841
−3.10	$\mu - 3.10\sigma$	.0010	− .85	$\mu - .85\sigma$	.1977
−3.05	$\mu - 3.05\sigma$	.0011	− .80	$\mu - .80\sigma$	.2119
−3.00	$\mu - 3.00\sigma$	.0013	− .75	$\mu - .75\sigma$	.2266
−2.95	$\mu - 2.95\sigma$	.0016	− .70	$\mu - .70\sigma$	.2420
−2.90	$\mu - 2.90\sigma$	.0019	− .65	$\mu - .65\sigma$	.2578
−2.85	$\mu - 2.85\sigma$	.0022	− .60	$\mu - .60\sigma$	.2743
−2.80	$\mu - 2.80\sigma$	.0026	− .55	$\mu - .55\sigma$	.2912
−2.75	$\mu - 2.75\sigma$	.0030	− .50	$\mu - .50\sigma$	.3085
−2.70	$\mu - 2.70\sigma$	.0035	− .45	$\mu - .45\sigma$	.3264
−2.65	$\mu - 2.65\sigma$	.0040	− .40	$\mu - .40\sigma$	.3446
−2.60	$\mu - 2.60\sigma$	.0047	− .35	$\mu - .35\sigma$	.3632
−2.55	$\mu - 2.55\sigma$	.0054	− .30	$\mu - .30\sigma$	.3821
−2.50	$\mu - 2.50\sigma$	.0062	− .25	$\mu - .25\sigma$	.4013
−2.45	$\mu - 2.45\sigma$	.0071	− .20	$\mu - .20\sigma$	.4207
−2.40	$\mu - 2.40\sigma$	.0082	− .15	$\mu - .15\sigma$	.4404
−2.35	$\mu - 2.35\sigma$	.0094	− .10	$\mu - .10\sigma$	.4602
−2.30	$\mu - 2.30\sigma$	.0107	− .05	$\mu - .05\sigma$	.4801
−2.25	$\mu - 2.25\sigma$	.0122			
−2.20	$\mu - 2.20\sigma$	.0139			
−2.15	$\mu - 2.15\sigma$	.0158	.00	μ	.5000
−2.10	$\mu - 2.10\sigma$	.0179			
−2.05	$\mu - 2.05\sigma$	.0202			
−2.00	$\mu - 2.00\sigma$	.0228	.05	$\mu + .05\sigma$	.5199
−1.95	$\mu - 1.95\sigma$	.0256	.10	$\mu + .10\sigma$	.5398
−1.90	$\mu - 1.90\sigma$	.0287	.15	$\mu + .15\sigma$	.5596
−1.85	$\mu - 1.85\sigma$	.0322	.20	$\mu + .20\sigma$	.5793
−1.80	$\mu - 1.80\sigma$	.0359	.25	$\mu + .25\sigma$	.5987
−1.75	$\mu - 1.75\sigma$	.0401	.30	$\mu + .30\sigma$	.6179
−1.70	$\mu - 1.70\sigma$	.0446	.35	$\mu + .35\sigma$	.6368
−1.65	$\mu - 1.65\sigma$	.0495	.40	$\mu + .40\sigma$	.6554
−1.60	$\mu - 1.60\sigma$	.0548	.45	$\mu + .45\sigma$	.6736
−1.55	$\mu - 1.55\sigma$	.0606	.50	$\mu + .50\sigma$	.6915
−1.50	$\mu - 1.50\sigma$	.0668	.55	$\mu + .55\sigma$	.7088
−1.45	$\mu - 1.45\sigma$	.0735	.60	$\mu + .60\sigma$	.7257
−1.40	$\mu - 1.40\sigma$	.0808	.65	$\mu + .65\sigma$	.7422
−1.35	$\mu - 1.35\sigma$	.0885	.70	$\mu + .70\sigma$	.7580
−1.30	$\mu - 1.30\sigma$	.0968	.75	$\mu + .75\sigma$	.7734
−1.25	$\mu - 1.25\sigma$	.1056	.80	$\mu + .80\sigma$	.7881
−1.20	$\mu - 1.20\sigma$	.1151	.85	$\mu + .85\sigma$	.8023
−1.15	$\mu - 1.15\sigma$	.1251	.90	$\mu + .90\sigma$	.8159
−1.10	$\mu - 1.10\sigma$	.1357	.95	$\mu + .95\sigma$	.8289
−1.05	$\mu - 1.05\sigma$	.1469	1.00	$\mu + 1.00\sigma$	.8413

Table 3. Cumulative Normal Distribution (Continued)

z	X	Area	z	X	Area
1.05	$\mu + 1.05\sigma$	.8531	−4.265	$\mu − 4.265\sigma$	.00001
1.10	$\mu + 1.10\sigma$	.8643	−3.719	$\mu − 3.719\sigma$	.0001
1.15	$\mu + 1.15\sigma$	.8749	−3.090	$\mu − 3.090\sigma$	.001
1.20	$\mu + 1.20\sigma$	.8849	−2.576	$\mu − 2.576\sigma$	.005
1.25	$\mu + 1.25\sigma$	.8944	−2.326	$\mu − 2.326\sigma$	.01
1.30	$\mu + 1.30\sigma$	.9032	−2.054	$\mu − 2.054\sigma$	.02
1.35	$\mu + 1.35\sigma$	.9115	−1.960	$\mu − 1.960\sigma$	.025
1.40	$\mu + 1.40\sigma$	.9192	−1.881	$\mu − 1.881\sigma$	.03
1.45	$\mu + 1.45\sigma$	.9265	−1.751	$\mu − 1.751\sigma$	.04
1.50	$\mu + 1.50\sigma$	.9332	−1.645	$\mu − 1.645\sigma$	.05
1.55	$\mu + 1.55\sigma$	.9394	−1.555	$\mu − 1.555\sigma$	.06
1.60	$\mu + 1.60\sigma$	.9452	−1.476	$\mu − 1.476\sigma$	.07
1.65	$\mu + 1.65\sigma$	.9505	−1.405	$\mu − 1.405\sigma$	.08
1.70	$\mu + 1.70\sigma$	.9554	−1.341	$\mu − 1.341\sigma$	.09
1.75	$\mu + 1.75\sigma$	.9599	−1.282	$\mu − 1 282\sigma$	.10
1.80	$\mu + 1.80\sigma$	.9641	−1.036	$\mu − 1.036\sigma$	.15
1.85	$\mu + 1.85\sigma$	.9678	− .842	$\mu − .842\sigma$	.20
1.90	$\mu + 1.90\sigma$	.9713	− .674	$\mu − .674\sigma$	.25
1.95	$\mu + 1.95\sigma$	.9744	− .524	$\mu − .524\sigma$	.30
2.00	$\mu + 2.00\sigma$	.9772	− .385	$\mu − .385\sigma$	.35
2.05	$\mu + 2.05\sigma$	.9798	− .253	$\mu − .253\sigma$	.40
2.10	$\mu + 2.10\sigma$	.9821	− .126	$\mu − .126\sigma$	.45
2.15	$\mu + 2.15\sigma$	.9842	0	μ	.50
2.20	$\mu + 2.20\sigma$	.9861	.126	$\mu + .126\sigma$	.55
2.25	$\mu + 2.25\sigma$	.9878	.253	$\mu + .253\sigma$	.60
2.30	$\mu + 2.30\sigma$	.9893	.385	$\mu + .385\sigma$	.65
2.35	$\mu + 2.35\sigma$	.9906	.524	$\mu + .524\sigma$	.70
2.40	$\mu + 2.40\sigma$	.9918	.674	$\mu + .674\sigma$	.75
2.45	$\mu + 2.45\sigma$	.9929	.842	$\mu + .842\sigma$	.80
2.50	$\mu + 2.50\sigma$	.9938	1.036	$\mu + 1.036\sigma$	.85
2.55	$\mu + 2.55\sigma$	.9946	1.282	$\mu + 1.282\sigma$	.90
2.60	$\mu + 2.60\sigma$	.9953	1.341	$\mu + 1.341\sigma$	.91
2.65	$\mu + 2.65\sigma$	.9960	1.405	$\mu + 1.405\sigma$	.92
2.70	$\mu + 2.70\sigma$	.9965	1.476	$\mu + 1.476\sigma$	.93
2.75	$\mu + 2.75\sigma$	.9970	1.555	$\mu + 1.555\sigma$	.94
2.80	$\mu + 2.80\sigma$	.9974	1.645	$\mu + 1.645\sigma$	.95
2.85	$\mu + 2.85\sigma$	.9978	1.751	$\mu + 1.751\sigma$	.96
2.90	$\mu + 2.90\sigma$	.9981	1.881	$\mu + 1.881\sigma$	.97
2.95	$\mu + 2.95\sigma$	.9984	1.960	$\mu + 1.960\sigma$	.975
3.00	$\mu + 3.00\sigma$	.9987	2.054	$\mu + 2.054\sigma$	.98
3.05	$\mu + 3.05\sigma$	.9989	2.326	$\mu + 2.326\sigma$	.99
3.10	$\mu + 3.10\sigma$	.9990	2.576	$\mu + 2.576\sigma$	.995
3.15	$\mu + 3.15\sigma$	.9992	3.090	$\mu + 3.090\sigma$	.999
3.20	$\mu + 3.20\sigma$	.9993	3.719	$\mu + 3.719\sigma$	.9999
3.25	$\mu + 3.25\sigma$	.9994	4.265	$\mu + 4.265\sigma$	.99999

[a]*Source*: From *Introduction to Statistical Analysis* by W. Dixon and F. Massey. Copyright 1969 by McGraw-Hill, Inc. Used with permission of McGraw-Hill Book Company.

Table 4. Percentiles of the t Distributions[a]

df	$t_{.60}$	$t_{.70}$	$t_{.80}$	$t_{.90}$	$t_{.95}$	$t_{.975}$	$t_{.99}$	$t_{.995}$
1	.325	.727	1.376	3.078	6.314	12.706	31.821	63.657
2	.289	.617	1.061	1.886	2.920	4.303	6.965	9.925
3	.277	.584	.978	1.638	2.353	3.182	4.541	5.841
4	.271	.569	.941	1.533	2.132	2.776	3.747	4.604
5	.267	.559	.920	1.476	2.015	2.571	3.365	4.032
6	.265	.553	.906	1.440	1.943	2.447	3.143	3.707
7.	.263	.549	.896	1.415	1.895	2.365	2.998	3.499
8	.262	.546	.889	1.397	1.860	2.306	2.896	3.355
9	.261	.543	.883	1.383	1.833	2.262	2.821	3.250
10	.260	.542	.879	1.372	1.812	2.228	2.764	3.169
11	.260	.540	.876	1.363	1.796	2.201	2.718	3.106
12	.259	.539	.873	1.356	1.782	2.179	2.681	3.055
13	.259	.538	.870	1.350	1.771	2.160	2.650	3.012
14	.258	.537	.868	1.345	1.761	2.145	2.624	2.977
15	.258	.536	.866	1.341	1.753	2.131	2.602	2.947
16	.258	.535	.865	1.337	1.746	2.120	2.583	2.921
17	.257	.534	.863	1.333	1.740	2.110	2.567	2.898
18	.257	.534	.862	1.330	1.734	2.101	2.552	2.878
19	.257	.533	.861	1.328	1.729	2.093	2.539	2.861
20	.257	.533	.860	1.325	1.725	2.086	2.528	2.845
21	.257	.532	.859	1.323	1.721	2.080	2.518	2.831
22	.256	.532	.858	1.321	1.717	2.074	2.508	2.819
23	.256	.532	.858	1.319	1.714	2.069	2.500	2.807
24	.256	.531	.857	1.318	1.711	2.064	2.492	2.797
25	.256	.531	.856	1.316	1.708	2.060	2.485	2.787
26	.256	.531	.856	1.315	1.706	2.056	2.479	2.779
27	.256	.531	.855	1.314	1.703	2.052	2.473	2.771
28	.256	.530	.855	1.313	1.701	2.048	2.467	2.763
29	.256	.530	.854	1.311	1.699	2.045	2.462	2.756
30	.256	.530	.854	1.310	1.697	2.042	2.457	2.750
40	.255	.529	.851	1.303	1.684	2.021	2.423	2.704
60	.254	.527	.848	1.296	1.671	2.000	2.390	2.660
120	.254	.526	.845	1.289	1.658	1.980	2.358	2.617
∞	.253	.524	.842	1.282	1.645	1.960	2.326	2.576
df	$-t_{.40}$	$-t_{.30}$	$-t_{.20}$	$-t_{.10}$	$-t_{.05}$	$-t_{.025}$	$-t_{.01}$	$-t_{.005}$

[a]*Source*: This table is taken from Table III of Fisher and Yates, *Statistical Tables for Biological, Agricultural and Medical Research*, published by Longman Group Ltd., London (previously published by Oliver & Boyd; Edinburgh). Used by permission of the authors and publishers. When the table is read from the foot, the tabled values are to be prefixed with a negative sign. Interpolation should be performed using the reciprocals of the degrees of freedom.

Table 5. Percentiles of the Chi Square Distributions[a]

df	$P_{0.5}$	P_{01}	$P_{02.5}$	P_{05}	P_{10}	P_{90}	P_{95}	$P_{97.5}$	P_{99}	$P_{99.5}$
1	.000039	.00016	.00098	.0039	.0158	2.71	3.84	5.02	6.63	7.88
2	.0100	.0201	.0506	.1026	.2107	4.61	5.99	7.38	9.21	10.60
3	.0717	.115	.216	.352	.584	6.25	7.81	9.35	11.34	12.84
4	.207	.297	.484	.711	1.064	7.78	9.49	11.14	13.28	14.86
5	.412	.554	.831	1.15	1.61	9.24	11.07	12.83	15.09	16.75
6	.676	.872	1.24	1.64	2.20	10.64	12.59	14.45	16.81	18.55
7	.989	1.24	1.69	2.17	2.83	12.02	14.07	16.01	18.48	20.28
8	1.34	1.65	2.18	2.73	3.49	13.36	15.51	17.53	20.09	21.96
9	1.73	2.09	2.70	3.33	4.17	14.68	16.92	19.02	21.67	23.59
10	2.16	2.56	3.25	3.94	4.87	15.99	18.31	20.48	23.21	25.19
11	2.60	3.05	3.82	4.57	5.58	17.28	19.68	21.92	24.73	26.76
12	3.07	3.57	4.40	5.23	6.30	18.55	21.03	23.34	26.22	28.30
13	3.57	4.11	5.01	5.89	7.04	19.81	22.36	24.74	27.69	29.82
14	4.07	4.66	5.63	6.57	7.79	21.06	23.68	26.12	29.14	31.32
15	4.60	5.23	6.26	7.26	8.55	22.31	25.00	27.49	30.58	32.80
16	5.14	5.81	6.91	7.96	9.31	23.54	26.30	28.85	32.00	34.27
18	6.26	7.01	8.23	9.39	10.86	25.99	28.87	31.53	34.81	37.16
20	7.43	8.26	9.59	10.85	12.44	28.41	31.41	34.17	37.57	40.00
24	9.89	10.86	12.40	13.85	15.66	33.20	36.42	39.36	42.98	45.56
30	13.79	14.95	16.79	18.49	20.60	40.26	43.77	46.98	50.89	53.67
40	20.71	22.16	24.43	26.51	29.05	51.81	55.76	59.34	63.69	66.77
60	35.53	37.48	40.48	43.19	46.46	74.40	79.08	83.30	88.38	91.95
120	83.85	86.92	91.58	95.70	100.62	140.23	146.57	152.21	158.95	163.64

[a]*Source*: From *Introduction to Statistical Analysis* by W. Dixon and F. Massey. Copyright 1969 by McGraw-Hill, Inc. Used with permission of McGraw-Hill Book Company.

Table 6. F Distribution, Upper 5 Percent Points (F_{95})[a]

DEGREES OF FREEDOM FOR NUMERATOR

	1	2	3	4	5	6	7	8	9	10	12	15	20	24	30	40	60	120	∞
1	161	200	216	225	230	234	237	239	241	242	244	246	248	249	250	251	252	253	254
2	18.5	19.0	19.2	19.2	19.3	19.3	19.4	19.4	19.4	19.4	19.4	19.4	19.4	19.5	19.5	19.5	19.5	19.5	19.5
3	10.1	9.55	9.28	9.12	9.01	8.94	8.89	8.85	8.81	8.79	8.74	8.70	8.66	8.64	8.62	8.59	8.57	8.55	8.53
4	7.71	6.94	6.59	6.39	6.26	6.16	6.09	6.04	6.00	5.96	5.91	5.86	5.80	5.77	5.75	5.72	5.69	5.66	5.63
5	6.61	5.79	5.41	5.19	5.05	4.95	4.88	4.82	4.77	4.74	4.68	4.62	4.56	4.53	4.50	4.46	4.43	4.40	4.37
6	5.99	5.14	4.76	4.53	4.39	4.28	4.21	4.15	4.10	4.06	4.00	3.94	3.87	3.84	3.81	3.77	3.74	3.70	3.67
7	5.59	4.74	4.35	4.12	3.97	3.87	3.79	3.73	3.68	3.64	3.57	3.51	3.44	3.41	3.38	3.34	3.30	3.27	3.23
8	5.32	4.46	4.07	3.84	3.69	3.58	3.50	3.44	3.39	3.35	3.28	3.22	3.15	3.12	3.08	3.04	3.01	2.97	2.93
9	5.12	4.26	3.86	3.63	3.48	3.37	3.29	3.23	3.18	3.14	3.07	3.01	2.94	2.90	2.86	2.83	2.79	2.75	2.71
10	4.96	4.10	3.71	3.48	3.33	3.22	3.14	3.07	3.02	2.98	2.91	2.85	2.77	2.74	2.70	2.66	2.62	2.58	2.54
11	4.84	3.98	3.59	3.36	3.20	3.09	3.01	2.95	2.90	2.85	2.79	2.72	2.65	2.61	2.57	2.53	2.49	2.45	2.40
12	4.75	3.89	3.49	3.26	3.11	3.00	2.91	2.85	2.80	2.75	2.69	2.62	2.54	2.51	2.47	2.43	2.38	2.34	2.30
13	4.67	3.81	3.41	3.18	3.03	2.92	2.83	2.77	2.71	2.67	2.60	2.53	2.46	2.42	2.38	2.34	2.30	2.25	2.21
14	4.60	3.74	3.34	3.11	2.96	2.85	2.76	2.70	2.65	2.60	2.53	2.46	2.39	2.35	2.31	2.27	2.22	2.18	2.13
15	4.54	3.68	3.29	3.06	2.90	2.79	2.71	2.64	2.59	2.54	2.48	2.40	2.33	2.29	2.25	2.20	2.16	2.11	2.07
16	4.49	3.63	3.24	3.01	2.85	2.74	2.66	2.59	2.54	2.49	2.42	2.35	2.28	2.24	2.19	2.15	2.11	2.06	2.01
17	4.45	3.59	3.20	2.96	2.81	2.70	2.61	2.55	2.49	2.45	2.38	2.31	2.23	2.19	2.15	2.10	2.06	2.01	1.96
18	4.41	3.55	3.16	2.93	2.77	2.66	2.58	2.51	2.46	2.41	2.34	2.27	2.19	2.15	2.11	2.06	2.02	1.97	1.92
19	4.38	3.52	3.13	2.90	2.74	2.63	2.54	2.48	2.42	2.38	2.31	2.23	2.16	2.11	2.07	2.03	1.98	1.93	1.88
20	4.35	3.49	3.10	2.87	2.71	2.60	2.51	2.45	2.39	2.35	2.28	2.20	2.12	2.08	2.04	1.99	1.95	1.90	1.84
21	4.32	3.47	3.07	2.84	2.68	2.57	2.49	2.42	2.37	2.32	2.25	2.18	2.10	2.05	2.01	1.96	1.92	1.87	1.81
22	4.30	3.44	3.05	2.82	2.66	2.55	2.46	2.40	2.34	2.30	2.23	2.15	2.07	2.03	1.98	1.94	1.89	1.84	1.78
23	4.28	3.42	3.03	2.80	2.64	2.53	2.44	2.37	2.32	2.27	2.20	2.13	2.05	2.01	1.96	1.91	1.86	1.81	1.76
24	4.26	3.40	3.01	2.78	2.62	2.51	2.42	2.36	2.30	2.25	2.18	2.11	2.03	1.98	1.94	1.89	1.84	1.79	1.73
25	4.24	3.39	2.99	2.76	2.60	2.49	2.40	2.34	2.28	2.24	2.16	2.09	2.01	1.96	1.92	1.87	1.82	1.77	1.71
30	4.17	3.32	2.92	2.69	2.53	2.42	2.33	2.27	2.21	2.16	2.09	2.01	1.93	1.89	1.84	1.79	1.74	1.68	1.62
40	4.08	3.23	2.84	2.61	2.45	2.34	2.25	2.18	2.12	2.08	2.00	1.92	1.84	1.79	1.74	1.69	1.64	1.58	1.51
60	4.00	3.15	2.76	2.53	2.37	2.25	2.17	2.10	2.04	1.99	1.92	1.84	1.75	1.70	1.65	1.59	1.53	1.47	1.39
120	3.92	3.07	2.68	2.45	2.29	2.18	2.09	2.02	1.96	1.91	1.83	1.75	1.66	1.61	1.55	1.50	1.43	1.35	1.25
∞	3.84	3.00	2.60	2.37	2.21	2.10	2.01	1.94	1.88	1.83	1.75	1.67	1.57	1.52	1.46	1.39	1.32	1.22	1.00

DEGREES OF FREEDOM FOR DENOMINATOR

[a]Source: By permission of Prof. E. S. Pearson from Merrington, M., and Thompson, C. M. "Tables of Percentage Points of the Inverted Beta (F) Distribution," *Biometrika* 33 (1943):73. Interpolation should be performed using reciprocals of the degrees of freedom.

Table 7. F Distribution, Upper 1 Percent Points (F_{99})[a]

DEGREES OF FREEDOM FOR NUMERATOR

Denominator df	1	2	3	4	5	6	7	8	9	10	12	15	20	24	30	40	60	120	∞
1	4,052	5,000	5,403	5,625	5,764	5,859	5,928	5,982	6,023	6,056	6,106	6,157	6,209	6,235	6,261	6,287	6,313	6,339	6,366
2	98.5	99.0	99.2	99.2	99.3	99.3	99.4	99.4	99.4	99.4	99.4	99.4	99.4	99.5	99.5	99.5	99.5	99.5	99.5
3	34.1	30.8	29.5	28.7	28.2	27.9	27.7	27.5	27.3	27.2	27.1	26.9	26.7	26.6	26.5	26.4	26.3	26.2	26.1
4	21.2	18.0	16.7	16.0	15.5	15.2	15.0	14.8	14.7	14.5	14.4	14.2	14.0	13.9	13.8	13.7	13.7	13.6	13.5
5	16.3	13.3	12.1	11.4	11.0	10.7	10.5	10.3	10.2	10.1	9.89	9.72	9.55	9.47	9.38	9.29	9.20	9.11	9.02
6	13.7	10.9	9.78	9.15	8.75	8.47	8.26	8.10	7.98	7.87	7.72	7.56	7.40	7.31	7.23	7.14	7.06	6.97	6.88
7	12.2	9.55	8.45	7.85	7.46	7.19	6.99	6.84	6.72	6.62	6.47	6.31	6.16	6.07	5.99	5.91	5.82	5.74	5.65
8	11.3	8.65	7.59	7.01	6.63	6.37	6.18	6.03	5.91	5.81	5.67	5.52	5.36	5.28	5.20	5.12	5.03	4.95	4.86
9	10.6	8.02	6.99	6.42	6.06	5.80	5.61	5.47	5.35	5.26	5.11	4.96	4.81	4.73	4.65	4.57	4.48	4.40	4.31
10	10.0	7.56	6.55	5.99	5.64	5.39	5.20	5.06	4.94	4.85	4.71	4.56	4.41	4.33	4.25	4.17	4.08	4.00	3.91
11	9.65	7.21	6.22	5.67	5.32	5.07	4.89	4.74	4.63	4.54	4.40	4.25	4.10	4.02	3.94	3.86	3.78	3.69	3.60
12	9.33	6.93	5.95	5.41	5.06	4.82	4.64	4.50	4.39	4.30	4.16	4.01	3.86	3.78	3.70	3.62	3.54	3.45	3.36
13	9.07	6.70	5.74	5.21	4.86	4.62	4.44	4.30	4.19	4.10	3.96	3.82	3.66	3.59	3.51	3.43	3.34	3.25	3.17
14	8.86	6.51	5.56	5.04	4.70	4.46	4.28	4.14	4.03	3.94	3.80	3.66	3.51	3.43	3.35	3.27	3.18	3.09	3.00
15	8.68	6.36	5.42	4.89	4.56	4.32	4.14	4.00	3.89	3.80	3.67	3.52	3.37	3.29	3.21	3.13	3.05	2.96	2.87
16	8.53	6.23	5.29	4.77	4.44	4.20	4.03	3.89	3.78	3.69	3.55	3.41	3.26	3.18	3.10	3.02	2.93	2.84	2.75
17	8.40	6.11	5.19	4.67	4.34	4.10	3.93	3.79	3.68	3.59	3.46	3.31	3.16	3.08	3.00	2.92	2.83	2.75	2.65
18	8.29	6.01	5.09	4.58	4.25	4.01	3.84	3.71	3.60	3.51	3.37	3.23	3.08	3.00	2.92	2.84	2.75	2.66	2.57
19	8.19	5.93	5.01	4.50	4.17	3.94	3.77	3.63	3.52	3.43	3.30	3.15	3.00	2.92	2.84	2.76	2.67	2.58	2.49
20	8.10	5.85	4.94	4.43	4.10	3.87	3.70	3.56	3.46	3.37	3.23	3.09	2.94	2.86	2.78	2.69	2.61	2.52	2.42
21	8.02	5.78	4.87	4.37	4.04	3.81	3.64	3.51	3.40	3.31	3.17	3.03	2.88	2.80	2.72	2.64	2.55	2.46	2.36
22	7.95	5.72	4.82	4.31	3.99	3.76	3.59	3.45	3.35	3.26	3.12	2.98	2.83	2.75	2.67	2.58	2.50	2.40	2.31
23	7.88	5.66	4.76	4.26	3.94	3.71	3.54	3.41	3.30	3.21	3.07	2.93	2.78	2.70	2.62	2.54	2.45	2.35	2.26
24	7.82	5.61	4.72	4.22	3.90	3.67	3.50	3.36	3.26	3.17	3.03	2.89	2.74	2.66	2.58	2.49	2.40	2.31	2.21
25	7.77	5.57	4.68	4.18	3.86	3.63	3.46	3.32	3.22	3.13	2.99	2.85	2.70	2.62	2.53	2.45	2.36	2.27	2.17
30	7.56	5.39	4.51	4.02	3.70	3.47	3.30	3.17	3.07	2.98	2.84	2.70	2.55	2.47	2.39	2.30	2.21	2.11	2.01
40	7.31	5.18	4.31	3.83	3.51	3.29	3.12	2.99	2.89	2.80	2.66	2.52	2.37	2.29	2.20	2.11	2.02	1.92	1.80
60	7.08	4.98	4.13	3.65	3.34	3.12	2.95	2.82	2.72	2.63	2.50	2.35	2.20	2.12	2.03	1.94	1.84	1.73	1.60
120	6.85	4.79	3.95	3.48	3.17	2.96	2.79	2.66	2.56	2.47	2.34	2.19	2.03	1.95	1.86	1.76	1.66	1.53	1.38
∞	6.63	4.61	3.78	3.32	3.02	2.80	2.64	2.51	2.41	2.32	2.18	2.04	1.88	1.79	1.70	1.59	1.47	1.32	1.00

DEGREES OF FREEDOM FOR DENOMINATOR

[a]Source: By permission of Prof. E. S. Pearson from Merrington, M., and Thompson, C. M. "Tables of Percentage Points of the Inverted Beta (F) Distribution," *Biometrika* 33 (1943):73. Interpolation should be performed using reciprocals of the degrees of freedom.

269

Bibliography

CHAPTER 1 EMERGENCE OF QUANTITATIVE ANALYSIS IN EDUCATION

Alkin, Marvin C., and Bruno, James E. "Systems Approaches to Educational Planning," Part IV. In *Social and Technological Change: Implications for Education*, edited by Philip K. Piele, T. Eidell, and S. Smith. Eugene, Oregon: Center for the Advanced Study of Educational Administration, 1970.

Averch, Harvey; Carroll, S.; Donaldson, T.; Kiesling, H.; and Pincus, J. "How Effective is Schooling?" R956 PCSF/RC RAND Corporation, March 1972.

Ayres, Leonard. *Laggards in Our Schools*. New York: Kelley, 1909.

Banghart, Frank W. *Educational System Analysis*. New York: Macmillan, 1969.

Blaug, Mark. "Cost-Benefit and Cost-Effectiveness Analysis of Education." In *Budgeting, Program Analysis, and Cost-Effectiveness in Educational Planning*, edited by OECD. Paris: Organisation for Economic Cooperation and Development, 1968.

Boulay, Peter C. "Systems Analysis: Tonic or Toxic." *Arizona Teacher* 57 (1969):6-9.

Boulding, Kenneth E. "The Schooling Industry as a Possibly Pathological Section of the American Economy." *Review of Educational Research* **40** (1972):129-143.

Bruno, James E. *Emerging Issues in Education.* Lexington, Massachusetts: D. C. Heath, 1973.

Bruno, James E., and Fox, Norman. "Quantitative Analysis in Administrative Preparation," Monograph #7. Eugene, Oregon: ERIC Clearinghouse, 1973.

Callahan, Raymond E. *Education and the Cult of Efficiency.* Chicago: The University of Chicago Press, 1962.

Coleman, James E.; Campbell, E.; Hobson, C.; Partland, J.; Mood, A.; Weinfeld, F.; and York, R. *Equality of Educational Opportunity.* Washington, D. C.: U.S. Government Printing Office, 1966.

Committee for Economic Development. *Innovation in Education: New Directions for the American.* New York: CED, 1968.

Conner, Forrest E. Foreword to *Administrative Technology and the School Executive,* edited by Stephen J. Knezevich. Washington, D.C.: Commission on Administrative Technology, American Association of School Administrators, 1969.

Coombs, Philip M., and Hallak, Jacques. *Managing Educational Costs.* New York: Oxford University Press, 1972.

Cronbach, L. J., and Snow, R. E. "Individual Differences in Learning Ability as a Function of Instructional Variables." Final Report OEC 4-6-061269-1217, Bethesda, Maryland, 1969.

Cubberly, Ellwood P. *Public School Administration.* Boston: Houghton Mifflin, 1916.

Culbertson, Jack A.; Farquhar, Robin H.; Gaynor, Alan K.; and Shibles, M. R. *Preparing Educational Leaders for the Seventies,* Final Report. Columbus, Ohio: University Council for Educational Administration, 1969.

Davis, Donald E., and Hendrix, Vernon L. *Systems Analysis in Educational Administration.* Minneapolis: University of Minnesota and University Council for Educational Administration, 1966.

Dror, Yehezkel. "Policy Analysis: A New Professional Role in Government Service." *Public Administration Review* **27** (1967):197-203.

Dror, Yehezkel. *Review of Educational Planning-Programming-Budgeting: A Systems Approach by Harry J. Hartley.* Santa Monica, California: The RAND Corporation, 1969.

Durstine, Richard M. "Technical Trends in Educational Management: Opportunities and Hazards." Papers and Proceedings: Annual Conference of the Comparative and International Education Society, Atlanta, Georgia, March 22-24, 1970. *Comparative Education Review* **14** (1970):327-334.

Enthoven, Alain. "Systems Analysis and the Navy." In *Planning Programming Budgeting: A Systems Approach to Management,* edited by Fremont J. Lyden and Ernest G. Miller. Chicago: Markham Publishing Company, 1968.

Erickson, Donald A. "Foreword." *Review of Educational Research* **37** (1967):376.

Farmer, James. *Why Planning, Programming, Budgeting Systems for Higher Education?* Boulder, Colorado: Western Interstate Commission for Higher Education, 1970.

Froomkin, Joseph. "Cost/Effectiveness and Cost/Benefit Analyses of Educational Programs." In *Proceedings of the Symposium on Operations Analysis of Education.* A conference sponsored by the National Center for Educational Statistics, Office of Education, U.S. Department of Health, Education, and Welfare, Washington, D.C., November 19-22, 1967. *Socio-Economic Planning Sciences* 2 (1969):381-387.

Harmes, H. M. "Improvement in Education: Criteria for Change." *Educational Technology* 10 (1970):46-50.

Hartley, Harry J. "Economic Rationality in Urban School Planning: The Program Budget." *Urban Education* 3 (1967):39-51.

Hartley, Harry J. *Educational Planning, Programming, Budgeting: A Systems Approach.* Englewood Cliffs, New Jersey: Prentice-Hall, 1968.

Hinds, Richard H. "Educational Program Planning and Related Techniques Annotated Bibliography." Unpublished Report, Miami, Florida: Dade County Public Schools, 1969.

Hirsch, Werner Z. "The Budget as an Instrument for Medium and Long-Range Planning and Programming of Education." In *Budgeting, Program Analysis, and Cost-Effectiveness in Educational Planning,* edited by OECD. Paris: Organisation for Economic Cooperation and Development, 1968.

Hogan, John. "Law and the Schools." Ph.D. dissertation, UCLA, 1972.

Hovey, Harold A. *The Planning-Programming-Budgeting Approach to Government Decision-Making.* New York: Frederick A. Praeger, 1968.

James, H. Thomas. "The Impending Revolution in School Business Management." Paper presented at the Association of School Business Officials, Houston, Texas, October 22-24, 1968.

James, H. Thomas. "The Cult of Efficiency and Education." Horace Mann Lecture 1968. Pittsburgh: University of Pittsburgh Press, 1969.

Kaufman, Roger. "Systems Approaches to Education: Discussion and Integration," Part III. In *Social and Technological Change: Implications for Education,* edited by Philip K. Piele, T. Eidell, and S. Smith. Eugene, Oregon: Center for the Advanced Study of Educational Administration, 1970.

Kaufman, Roger A. *Educational System Planning.* Englewood Cliffs, New Jersey: Prentice-Hall, 1972.

Keppel, Francis. "Operations Analysis—The Promise and the Pitfalls." In *Proceedings of the Symposium on Operations Analysis of Education.* A conference sponsored by the National Center for Educational Statistics, Office of Education, U.S. Department of Health, Education, and Welfare, Washington, D.C., November 19-22, 1967. *Socio-Economic Planning Sciences* 2 (1969):121-125.

Kiesling, Herbert J. *Multivariate Analysis of Schools and Educational Policy.* Santa Monica, California: The RAND Corporation, 1971.

Knezevich, Stephen J. "The Systems Approach to School Administration: Some Perceptions on the State of the Art in 1967." In *Proceedings of the*

Symposium on Operations Analysis of Education. A conference sponsored by the National Center for Educational Statistics, Office of Education, U.S. Department of Health, Education, and Welfare, Washington, D.C., November 19-22, 1967. *Socio-Economic Planning Sciences* 2 (1969):127-133.

Knezevich, Stephen J., ed. *Administrative Technology and the School Executive.* Washington, D.C.: Commission on Administrative Technology, American Association of School Administrators, 1969.

Kraft, Richard H. P., and Latta, Raymond F., eds. Special issue on "Systems Techniques in Educational Planning and Management." *Education Technology* 12 (1972):5-79.

Levin, Henry M., and Snow, Richard E. "The Emerging Intersection of Economics and Psychology in Educational Research," Chapter 14. In *Emerging Issues in Education,* edited by James E. Bruno. Lexington, Massachusetts: D. C. Heath, 1973.

McNamara, James F. "Mathematical Programming Models in Educational Planning." *Review of Educational Research* 41 (1971):419-446.

McNamara, James F. "Mathematics and Educational Administration." *Journal of Educational Administration* X (1972):164-183.

Mood, Alexander M., and Stoller, David S. "USOE is Knee-Deep in Operational Analysis." *Nation's Schools* 80 (1967):74-77.

Operation PEP. *Symposium on the Application of Systems Analysis and Management Techniques to Educational Planning in California* (Chapman College, Orange, California, June 12-13, 1967). Burlingame, California, 1967.

Organisation for Economic Cooperation and Development (OECD). *Budgeting, Program Analysis, and Cost-Effectiveness in Educational Planning.* Paris: OECD, 1968.

Organisation for Economic Cooperation and Development (OECD). *Efficiency in Resource Utilization in Education.* Paris: OECD, 1969.

Organisation for Economic Cooperation and Development (OECD). *Systems Analysis for Educational Planning: Selected Annotated Bibliography.* Paris: OECD, 1969.

Peat, Marwick, Mitchell, and Co. *Educational Planning and Evaluation Guide for California School Districts.* Sacramento, California: California State Advisory Commission on School District Budgeting and Accounting, 1972.

Pfeiffer, John. *New Look at Education: Systems Analysis in Our Schools and Colleges.* New York: Odyssey Press, 1968.

Phi Delta Kappa. *Educational Goals and Objectives: Model Program for Community and Professional Involvement.* Bloomington, Illinois, n.d.

Schultze, Charles L. "Why Benefit-Cost Analysis?" In *Program Budgeting a Benefit-Cost Analysis,* edited by Harley H. Hinichs and Graeme M. Taylor. Pacific Palisades, California: Goodyear Publishing Company, Inc., 1969.

Simon, Herbert A. *The Shape of Automation for Men and Management.* New York: Harper and Row, 1966.

Sisson, Roger L. "Can We Model the Educational Process?" In *Proceedings of the Symposium on the Operations Analysis of Education.* A conference sponsored by the National Center for Educational Statistics, Office of Education, U.S. Department of Health, Education, and Welfare, Washington, D.C., November 19–22, 1967. *Socio-Economic Planning Sciences* 2 (1969):109–119.

Sisson, Roger L. "Operations Analysis: Some Definitions and an Evaluation." Proceedings of American Association of Collegiate Registrars and Admissions Officers, Annual Meeting. *College and University* 45 (1970): 669–685.

Stoller, David S. Foreword to *Proceedings of the Symposium on Operations Analysis of Education.* A conference sponsored by the National Center for Educational Statistics, Office of Education, U.S. Department of Health, Education, and Welfare, Washington, D.C., November 19–22, 1967. *Socio-Economic Planning Sciences* 2 (1969):105–107.

Stoller, David S., and Dorfman, William, conference eds. *Proceedings of the Symposium on Operations Analysis of Education.* A conference sponsored by the National Center for Educational Statistics, Office of Education, U.S. Department of Health, Education, and Welfare, Washington, D.C., November 19–22, 1967. *Socio-Economic Planning Sciences* 2 (1969).

Tanner, C. Kenneth. *Designs for Educational Planning: A Systematic Approach.* Lexington, Massachusetts: Heath, Lexington Books, 1971.

Thomas, J. Allen. "Efficiency Criteria in Urban School Systems." Paper presented at the Annual Meeting of the American Educational Research Association, New York, February 1967.

Thomas, J. Allen. *The Productive School: A Systems Analysis Approach to Educational Administration.* New York: Wiley, 1971.

Thompson, Robert B. *A Systems Approach to Instruction.* Hamden, Connecticut: The Shoe String Press, 1971.

Van Dusseldorp, Ralph A.; Richardson, Duane E.; and Foley, Walter J. *Educational Decision-Making Through Operations Research.* Boston: Allyn and Bacon, 1971.

Van Gigh, John P., and Hill, Richard F. *Using Systems Analysis to Implement Cost-Effectiveness and Program Budgeting in Education.* Englewood Cliffs, New Jersey: Educational Technology Publication, 1971.

Weisbrod, Burton A. *External Benefits of Public Education: An Economic Analysis.* Princeton, New Jersey: Industrial Relations Section, Department of Economics, Princeton University, 1964.

Wildavsky, Aaron, "Rescuing Policy Analysis from PPBS (PPBS re-examined)." *Public Administration Review* 29 (1969):189–202. Reprinted in *Educational Investment in an Urban Society*, edited by Melvin R. Levin and Alan Shank. New York: Teachers College Press, 1970.

Wright, Chester. "The Concept of a Program Budget." In *Program Budgeting and Benefit-Cost Analysis*, edited by Harley H. Hinrichs and Graeme M. Taylor. Pacific Palisades, California: Goodyear Publishing Company, Inc., 1969.

CHAPTER 2 UNIVARIATE AND BIVARIATE ANALYSIS

Afifi, A. A., and Azen, S. P. *Statistical Analysis, A Computer Oriented Approach.* New York: Academic Press, 1972.

Blalock, H. *Social Statistics.* New York: McGraw-Hill, 1972.

Dixon, Wilford, and Massey, Frank J. *Introduction to Statistical Analysis.* New York: McGraw-Hill, 1969.

Elzey, Freeman F. *A Programmed Introduction to Statistics.* Belmont, California: Wadsworth Publishing Co., Inc., 1966.

Gotkin, L. G., and Goldstein, L. *Descriptive Statistics, A Programmed Textbook.* Vol. I and II. New York: Wiley, 1967.

Kirk, Roger E. *Experimental Design: Procedures for the Social Sciences.* Belmont, California: Wadsworth Publishing Co., 1968.

Phillips, John L. *Statistical Thinking.* San Francisco: W. H. Freeman and Company, 1973.

Popham, W. J. *Educational Statistics.* New York: Harper and Row, 1967.

Popham, W. J., and Sirotnick, Kenneth. *Educational Statistics,* second edition. New York: Harper and Row Publishers, 1973.

Popham, W. J., and Trimble, R. R., "The Minnesota Teacher Attitude Inventory as an Index of General Teaching Competence." *Educational and Psychological Measurement* 20 (1960):509-512.

Siegel, Sidney. *Non-Parametric Statistics.* New York: McGraw-Hill, 1956.

Williams, Frederick. *Reasoning with Statistics.* New York: Holt, Rinehart and Winston, 1968.

CHAPTER 3 MULTIPLE LINEAR REGRESSION

Amick, Daniel James. "A Multivariate Statistical Analysis of the Use of a Scientific Computer Based Current Awareness Information Retrieval System." *Journal of the American Society for Information Science* 21 (1970):171-178.

Brandt, E. G. *The Abuse of Stepwise Regression or: Experiments in Fishing,* p. 4260. Santa Monica, California: The RAND Corporation, February 1970.

Cooley, William W., and Lohnes, Paul R. *Multivariate Procedures for the Behavioral Sciences.* New York: John Wiley & Sons, 1962.

Crow, E.; Davis, F.; and Maxfield, M. *Statistics Manual.* New York: Dover Publications, Inc., 1960.

Dei Rossi, James A., and Sumner, Gerald C. *Exploring the Effects of Distorting Classical Linear Regression Assumptions,* p. 4103. Santa Monica, California: The RAND Corporation, August 1969.

Dixon, W. J. *Bio-Medical Computer Programs.* Los Angeles, California: Health Sciences Computing Facility, University of California at Los Angeles, September 1965.

Ezekiel, Mordecai, and Fox, Karl A. *Methods of Correlation and Regression Analysis*. New York: John Wiley & Sons, 1959.

Flathman, Dave. *Hypothesis Testing with Multiple Regression* (paper). Alberta: Educational Research Services, University of Alberta, Edmonton, Canada, November 1968.

Gordon, Robert A. "Issues in Multiple Regression." *The American Journal of Sociology* 73 (1968):592–616.

International Business Machines. *Catalog of Programs for IBM 704-709-7040-7044-7090 and 7094 Data Processing Systems*. White Plains, New York: Program Information Department, International Business Machines, October 1964.

International Business Machines. *Concepts and Applications of Regression Analysis*, E20-01800-1. White Plains, New York: International Business Machines Corporation, 1966.

International Business Machines. *Outlines of Statistical Techniques, Applications and Programs for Industry, Engineering and Science*, C20-1645-0. White Plains, New York: International Business Machines Corporation, 1967.

International Business Machines. *System/360 Scientific Subroutine Package (360-CM-03X) Version III: Programmers Manual*, H20-0205-3. White Plains, New York: International Business Machines Corporation, 1969.

Jelinck, Richard C., and Steffy, Wilbert. "Use of Multi-Variate Techniques for the Analysis of Work Measurement Data." *Journal of Industrial Engineering* 17 (1966):106–111.

Kelly, Francis J.; Beggs, D.; McNeil, K.; Eichelberger, T.; and Lyon, J. *Multiple Regression Approach*. Carbondale, Illinois: Southern Illinois University Press, 1969.

Leser, C. *Econometric Techniques and Problems*. New York: Hafner Publishing Co., 1966.

Pederson, Poul Ove. "Multivariate Models of Urban Development." *Socio-Economic Planning Sciences* 1 (1967):101–106.

Tintner, Gerhard. *Econometrics*, Science Edition. New York: John Wiley & Sons, 1970.

Wegner, P. "Relations Between Multivariate Statistics and Mathetical Programming." *Applied Statistics* 12 (1965):146–150.

Wonnacott, R., and Wonnacott, T. *Econometrics*. New York: John Wiley & Sons, 1970.

Educational Applications of Regression Analysis

Allen, Leslie R. "An Evaluation of Certain Cognitive Aspects of the Material Objects Unit of the Science Curriculum Improvement Study Elementary Science Program." *Journal of Research in Science Teaching* 7 (1970):277:281. The Science Curriculum Improvement Study (SCIS) elementary science program was supported by the National Science Foundation under development at the University of California at

Berkeley. The Material Objects unit teaches the first grade child the
fundamental concepts of (a) objects and their properties, and (b) material.
The purpose of this study was to investigate whether participation in the
SCIS elementary science program at grade 1 level results in a performance
superior to that of grade 1 nonparticipants in the program when certain
SCIS objectives are considered.

Averch, Harvey, and Kiesling, Herbert J. *The Relationship of School and
Environment to Student Performance: Some Simultaneous Models for the
Project Talent High Schools.* Santa Monica, California: The RAND
Corporation (forthcoming). This study compares ordinary and two-stage
least-squares techniques for models of pupil performance using grades 9
and 11 in the 775 public Project Talent high schools.

Bowles, Samuel, *Educational Production Function*, Final Report, U.S. Office
of Education, U.S. Department of Health, Education, and Welfare,
Washington, D.C. OEC-1-7-00451-2651, ED 037 590. Cambridge, Massachusetts: Harvard University, February 1969. This is a study of the
performance of Black twelfth graders; it includes findings from two data
sets: Project Talent high schools and the U.S. Office of Education's Equal
Opportunity Survey (EOS). Bowles' study is treated as two studies here,
with the findings from the Talent high schools labeled (a) and the EOS
data (b). The results of the Project Talent study can be found in W. Lee
Hansen, ed. *Education, Income, and Human Capital*, Studies in Income
and Wealth No. 35, pp. 11-61. New York: National Bureau of Economic
Research, Columbia University Press, 1970.

Burkhead, Jesse; Fox, Thomas G.; and Holland, John W. *Input and Output in
Large City High Schools.* Syracuse, New York: Syracuse University Press,
1967. This is a study of high schools in Chicago, Atlanta, and a selected
sample of Project Talent high schools.

Christal, Raymond E. "Selecting a Harem—and Other Applications of the
Policy-Capturing Model." *Journal of Experimental Education* 36
(1968):35-41. This study was undertaken to determine the appropriate
distribution of a sample of grades for jobs in various officer specialities
and fields. Using a sample of board ratings and establishing the variables,
a multiple linear regression model was employed to simulate board action.

Cohn, Elchanan. "Economics of Scale in Iowa High School Operations."
Journal of Human Resources 3 (1968):422-434. A study of 377 Iowa
high schools.

Coleman, J.; Campbell, E.; Hobson, C.; McPartland, J.; Mood, A.; Weinfeld, F.;
and York, R. *Equality of Educational Opportunity*. Washington, D.C.: U.S.
Government Printing Office, 1966.

Danish, Steven. "Factors Influencing Changes in Empathy Following a Group
Experience." *Journal of Counseling Psychology* 18 (1971):262-267.
Among the variables hypothesized as important in producing change in
empathy are counselor warmth and empathy, client's motivation to
change, and the quality of the client–counselor relationship. The purpose
of the study was to determine the relationship between these variables
and to study the separate effects of each.

Fox, Thomas G. "School System Resource Use in Production of Interdependent Educational Outputs." Mimeographed. Paper read at The Joint National Meeting, American Astronautical Society and Operations Research Society in 1969 at Denver, Colorado. Additional studies done within a simultaneous equation framework of the Chicago high school data used by Burkhead (above).

Hanushek, Eric A. *The Education of Negroes and Whites*. Ph.D. dissertation. Microfilm. Massachusetts Institute of Technology, 1968. A study of the relative effects of school and background characteristics of Whites in 471 schools and Blacks in 242 schools, using data gathered by the U.S. Office of Education's Equal Opportunity Survey.

Hanushek, Eric A. *The Value of Teachers in Teaching*, RM-6362-CC/RC. Santa Monica, California: The RAND Corporation, December 1970. This is a study of the relationship of second and third grade pupils in a medium-sized California school district that is unique in that pupils were matched to individual teachers. Caucasian and Spanish-surnamed children were studied separately.

Herbert, David, and Latwack, Lawrence. "Prediction of Recidivism Among Juvenile Delinquents." *Journal of Educational Research* 61 (1967):74–75. This study develops a predictive measure of recidivism among institutionalized juvenile delinquents. A follow-up study of 100 boys 5 years after they were paroled provided information on 10 variables to be studied in the predictive equation.

Katzman, M. T. "Distribution and Production in a Big City Elementary School System." Ph.D. dissertation, Yale University. This is a study of schools within the Boston school system.

Kiesling, Herbert J. *The Relationship of School Inputs to Public School Performance in New York State*, P-4211. Santa Monica, California: The RAND Corporation, October 1969. A study of the data for New York State school districts gathered in 1958, 1959, and 1960. Grades 4, 5, and 6 were studied. Meaningful relationships were found for 46 of the 89 urban districts studied, and these were used for the results described.

Kiesling, Herbert J. *A Study of the Cost and Quality of New York School Districts*, Final Report, Bloomington, Indiana, Project No. 8-0264. Washington, D.C: U.S. Department of Health, Education, and Welfare, U.S. Office of Education, 1970. A study of grades 5 and 8 from a sample of 86 school districts in New York State for which data were gathered in 1965.

Levin, Henry M. "A New Model of School Effectiveness." *Do Teachers Make a Difference?*, OE-58042, pp. 55–78. Washington, D.C.: U.S. Department of Health, Education, and Welfare, U.S. Office of Education, 1970. A study of pupil data for schools in a large eastern city gathered by the Equal Opportunity Survey. It contains the first use of simultaneous equation techniques in educational model building.

Michelson, Stephan. "The Association of Teacher Resourcefulness with Children's Characteristics." *Do Teachers Make a Difference?*, OE-58042, pp. 120–168. Washington, D.C.: U.S. Department of Health, Education, and

Welfare, U.S. Office of Education, 1970. This contains further research with the data used by Levin generated by the Equal Opportunity Survey for a large eastern city.

Mollenkopf, William G. *A Study of Secondary School Characteristics as Related to Test Scores*, Research Bulletin RB-56-6. Princeton, New Jersey: Educational Testing Service, 1956. This study relates variables obtained from a questionnaire sent to secondary schools to pupil aptitude and achievement performance.

Spuck, D. W. "Reward Structures in the Public High School." *Education Administration Quarterly* 10 (1974):18-34.

Thomas, James Alan. "Efficiency in Education: A Study of the Relationship Between Selected Inputs and Mean Test Scores in a Sample of Senior High Schools." Microfilm. Ph.D. dissertation, Stanford University Library, 1962. A study of 206 Project Talent high schools found in communities with populations between 2,500 and 25,000.

Walberg, Herbert J., and Rasher, Sue Pinzur. "Public School Effectiveness and Equality: New Evidence and Its Implications." *Phi Delta Kappan* LVI (1974):3-9.

CHAPTER 4 DISCRIMINANT ANALYSIS

General References

Amick, Daniel James. "A Multivariate Statistical Analysis of the Use of a Scientific Computer Based Current-Awareness Information Retrieval System." *Journal of the American Society for Information Science* 21 (1970):171-178.

Cherukupalle, Nirmala. "Classification Techniques in Planning Analysis." *Journal of Socio-Economic Planning Sciences* 4 (1970):395-406.

Cooley, William W., and Lohnes, Paul R. *Multivariate Procedures for the Behavioral Sciences*. New York: John Wiley & Sons, 1962.

Dixon, W. J *Bio-Medical Computer Programs*. Los Angeles: Health Sciences Computing Facility, University of California at Los Angeles, 1965.

Eisenbeis, Robert A., and Avery, Robert B. *Discriminant Analysis and Classification Procedures*. Lexington, Massachusetts: Lexington Books, D. C. Heath & Co. 1972.

International Business Machines. *Outlines of Statistical Techniques, Applications and Programs for Industry, Engineering and Science*, C20-1645-0. White Plains, New York: International Business Machines Corporation, 1967.

International Business Machines. *System/360 Scientific Subroutine Package (360-CM-03X) Version III: Programmers Manual*, H20-0205-3. White Plains, New York: International Business Machines Corporation, 1966.

Kelly, Francis J.; Beggs, D.; McNeil, K.; Eichelberger, T.; and Lyon, J. *Multiple Regression Approach*. Carbondale, Illinois: Southern Illinois University Press, 1969.

Kerlinger, Fred N. *Foundations of Behavioral Research*. New York: Holt, Rinehart and Winston, 1973.

Neuwirth, Sidney I., and Shegda, Michael. "Discriminant Analysis." *Management Services* 1 (1964):28-30.

Nie, Norman; Bent, D.; and Hall, C. H. *Statistical Package for the Social Sciences*. New York: McGraw-Hill, 1970.

Rao, C. R. *Advanced Statistical Methods in Biometric Research*. New York: John Wiley, 1952.

Rao, C. R., and Slater, P. "Multivariate Analysis Applied to Differences Between Neurotic Groups." *British Journal of Psychology, Statistical Section* 2 (1949):17-29.

Rettig, Salomon, "Multiple Discriminant Analysis, An Illustration." *American Sociological Review* 29 (1964):398-406.

Tintner, Gerhard. *Econometrics*, Science Edition. New York: John Wiley and Sons, 1970.

Van de Geer, John. *Introduction to Multivariate Analysis for Social Sciences*. San Francisco, California: W. H. Freeman & Co., 1971.

Waugh, F. V. "Regressions Between Sets of Variables." *Econometrica* 10 (1942):290.

Educational Applications of Discriminant Analysis

Asher, William, and Shively, Joseph E. "Technique of Discriminant Analysis: A Reclassification of Harbison and Myers Seventy Five Countries." *Comparative Education Review* 13 (1969):180-186.

Astin, Helen, "Career Development of Girls During the High School Years." *Journal of Counseling Psychology* 15 (1968):536-540. This study was designed to explore the career development of girls during their high school years. Specific goals were (1) to identify personal qualities of ninth grade girls that predict their vocational choices 3 years later in the twelfth grade; (2) to identify some of the personal qualities associated with choices of particular kinds of occupations.

Astin, H., and Myint, T. "Career Development of Young Women During the Post High School Years." *Journal of Counseling Psychology* 18 (1971):369-393. The purpose of the study was to explore the career development of women during the 5-year period after high school. The study concerns itself with identifying which of 36 personal variables obtained in the women's senior year of high school best predicts later career choice.

Bean, Andrew G., and Covert, Robert W. "Prediction of College Persistence, Withdrawal, and Academic Dismissal: A Discriminant Analysis." *Educational and Psychological Measurement* 33 (1973):407-411.

Bruno, James E., and Nelkin, Ira M. "An Empirical Analysis of Teacher Militancy." *Educational Administration Quarterly* 12 (1975).

Dunteman, G. H. "A Discriminant Analysis of the MMPI for Female College Students in Health and Education." *The Journal of Experimental Education* 35 (1967):85-90.

Herrmann, Robert W. "Classroom Status and Teacher Approval and Disapproval—A Study in Children's Perceptions." *Journal of Experimental Education* 41 (1972):32-39.

Keenen, Charles B., and Holmes, June E. "Predicting Graduation, Withdrawal and Failure in College by Multiple Discriminant Analysis." *Journal of Educational Measurement* 7 (1970):91-95. An illustration of using multiple discriminant analysis and nonintellective data in predicting graduation, withdrawal, and failure in a college of liberal arts. The nonintellective factors are qualitative content categories derived from candidates' personal application statements.

Simon, A., and Ward, Lionel. "The Performance of High and Low Ability Groups on Two Measures of Creativity." *Journal of Education Research* 2 (1973):70-73.

Tatsuoka, Maurice. *Selected Topics in Advanced Statistics, An Elementary Approach. No. 6.* Champaign, Illinois: Institute for Personality and Ability Testing, 1970. A study of personality traits and how they affect college major choices. Data taken from 150 college juniors and seniors who were in three major fields: (1) science, (2) art, and (3) psychology.

Wang, Margaret C. "The Use of Canonical Correlation Analysis in An Investigation of Pupils Rate of Learning in School." *Journal of Educational Research* 64 (1970):35-45.

CHAPTER 5   FOUNDATIONS OF MICROECONOMIC THEORY

General References to the Economics of Education

Anderson, C. A., and Bowman, M. J., eds. *Education and Economic Development.* Chicago: Aldine, 1965.

Becker, Gary S. *Human Capital.* New York: National Bureau of Economic Research, 1964.

Blaug, M. "Approaches to Educational Planning." *The Economic Journal* 77, (1967):262-187.

Blaug, M., ed. *Economics of Education 1.* Baltimore, Maryland: Penguin, 1968.

Blaug, M., ed. *Economics of Education 2.* Baltimore, Maryland: Penguin, 1969.

Blaug, M. ed. *Economics of Education: A Selected Annotated Bibliography.* New York: Pergamon, 1970. (This provides the most current and complete reference to works in the field; over 1,300 entries.)

Bowman, M. J. "Economics of Education." *Review of Educational Research* 39 (1969):641-670.

Bowman, M. J., ed. *Readings in the Economics of Education.* Paris: UNESCO, 1968.

Carnoy, Martin. *Schooling in a Corporate Society.* New York: David McKay Company, 1972.

Davis, Ronnie J., and Merrall, John F. *Evaluating Educational Investment.* Lexington, Massachusetts: Lexington Books, D. C. Heath, 1974.

Hall, R., and Lauwerys, J. A., eds. *The Yearbook of Education: Education and Economics.* New York: World Book, 1965.

Halsey, A. H.; Floud, J.; and Anderson, C. A., eds. *Education, Economy and Society.* Glencoe, Illinois: Free Press, 1961.

Hansen, W. Lee. "Total and Private Rates of Return to Investment in Schooling." *Journal of Political Economy* 71 (1963):128-140.

Hirshleifer, J. *Investment, Interest and Capital.* Englewood Cliffs, New Jersey: Prentice-Hall, 1970.

Kruger, A. O. "Factor Endowment and Per Capita Income Differences Among Countries." *The Economic Journal* 78 (1968):641-659.

Machlup, Fritz. *Education and Economic Growth.* Lincoln, Nebraska: University of Nebraska Press, 1970.

Nicholson, Walter. *Microeconomic Theory Basic Principles and Extensions.* Hinsdale, Illinois: Dryden Press, 1972.

Robinson, E. A. G., and Vaizey, J., eds. *The Economics of Education.* New York: St. Martins, 1966.

Rogers, Daniel C., and Rucklin, Hirsch S. *Economics and Education.* New York: Free Press, 1971.

Sanders, D., and Barth, P. "Education and Economic Development." *Review of Educational Research* 38 (1968):213-230.

Schultz, T. *The Economic Value of Education.* New York: Columbia University Press, 1963.

Economics in Educational Planning

Beeby, C. E., ed. *Qualitative Aspects of Educational Planning.* Paris: UNESCO, IIEP, 1969.

Bowles, S. *Planning Educational Systems for Economic Growth.* Cambridge, Massachusetts: Harvard University Press, 1969.

Coombs, P. H. *The World Educational Crisis: A Systems Analysis.* New York: Oxford University Press, 1968.

Correa, H. *Quantitative Methodologies of Educational Planning.* Scranton, Pennsylvania: International Textbook, 1969.

Hagen, E. E. *On the Theory of Social Change: How Economic Growth Begins.* Homewood, Illinois: Dorsey, 1962.

Hall, R., and Lauwerys, J. A., eds. *The Yearbook of Education: Educational Planning.* New York: World Book, 1967.

McClelland, D. C. *The Achieving Society.* Princeton, New Jersey: Van Nostrand, 1961.

Educational Production Function Studies

Hanushek, Eric. *The Value of Teachers in Teaching,* RM-6362-CC/RC. Santa Monica, California: The RAND Corporation, December 1970. (Production function techniques applied in an effort to determine the impact of teachers and school-related factors on educational achievement.)

Kiesling, Herbert J. *Multivariate Analysis of Schools and Educational Policy*, P-4595. Santa Monica, California: The RAND Corporation, March 1971. (Overview and review of production function studies in education.)

Thomas, J. Alan. *The Productive School*. New York: John Wiley and Sons, 1971.

Multivariate Studies

Bowles, Samuel. *Educational Production Function*, Final Report, U.S. Department of Health, Education, and Welfare, U.S. Office of Education, OEC-1-7-00451-2651, ED 037 590. Cambridge, Massachusetts: Harvard University, February 1969.

Burkhead, Jesse; Fox, Thomas G.; and Holland, John W. *Input and Output in Large City High Schools*. Syracuse, New York: Syracuse University Press, 1967.

Cohn, Elchanan. "Economics of Scale in Iowa High School Operations." *Journal of Human Resources* 3 (1968):422–434.

Fox, Thomas G. "School System Resource Use in Production of Interdependent Educational Outputs." Mimeographed. Paper presented at The Joint National Meeting, American Astronautical Society and Operations Research Society at Denver, Colorado in 1969.

Hanusek, Eric. "The Education of Negroes and Whites." Microfilm. Ph.D. dissertation, Massachusetts Institute of Technology, 1968.

Hanusek, Eric. *The Value of Teachers in Teaching*, RM-6362-CC/RC. Santa Monica, California: The RAND Corporation, December 1970.

Ketsman, N. T. "Distribution and Production in a Big City Elementary School System." Ph.D. dissertation, Department of Economics, Yale University, 1969.

Kiesling, Herbert J. *The Relationship of School Inputs to Publich School Performance in New York State*, P-4211. Santa Monica, California: The RAND Corporation, October 1969.

Kiesling, Herbert J. *A Study of the Cost and Quality of New York School Districts*, Final Report, Bloomington, Indiana, Project No. 8-0264. Washington, D.C.: U.S. Office of Education, 1970.

Levin, Henry M. "A New Model of School Effectiveness." *Do Teachers Make a Difference?*, OE-58042, 1970. Washington, D.C.: U.S. Department of Health, Education, and Welfare, U.S. Office of Education, pp. 55–78.

Mellenkopf, William G. *A Study of Secondary School Characteristics as Related to Test Scores*. Research Bulletin RB-56-6. Princeton, New Jersey: Educational Testing Service, 1956.

Thomas, James Alan. "Efficiency in Education: A Study of the Relationship Between Selected Inputs and Mean Test Scores in a Sample of Senior High Schools." Microfilm. Ph.D. dissertation, Stanford University, 1962.

CHAPTER 6 PROGRAM EVALUATION AND REVIEW TECHNIQUES (PERT)

General References

Avotts, I. "The Management Side of PERT." *California Management Review* 4 (1962):16-27.

Cook, Desmond L. *An Introduction to PERT.* Columbus, Ohio: Bureau of Educational Research and Service, The Ohio State University, 1964.

Federal Electric Company. *Programmed Introduction to PERT.* New York: John Wiley and Sons, 1963.

Hansen, B. J. *Practical PERT, Including Critical Path Method.* Washington, D.C.: America House, 1965.

Healey, T. L. "Activity Subdivision and PERT Probability Statements." *Operations Research* 9 (1961):341-350.

Kelly, J. E., and Walker, M. B. "Critical Path Planning and Scheduling." In *Proceedings of the Eastern Joint Computer Conference,* 1959, pp. 160-170. Paper presented at the Eastern Joint Computer Conference, December 1-3, 1959, at Boston, Massachusetts.

MacCrimmon, K. R., and Ryavec, C. A. *An Analytical Study of PERT Assumptions,* RM 3408. Santa Monica, California: The RAND Corporation, 1962.

Van Slyke, R. *Uses of Monte Carlo in PERT,* MB 3367 PR. Santa Monica, California: The RAND Corporation, 1963.

Educational Applications

Case, Marston C. "The Application of PERT to Large Scale Educational Research and Evaluation Studies." *Educational Technology* 9 (1969):79-83.

Cochran, Leslie. "PERT: A Technique in Educational Research." *Journal of Educational Research* 63 (1969):19-25.

Cook, Desmond. *PERT Applications in Education,* USGPO 0E12024. Washington, D.C.: U.S. Department of Health, Education, and Welfare, 1966.

Justus, John. "PERT." *School Management* 11 (1967):24-29.

Liebeskuind, Morris. "Design and Construction of School Buildings: Critical Path Method." *Proceedings of the Association of School Business Officials of the U.S. and Canada* 50 (1964):151.

Mackay, D. A. "Application of the Critical Path Method to Educational Research Projects." *Alberta Journal of Educational Research* 14 (1968):15-22.

Pratzner, F. C., "Estimates of Teaching—Learning Time." *Educational Technology* 12 (1972):58-62.

Pullis, Joe M., and Rice, Philip F. "Application of PERT to Research in Business Education." *The Delta Pi Epsilon Journal* 14 (1972):25-33.

CHAPTER 7   LINEAR PROGRAMMING

General References

Charnes, A.; Cooper, W. W.; and Henderson, A. *An Introduction to Linear Programming.* New York: John Wiley and Sons, 1953.

Wegner, P. "Relations Between Multivariate Statistics and Mathematical Programming." *Applied Statistics* 12 (1965):146–150.

Educational References

Ackoff, R. L. "Toward Strategic Planning of Education." *Efficiency in Resource Utilization in Education.* Paris: OECD, 1969.

Adelman, I. "A Linear Programming Model of Educational Planning: A Case Study of Argentina." In *The Theory and Design of Economic Development,* edited by Irma Adelman and Erick Thorbecke. Baltimore, Maryland: Johns Hopkins Press, 1964.

Balinsky, W. L. "Some Manpower Planning Models Based on Educational Attainment," Technical Memorandum No. 185. Cleveland, Ohio: Department of Operations, Case Western Reserve University, June 1970.

Banghart, F. W. *Educational Systems Analysis.* Toronto: Collier-Macmillan, 1969.

Besel, Ronald. "A Linear Model for the Allocation of Instructional Resources." *Socio-Economic Planning Science* 6 (1972):501–506.

Bowles, S. "The Efficient Allocation of Resources in Education." *Quarterly Journal of Economics* 81 (1967):189–219.

Bowles, S. "Towards an Educational Production Function." In *Education, Income, and Human Capital,* edited by W. L. Hensen. A report of the National Bureau of Economic Research. New York: Columbia University Press, 1970.

Bruno, J. E. "An Alternative to the Use of Simplistic Formulas for Determining State Resource Allocation in School Finance Programs." *American Educational Research Journal* 6 (1969):479–514.a

Bruno, J. E. *A Linear Programming Approach to Position-Salary Evaluation in School Personnel Administration,* research memorandum. Santa Monica, California: The RAND Corporation, February 1969.b

Bruno, J. E. "A Mathematical Programming Approach to School System Finance." *Socio-Economic Planning Sciences* 3 (1969):1–12. (c)

Bruno, J. E. "Using Linear Programming Salary Evaluation Models in Collective Bargaining Negotiations with Teacher Unions." *Socio-Economic Planning Sciences* 3 (1969):103–118. (d)

Bruno, J. E. "An Alternative to Uniform Expenditure Reductions in Resource State Finance Programs." *Management Science: Applications* 17 (1971): 386–398.

Campbell, Hugh G., and Ignizio, James P. "Using Linear Programming for Predicting Student Performance." *Educational and Psychological Measurement* 32 (1972):397–401.

Clarke, S., and Surkis, J. "An Operations Research Approach to Racial Desegregation of School Systems." *Socio-Economic Planning Sciences* I (1968):259-272.

Harding, R. E. "The Linear Programming Approach to Master Time Schedule Generation in Education." In *Optimal Scheduling in Educational Institutions*, edited by A. G. Holtzman & W. R. Turkes, Cooperative Research Project No. 1323. U.S. Department of Health, Education, and Welfare, Office of Education. Pittsburgh: University of Pittsburgh, 1964.

Heckman, L. B., and Taylor, H. M. "School Rezoning to Achieve Racial Balance: A Linear Programming Approach." *Socio-Economic Planning Sciences* 3 (1969):127-133.

Heckman, L. B., and Taylor, H. M. *Designing School Attendance Zones by Linear Programming.* Ithaca, New York: Department of Environmental Systems Engineering, Cornell University, January 1970.

Holtman, A. G. "Linear Programming and the Value of an Input to a Local Public School System." *Public Finance* 23 (1968):429-440.

Lachene, R. "The Application of Operations Research to Educational Planning." *Efficiency in Resource Utilization in Education.* Paris: OECD, 1969.

Lawrie, N. L. "An Integer Linear Programming Model of a School Time-Tabling Problem." *The Computer Journal* 12 (1969):307-316.

McNamara, J. F. *A Mathematical Programming Model for the Efficient Allocation of Vocational Technical Education Funds.* Harrisburg, Pennsylvania: Pennsylvania Department of Education, 1970.

McNamara, J. F. "A Mathematical Programming Approach to State-Local Program Planning in Vocational Education." *American Educational Research Journal* 8 (1971):336-363.

Shapley, R. P.; Fulkerson, D.; Havelick, A.; and Weiler, D. *A Transportation Program for Filling Idle Classrooms in Los Angeles*, P-3 405. Santa Monica, California: The RAND Corporation, July 1966.

CHAPTER 8 LORENZ CURVE ANALYSIS

Alker, Hayward R. *Mathematics and Politics.* New York: Macmillan Co., 1965.

Alker, Hayward R. "Measuring Inequality." *The Quantitative Analysis of Social Problems*, edited by Edward R. Tufte. Reading, Massachusetts: Addison-Wesley Publishing, 1970.

Alker, H. R., and Rusett, B. M. "On Measuring Inequality." *Behavioral Science* 9 (1964):207-218.

Hacker, Andrew. *Congressional Redistricting the Issue of Equal Representation.* Washington, D.C.: Brookings Institute, 1953.

Schubert, Glendon, and Puss, Charles. "Measuring Malapportionment." *American Political Science Review* LVIII (1964):302-327.

Silva, Ruth. "Apportionment of the New York State Legislature." *American Political Science Review* LV (1961):870-881.

CHAPTER 9 DELPHI TECHNIQUES

Adelson, Marvin; Alkin, Marvin; Carey, Charles; and Helmer, Olaf. "Planning Education for the Future: Comments on a Pilot Study." *American Behavioral Scientist* 10 (1967):1–31.

Brown, Bernice B. *Delphi Process: A Methodology Used for the Elicitation of Opinions of Experts*, P-3925. Unpublished paper. Santa Monica, California: The RAND Corporation, September 1968.

Brown, B.; Cochran, S.; and Dalkey, N. *The Delphi Method II: Structure of Experiments*, RM-5957-PR. Santa Monica, California: The RAND Corporation, June 1969.

Campbell, Robert M., and Hitchin, David. "The Delphi Technique: Implementation in the Corporate Environment." *Management Services* 5 (1968):37–42.

Cyphert, F. R., and Gant, W. L. "The Delphi Technique: A Case Study." *Phi Delta Kappan* 52 (1971):272–273.

Dalkey, Norman C. *Delphi*, P-3704. Santa Monica, California: The RAND Corporation, October 1967.

Dalkey, Norman C. *Delphi*, P-3704. Unpublished paper. The RAND Corporation, October 1967.

Dalkey, N. *Experiments in Group Prediction*, P-3820, Santa Monica, California: The RAND Corporation, March 1968. (a)

Dalkey, N. *Predicting the Future*, P-3948. Santa Monica, California: The RAND Corporation, October 1968. (b)

Dalkey, N. *The Delphi Method: An Experimental Study of Group Opinion*, RM-5888-PR. Santa Monica, California: The RAND Corporation, June 1969.

Dalkey, N., and Helmer, O. "An Experimental Application of the Delphi Method to the Use of Experts." *Management Science* 9 (1963):459–467.

Dalkey, N., and Rourke, Daniel. *Experimental Assessment of Delphi Procedures with Group Value Judgments*, R-612. Santa Monica, California: The RAND Corporation, February 1971.

Dalkey, N.; Borwn, B.; and Cochran, S. *The Delphi Method III: Use of Self-Ratings to Improve Group Estimates*, RM-6115-PR. Santa Monica, California: The RAND Corporation, November 1970. (a)

Dalkey, N.; Brown, B.; and Cochran, S. *The Delphi Method IV: Effect of Percentile Feedback and Feed-In of Relevant Facts*, RM-6118-PR. Santa Monica, California: The RAND Corporation, March 1970. (b)

Dalkey, Norman C.; Rourke, D.; Lewis, R.: and Snyder, D. *Studies in the Quality of Life*. Lexington, Massachusetts: Lexington Books, D. C. Heath and Company, 1972.

Fuller, R. Buckminister. *Intuition*. Garden City, New York: Doubleday and Company, Inc., 1972.

Haydon, Brownlee. *The Year 2000*, P-3571. Unpublished paper. The RAND Corporation, March 1967.

Helmer, O. *Convergence of Expert Consensus Through Feedback*, P-2973. Santa Monica, California: The RAND Corporation, September 1964.

Helmer, O. *The Use of the Delphi Technique in Problems of Educational Innovations*, P-3499. Santa Monica, California: The RAND Corporation, December 1966.

Helmer, Olaf. *Analysis of the Future: The Delphi Method*, P-3558. Santa Monica, California: The RAND Corporation, March 1967.

Helmer, O. "A New Intellectual Climate: A Civilized Pattern of Behavior." *Vital Speeches of the Day* 33 (June 1, 1967). Speech delivered at the National Industrial Conference Board's 3rd Annual Public Affairs Conference, April 20, 1967 at New York.

Helmer, Olaf. *The Future of Science*, P-3607. Unpublished paper. The RAND Corporation, May 1967.

Helmer, O. *Systematic Use of Expert Opinions*, P-3721. Santa Monica, California: The RAND Corporation, November 1967.

Helmer, O., and Rescher, Nicholas. "On the Epistomology of the Inexact Sciences." *Management Sciences* 6 (1959):25-52.

Huckfeldt, Vaughn. *Imaging Future Organization in Higher Education*. Paper presented at UCEA Career Development Seminar October 29–November 1, 1972, at St. Paul, Minnesota.

McLean, Robert. *An Outline and Justification for the Use of the Delphi Method in Corrections Planning*, Internal Notes. New York City Rand Institute, February 19, 1971.

Quade, E. S. *Cost-Effectiveness: Some Trends in Analysis*, P-3529-1. Santa Monica, California: The RAND Corporation, March 1970.

Turoff, M. "Delphi and Its Potential Impact on Information Systems." Paper presented to Joint Computer Conference, Las Vegas, Nevada, Fall 1971. In *Proceedings of the Joint Computer Conference* 1971, pp. 317–326.

Index